T0248377

LINCOLN'S CONSERVATIVE ADVISOR

LINCOLN'S CONSERVATIVE ADVISOR

ATTORNEY GENERAL EDWARD BATES

Mark A. Neels

Southern Illinois University Press | Carbondale

Southern Illinois University Press
www.siupress.com

Copyright © 2024 by the Board of Trustees,
Southern Illinois University
All rights reserved
Printed in the United States of America

First printed August 2024.

Cover illustration: Full length portrait of Edward Bates, 1860 Republican
presidential nominee and attorney general under President Abraham
Lincoln, painted by William F. Cogswell. Missouri Historical Society.

ISBN 978-0-8093-3949-5 (paperback)
ISBN 978-0-8093-3950-1 (cloth)
ISBN 978-0-8093-3951-8 (ebook)
This book has been catalogued with The Library of Congress.

Printed on recycled paper ♻

SIU
Southern Illinois University System

To Wally, who always wondered if I had found a title.

CONTENTS

Gallery of illustrations beginning on page 91

ACKNOWLEDGMENTS

This book is the culmination of over a decade of research in primary and secondary sources on Bates and his time. Several friends were instrumental in its completion. My master's thesis adviser, Louis S. Gerteis, first set me on the task. Jason Stacy took up the baton as adviser on my dissertation while Erik Alexander served as a committee member and made important contributions to that manuscript. Friends Paul Balfe, Michael Beatty, Tim Callahan, Tom Day, Kim Farley, Steve Gietschier, Boyd Murphree, Dana Pertermann, Terry Pfizer, and Paul Shultz offered to read sections of the book. Their comments and suggestions made the final product infinitely better. Dorris Keeven-Franke also served as a reader and, alongside Dan Fuller of Bellefontaine Cemetery and Arboretum, helped "connect the dots" regarding the mystery of Bates's interment there. The archivists at the Missouri History Museum Library and Research Center were incredibly helpful and generous with my requests to locate and photograph papers pertaining to Bates's life and times; my research assistant, Liz Bird, meticulously transcribed Bates letters and memoranda, and my editor at SIU Press, Sylvia Frank Rodrigue, consistently offered gentle and encouraging advice throughout the writing and editing process—as did my parents, Bill and Dee Dee Neels, my aunt, Nancy Eaves, and my mother-in-law, Pam Berkowitz. Lastly, and most importantly, my wife, Lauren, and my sons, Lincoln and Sam, were there through the peaks and valleys, for which I will forever be grateful.

A NOTE ON STYLE

Before proceeding with the narrative, I must mention a stylistic choice that appears early in the text. As a rule, I refer to Edward Bates throughout the book as "Bates." The exception to this is in chapter 1, when I discuss how he navigated the same circles as his older brother, Frederick. As Bates moved out of his brother's shadow and came into his own, reference to him in the narrative switches to the more common "Bates" and continues as such until the conclusion. Only in instances when he is referenced alongside another member of the Bates family does the narrative revert to the use of first name only.

LINCOLN'S CONSERVATIVE ADVISOR

Introduction

In July 1864, residents of Washington, D.C., assembled at the White House for the unveiling of artist Francis Bicknell Carpenter's newest work: *The First Reading of the Emancipation Proclamation of Abraham Lincoln*. The painting was monumental. Measuring nine feet tall by fifteen feet wide, it received general praise for its depiction of a watershed moment in American history. On second glance, however, it becomes clear that the artist captured something else as well. Through his careful placement of key figures, Carpenter touched upon the fragmentary nature of the administration—a phenomenon he witnessed firsthand during his six months in residence at the White House.

Lincoln sits in the foreground, left of center—a position that speaks to his place in history as the "Great Emancipator." Flanking him on his right and left, respectively, sit Secretary of War Edwin Stanton and Secretary of State William Seward. Treasury Secretary Salmon P. Chase, meanwhile, stands behind Lincoln with arms crossed. The placement of these men emphasizes their importance in carrying out the policy of emancipation. Perhaps the most telling, though, is the position of the rest of the cabinet. Right of center sits Secretary of the Navy Gideon Welles, and behind him stands Interior Secretary Caleb Smith and Postmaster General Montgomery Blair. The three men are separated from Lincoln and the aforementioned trio by the cabinet table, which serves as a literal representation of the ideological barrier existing between them. Lastly, at the far right, away from everyone else and nearly enveloped by shadows, sits Attorney General Edward Bates with arms crossed—a mirror image of Chase, but bearing an expression of disappointment and resignation.

Why does Bates seem so unenthusiastic about Lincoln's crowning achievement? Did he possess a certain philosophical conviction missing among Lincoln's other advisors? This book sets out to answer these questions by examining Bates's life and, particularly, his role as a conservative advisor to Abraham Lincoln. In the end, more than simply highlighting the conflict within Lincoln's administration, Bates's example lays bare the strong philosophical divisions within the Republican Party during the Civil War era. These divisions were present at the party's founding, crystallized during the war, and ultimately sparked a political realignment during Reconstruction. Bates was at the center of this divide for most of its existence, and in some cases he assisted in its promulgation. This is his story.

This study joins a seventy-year-long conversation around the role of ideology in American politics. At midcentury, Richard Hofstadter believed that American political parties, the politicians who represented them, and the people who supported them possessed no discernable ideological differences from one another. T. Harry Williams concurred, arguing that politicians in the Civil War era self-identified as conservative or radical not on ideological grounds but out of opposition to the agenda of the other party. Lee Benson took only a marginally different approach, noting that no ideology existed in the antebellum period, but also arguing that voters and politicians nurtured allegiances to political parties by harkening to voters' ethnic, socioeconomic, and religious characteristics.[1]

During the centennial of the Civil War and the bicentennial of American independence, historians began reevaluating these earlier arguments. Bernard Bailyn found that seventeenth-century ideas about power and liberty influenced Americans' understanding of the relationship between government and the governed during the Revolution. Lance Banning observed that, in the first two decades of the nineteenth century, Jeffersonians brought these revolutionary ideals of nonpartisanship and virtuous government into the political mainstream. And Joel H. Silbey and Jean Baker extended these arguments to include the Democrats of the antebellum and Civil War years, with Silbey arguing that Democrats possessed ideas and values that they refused to compromise even at the sake of electoral defeat while Baker traced the origins of those ideals to the populist persuasions of the Jacksonian era. Eric Foner, Michael F. Holt, and Daniel Walker Howe applied these methods to the Whigs and Republicans, observing that a person's residency North or South naturally created differences of opinion about the principle of republicanism that, in turn, led Americans, on the eve of war, to envision themselves as living within separate nations.[2]

The discourse over political ideology in American history has not let up in the last thirty years. In the 1980s, William Gienapp's pivotal study of the antebellum Republicans synthesized much of the work of earlier historians. For instance, he agreed with Foner and Holt that Republicans possessed a collective faith in classical republicanism, but he also echoed the midcentury scholars in observing that Republican leadership possessed a clear set of sectional values and strongly condemned the failure of the older political parties to provide solutions to major problems facing the nation. Lawrence Kohl made similar conclusions about the Jacksonian era, rejecting the notion that politics in this time was banal and finding that, as Americans built a new social order, political parties were integral to sorting out the ideals upon which that society would be built. In contrast, Aaron Astor, Joshua Lynn, and Adam I. P. Smith have each recently argued that the high-minded republican ideals to which antebellum conservatives clung were "imagined," thus failing them as they confronted the pressures of unfolding events. In the absence of a true set of ideals, conservatives in the border states were instead driven by opposition to wartime extremism and a desire to maintain the racial hierarchy of the antebellum period.[3]

At times, particularly early in his life, Edward Bates's political affiliation was guided more by reaction than principle. His father and brothers were Jeffersonian; therefore, he was too. By the Jacksonian era, however, Bates had developed a distinct political philosophy. As Joyce Appleby has observed, Bates's generation, born between 1776 and 1800, was forced by the destruction of their parents' world to build their own society anew. They were free to imagine what the new United States might become. In doing so, they relied on their peers, as opposed to their parents, as role models. In a sense, the separation from Great Britain—the irrevocable break from the past—made this generation feel that America was a blank slate. They could hold on to the values of the past, or they could discard them altogether. Whichever way members of this generation went determined the radicalism and conservatism of the mid-nineteenth century. By the time Bates's generation grew into their middle and sunset years, they had successfully built a society that valued limited government, a free-enterprise economy supported by fervent Christian ideals of hard work, and a caste system that allowed slavery to thrive alongside white economic prosperity. The establishment of these core values, however, left the next generation little room to exercise its own intellectual autonomy, and when that generation attempted to plot its own course, it was met with resistance from the older one. Indeed, a link exists between Bates's Whiggishness and the Burkean conservatism of eighteenth-century England in that both placed a premium on the maintenance of established political and social traditions, with only gradual change over time. These were strong values that he possessed the rest of his life and that drove him to battle what he perceived as the corruption of wartime Democrats and the radicalism of postwar Republicans.[4]

This book also joins a growing field of Lincoln studies that analyzes Lincoln's presidency through the eyes of his contemporaries. In 1936, J. G. Randall famously asked in the *American Historical Review*, "Is the Lincoln Myth Exhausted?" The response from the Lincoln community has been an emphatic "No." For almost twenty years now—since the publication of Doris Kearns Goodwin's *Team of Rivals* as well as the commemorations of the bicentennial of Lincoln's birth and the sesquicentennial of the Civil War—there has been a plethora of new works on Lincoln's cabinet secretaries. This is by no means a new phenomenon. The first biographies of Seward, Chase, and Stanton were published within years of their deaths. The early decades of the twentieth century also saw new biographies of these men, but the first truly scholarly examinations appeared in the leadup to the Civil War centennial. Burton Hendrick's *Lincoln's War Cabinet*, David Donald's *Lincoln's Herndon*, and Fletcher Pratt's *Stanton* paved the way for Benjamin Thomas and Harold Hyman's magisterial *Stanton*, Glyndon Van Deusen's *William Henry Seward*, and Marvin Cain's *Lincoln's Attorney General*—to this date, the only extant full-length biography of Edward Bates. John Niven gave Gideon Welles his own scholarly treatment in the 1970s, and new works on Salmon Chase by Niven and Frederick Blue were published in the mid-eighties and nineties.[5]

Since the Lincoln bicentennial, there have been a slew of new biographies on Lincoln contemporaries such as Mary Lincoln, Robert Todd

Lincoln, Frank Blair Jr., William Pitt Fessenden, and Edward Everett. New examinations of the cabinet secretaries have also appeared, including Walter Stahr's biographies of Seward, Stanton, and Chase, as well as Paul Kahan's life of Simon Cameron and William Marvel's recent life of Edwin Stanton. Even Lincoln's personal secretaries, John Hay and John Nicolay, have been the subject of at least two books in the past decade. These studies benefitted from an explosion of scholarship on the Civil War era since the sesquicentennial, as well as an abundance of newly available primary source material through digitization projects at the Library of Congress, the National Archives, and the Abraham Lincoln Presidential Library and Museum. Yet there is still work to be done. There has not been a new biography of Gideon Welles for the better part of fifty years, and this book humbly attempts to rectify a similar gap in scholarship on Bates.[6]

Thomas Fleming Bates Family Tree

Thomas Fleming Bates
11/01/1741–05/26/1805

Caroline Matilda Woodson Bates
10/17/1751–10/15/1845

1770s

Charles Fleming
05/10/1772–05/30/1808

Sarah
11/25/1773–08/12/1859

Tarlton
05/22/1775–01/08/1806

Frederick
06/23/1777–08/04/1825

Fleming
02/27/1779–12/26/1830

1780s

Richard
07/10/1781–05/03/1811

Susannah
04/21/1783–07/14/1805

Margaret
08/25/1785–?

James Woodson
08/25/1787–12/26/1846

Anna (Nancy)
02/07/1789–12/13/1813

1790s

Caroline
02/20/1791–10/16/1811

Edward
09/04/1793–03/25/1869

Edward Bates Family Tree

Edward Bates
09/04/1793–03/25/1869

Julia Davenport Coalter Bates
03/14/1807–10/15/1880

1820s	*1830s*	*1840s*	*1850s*
Joshua (Barton) 02/29/1824–12/27/1892	**Maria** 01/14/1831–03/28/1832	**Matilda** 01/21/1840	**Catherine** 03/12/1850–07/27/1850
Holmes 06/21/1826–07/28/1827	**Julian** 01/07/1833–07/20/1902	**Kora** 06/20/1841–11/06/1842	**Julia** 11/13/1852–09/26/1854
Nancy 12/11/1827–10/17/1872	**Fleming** 04/02/1834–12/08//1871	**John** 08/26/1842–02/04/1919	**David Coalter** 04/06/1856–01/29/1858
Fanny 04/11/1829–03/18/1830	**Richard** 12/12/1835–09/25/1879	**Charles** 08/26/1842 -02/01/1893	
	Edward 02/13/1838–11/16/1846	**Ben** 09/17/1847–10/07/1848	

1.
Son of Virginia, Father of Missouri

The James River, one of the mightiest waterways in Virginia, stretches from the Appalachian Mountains to the Chesapeake Bay. It is surpassed in size only by the Potomac and the Roanoke. But what it lacks in size, the James more than makes up in rich history. Here at Jamestown in 1607, England began its long march to empire. Within a generation, new villages such as Norfolk, Williamsburg, and Richmond sprouted up to the west. Not far from the river's banks, at Shadwell Plantation in Goochland County, Thomas Jefferson was born in 1743. And it was in this same county that Edward Bates, the youngest son of Thomas Fleming Bates and Caroline Woodson, was born on September 4, 1793.

Edward was descended from a long line of Virginians stretching back to John Bates, his fourth great-grandfather on his father's side, and John Woodson, his fourth great-grandfather on his mother's. Both men immigrated to the colony in 1624, where their offspring produced prosperous men of society. John Bates's son, John II, for instance, was known as "John the Quaker" for hosting large gatherings of the Society of Friends, and he counted among his possessions vast landholdings in York and New Kent Counties as well as over twenty enslaved people. John Woodson's son, Robert, similarly owned a large plantation near White Oak Swamp in York County.[1]

Large families with ten children on average were common in both Thomas's and Caroline's ancestral lines. When they were married on August 8, 1771, the happy couple hoped to continue the tradition. In quick succession, Caroline gave birth to three children—Charles Fleming in 1772, Sarah in 1773, and Tarleton in 1775. After Thomas moved the family to Goochland County in 1776 and established a farm named Belmont, they welcomed an additional nine children. Frederick was born in 1777, Fleming in 1779, Richard in 1781, Susannah in 1783, Margaret in 1785, James in 1787, Anna (known as Nancy) in 1789, Caroline in 1791, and finally Edward in 1793.[2]

Goochland was typical of the Virginia Piedmont. The primary crop before the Revolution was tobacco, which required a large, enslaved labor force for cultivation. Later, when farmers switched to wheat, many sold their excess enslaved workers to farmers in Virginia's southern counties, where the cotton boom put them in high demand. Still, as late as 1790, Goochland's enslaved population nearly equaled its free population—4,658 of Goochland's 9,053 residents were enslaved, and an additional 257 were "free persons" other than white. The Bates children were thus exposed to slavery—and its effects—from a young age.[3]

Thomas proved typical of enslavers in this region, being prosperous enough to have more than five enslaved laborers. Caroline herself was deeded six enslaved persons—a woman named Phillis and her three sons and two daughters—by her father, Charles Woodson, in 1781. The Bateses were also not above using violent means to coerce their enslaved laborers to work. Years later, Frederick remembered Caroline counseling her children to avoid enslaving others; not because of any moral scruples she held toward the institution but because "nothing but discipline could make [enslaved people] profitable."[4]

Despite the oppressive force of slavery in their midst, the Bates children thought warmly of their parents and their home at Belmont. Overlooking Thomas's status as an enslaver, Onward, Thomas's great-grandson, remembered him as "a man of peace, born and bred in the doctrines of the Quaker sect and so imbued with these doctrines that they were illustrated in his whole life and transmitted to his posterity." Indeed, Quakerism was a common thread among the Bates ancestors. Yet when the war came, Thomas departed from his pacifist ways to fight in the Battle of Yorktown.

Later, Caroline was dismissed from the Society of Friends for, Onward presumed, being an enslaver of Black servants. "Thoughtless descendants may undertake to be critical of one who was a slave holder and who was apparently turned out of the Quaker Church," Onward later wrote of his great-grandmother, "and I ask such to consider the conditions existing at the time and never forget that our grandmother Caroline was revered as a remarkable woman and very much beloved. . . ." Regardless of the occasion for their leaving the sect, the values of Quakerism—frugality, modesty, pacifism—remained central to their way of life.[5]

If, in their reminiscences, the Bates children chose to dismiss the detrimental effects of slavery on the family at Belmont, they also glossed over some of the harsh economic realities of life in post-Revolutionary Virginia. Thomas's mercantile career, in which he had been engaged ten years before Yorktown, was dealt a hard blow by trade restrictions and British general Charles Cornwallis's raids through the region. By October 1801, he was forced to sell off much of his property to satisfy his creditors. Still, Thomas never regretted his military service. Years later, he recalled: "It pleased heaven to grant us independence, at the price of ruin & devastation to many." Independence notwithstanding, Thomas's financial troubles meant that Edward and his brothers—unlike their illustrious ancestors—could rely on little in the way of inheritance to help establish them in life.[6]

Overall, as was common for the first generation after independence, the Bates sons managed to do quite well. For them, a new energy seemed to have been unleashed by the Revolution. Commercial and political opportunities were ripe for the taking by young men hungry to make something of themselves and, in turn, build a new society. Of Thomas and Caroline's eldest sons, Frederick achieved the greatest success and became the idol of young Edward. He first undertook the study of law in 1795, then became the postmaster of the Goochland County Court. In 1797, he was appointed to the quartermaster's department of the Army of the Northwest and moved to Detroit. There, he went into business as a merchant, and would have made a lasting career of it had a fire not consumed much of the town, and his goods with it, in June 1805. But Frederick soon realized that his talents were best suited for politics, and the family's affiliation with the rising Democratic-Republican Party accounted for his luck in that profession. As far back as Edward could remember, Jeffersonian republicanism had been a bedrock of his family's political faith. Much of his early education involved watching his father and his brothers work for Jefferson's election in 1800. In return, the president rewarded Frederick first with a position as receiver of the public monies at Detroit, and then—in quick succession—as territorial land commissioner, associate judge of the Michigan Territory; and, finally, in 1807, as secretary of the Louisiana Territory and recorder of deeds in the city of St. Louis. Shortly thereafter, Frederick left Detroit for his new home—a small French village on the west bank of the Mississippi River.[7]

While Frederick's star was rising in the West, back in Virginia, Thomas died on May 26, 1805, leaving the family, for a time, in dire straits. Twelve-year-old Edward was briefly tutored by his mother and sisters, but the young man may have been too much for a mother touched with grief, for she soon sent him to live with his uncle, Benjamin (Thomas's brother), in Hanover Courthouse. There, he studied mathematics, philosophy, and history before—once his late father's estate was settled—entering into further instruction in English and the classics at Charlotte Hall Academy in Maryland. Still, adventure, not academics, captured the young man's imagination. Realizing this, a friend of the family managed to get Edward an appointment as a midshipman in the navy, but Caroline forbade it. When war broke out again with England in June 1812, however, she could not keep her son from taking up his father's Revolutionary War musket and joining the Virginia militia.[8]

Edward's military career was brief. He was mustered into service in February 1813, assisted in the defense of Norfolk, and mustered out by October—missing by a year some of the most exciting action in that theater of the war. Left with few prospects at home, he drifted about for several months, pondering his future, before being inspired by Frederick's letters detailing the prosperity to be found in Missouri, as well as his own quick social advancements. With nothing to gain by staying in Virginia, in February 1814, Edward started west. He was twenty years old.[9]

St. Louis was an auspicious place to make a start. Established fifty years earlier as a French fur-trading post, the village was now capital of the Missouri Territory. Along its dirt streets and its wharves could be found, as Washington Irving later described, a melting pot of European and American cultures: "Here were to be seen about the river banks [sic], the hectoring, extravagant, bragging boatmen of the Mississippi, with the gay grimacing, singing, good-humored Canadian voyageurs. Vagrant Indians, of various tribes, loitered about the streets. Now and then, a stark Kentucky hunter, in leathern hunting-dress, with rifle on shoulder and knife in belt, strode along."[10]

Much of the whirl and rush that Irving described, however, was sustained by forced labor. In 1820, only six years after Edward arrived, St. Louis County was home to 1,800 enslaved people owned by a mere 10 percent of white families. But if only a small number of white people kept Black people captive, the desire to acquire enslaved people, combined with the fact that enslavers held a monopoly on political power, portended a rise in the enslaved population in the coming years. Indeed, within a decade, the number of enslaved people in St. Louis had doubled.[11]

Slavery here was markedly different from what Edward had known back in Virginia. In St. Louis, enslaved people enjoyed a certain amount of freedom denied to their counterparts on rural farms and plantations. Some were allowed to live in homes separate from those of their enslavers, much to the chagrin of rural white people who feared such liberties would only aggravate an underlying desire among the enslaved population for emancipation. Their concern was worsened by the fact that just across the Mississippi River, freedom beckoned in the form of the free territory of Illinois. To that end, St. Louis's white population maintained a strong grip on enslaved Black people through coercion and intimidation by police and vigilance committees. Indeed, public executions of captured fugitives from slavery were a common sight during this time.[12]

Upon arrival, Edward reconnected with Frederick. At the time, the older brother was deep in the political mire surrounding the trial for treason of former governor of Louisiana James Wilkinson in connection with the machinations of former vice president Aaron Burr. In 1807, Jefferson had sought to replace Wilkinson with a trustworthy administrator. He settled upon his personal secretary, Meriwether Lewis, but Lewis did not arrive to take up his post for nearly a full year after his appointment. Frederick, in the interim, was acting chief executive and, by all accounts, proved a fair and able administrator. Once Lewis arrived, however, Frederick ceded his authority to the tardy governor, who knew nothing of local issues and showed little interest in learning. Unable to control the various factions among the St. Louis gentry, Lewis became irascible and uncomfortable in social settings where he was not the center of attention—symptoms of the depression that may have led to his suicide in Nashville, Tennessee, in October 1809.[13]

Lewis's death paved the way for Frederick's second stint as acting governor. From October 1809 to April 1810, he carefully repaired the damage and, again, became renowned for his fair and balanced administration. Of particular concern was Lewis's failure to execute laws curbing land speculation. Frederick, in contrast, was so strict in his enforcement that, at one point, a St. Genevieve speculator who had profited from Lewis's mismanagement challenged him to a duel. Frederick wisely avoided the duel, and President James Madison eventually nominated a replacement—first, Benjamin Howard in 1810 and then, in 1812, Lewis's old fellow explorer, William Clark. Frederick then returned to his position as territorial secretary, where he remained until Missouri won its bid for statehood in 1821.[14]

For Edward, being the younger brother of such a prominent figure had its benefits, not least of which was the introductions it provided to powerful men of society. Both Frederick's enemies and his friends were worth knowing. His rivals, known as the St. Louis Junto, fiercely defended their claims to vast landholdings granted by the old Spanish government of Louisiana. Among the most prominent was Edward Hempstead, the one-time attorney general for the territory whom Frederick had forced from office in 1810 over Hempstead's attempt to award a patronage post to a corrupt former sheriff. Also of importance was Thomas Hart Benton, an up-and-coming attorney who had immigrated to Missouri from Tennessee, where he served for a time as a state senator and close military aide to General Andrew Jackson, with whom he had a falling out over Jackson's position as second in a duel involving Benton's brother, Jesse.[15]

Frederick's friends, like their Junto adversaries, were also young land speculators. Influential among them was David Barton, a veteran of the War of 1812 and Hempstead's successor as attorney general before he was promoted by Governor Clark to judge of the Northern District of Missouri. One of the most well-liked men in Missouri, Barton, in 1818, won election to the territorial legislature, where he was chosen speaker.[16]

Equally important was Rufus Easton, who served as chief clerk of the Louisiana Territory before being elevated by President Jefferson to the Territorial Supreme Court. In 1812, Easton ran unsuccessfully against Hempstead for a seat on the Territorial Legislative Council. Two years later, he won the race for nonvoting delegate to the U.S. House of Representatives. It was during his term in Congress, as he traveled back and forth between Washington and St. Louis, that Edward Bates asked Easton to tutor him in the law.[17]

Studying law involved reading legal tracts in an established attorney's private library. The sense of responsibility an attorney owed to society was the one universal characteristic imparted to his pupils. It was no surprise, then, that many attorneys later entered politics. At the end of his tutelage, the aspiring pupil took an examination administered by a council of judges who either approved or disapproved of his entry into this exclusive club. If he passed, the new attorney could then open shop.[18]

Edward was admitted to the bar in 1816 and, following in the footsteps of his tutor, soon built a reputation in Missouri as a capable land attorney. According to his friend, John F. Darby, he cut a striking figure: "His person was small; he was dressed in the habiliments characteristic of the legal profession of that day . . . ruffles, blue broadcloth coat and gilt buttons . . . some lingering marks of the vestments of the Revolution . . . his suavity of manner and smooth boyish face (as it was then) and bright black eyes made a telling impression on my fancy." For all his looks, his real gifts were oratory and an adeptness at trying cases involving Spanish and French land claims. In carrying out this work, like his older brother, he drew the attention of men of influence. Within the first years of Edward's legal career, Governor Clark appointed him circuit attorney for St. Charles, St. Louis, and Washington Counties. Later in 1820, after he opened his own private practice with his fellow law student Joshua Barton—brother of David Barton—Clark further rewarded him with appointment as attorney for the Northern District of Missouri. From there, he made connections with several more influential figures—including future Missouri governor Alexander McNair—who would have an impact on his later political career.[19]

While Edward's proximity to the St. Louis gentry provided him a level of refinement that he otherwise would have lacked living on the family farm in Virginia, it also provided him with a first-rate education in the volatility of nineteenth-century politics. Disease, accident, and murder were all causes of death on the frontier, but politics—as Frederick had already discovered—could be just as deadly. While the lower classes often settled disputes with fisticuffs, the pillars of the community—attorneys, politicians, businessmen—resolved their differences on the "field of honor."[20]

Dueling was introduced to America during the Revolution by European soldiers fighting in the Continental Army. In the decades since, the first generation of Americans shaped what had been a practice among aristocrats to solve disputes over women and gambling into a uniquely democratic means of resolving political disputes between men with a public image to defend. Whether lawyers, politicians, or newspaper editors, all were subject to the practice. As such, many of Edward's contemporaries engaged in it. Among them, Thomas Hart Benton was the best practiced. In 1816, a year after his arrival in St. Louis, Benton served as second in a duel between Thomas Hempstead—brother of Edward Hempstead—and Edward's law partner, Joshua Barton. In a bloodless confrontation, both parties met on a sandbar in the middle of the Mississippi River directly across from the city, fired their weapons, but failed to meet their mark. They agreed that they were satisfied and pledged each other no further ill will.[21]

Bloodless duels were common—for a man's honor to be restored among his peers, he need only fire his weapon—but because no one was injured in this face-off, Benton and Edward were obligated as witnesses to sign a testimonial stating that Hempstead and Barton had conducted themselves in a manner that was "honorable and correct." In essence, because there were no scars to prove it, both witnesses placed their own honor on the line in vouching for the characters of their friends.[22]

The next year, Benton was involved in another public quarrel—this time with fellow attorney Charles Lucas. Lucas accused Benton of not paying back taxes. Benton denied the claim and demanded satisfaction. The duel on August 12 was bloody, but not deadly. Benton was wounded in the knee while Lucas received a nonlethal wound to the throat. Honor had been satisfied, but not Lucas. A few weeks later, he started a rumor that Benton had left Tennessee in 1814 to escape criminal charges and a prison sentence. Benton, still heated from their previous engagement, again demanded satisfaction. This time, his bullet pierced Lucas's heart.[23]

Three years after the Benton-Lucas affair, in August 1820, Edward found himself in a similar situation. While arguing a case in court, the opposing attorney, Luke E. Lawless, insulted Edward's character. In reply, Edward questioned Lawless's intelligence. That evening, Edward received a hastily scribbled note from Lawless demanding satisfaction. Edward refused on the grounds that his public snipe was "more than justified by the provocation you had first given." Such a response could easily have escalated tensions, but unlike the Benton-Lucas affair, both sides settled their differences off the dueling grounds. Nonetheless, this episode, as well as the previous skirmishes to which Edward had been privy, highlighted the challenges of disentangling personal honor from professional matters in this rough-and-tumble town.[24]

Just as it exposed him to the frontier social dangers, Edward's profession also opened opportunities to participate in politics. The struggle for Missouri statehood, more than any event in his early adulthood, paved the way for his future political success. For two years starting in 1818, the Missouri Territory tried to win Congress's blessing for sovereignty. The first attempt failed after John Scott, Missouri's lone nonvoting delegate to Congress, was unable to convince the House to take up a statehood bill. The next year, easterners in the House passed Scott's bill, but only after ensuring its failure in the Senate by tacking onto it a rider denying the extension of slavery into the new state and mandating gradual emancipation for all enslaved people under the age of twenty-five. When the session ended on March 3, 1819, the matter was left unresolved.[25]

Missourians quickly lost patience with Congress. The extension of slavery was not, to them, a pressing issue. When the matter cropped up in the local press during the summer of 1819, it was rare, and most newspaper editors were surprisingly antislavery in their sentiments. What, then, could be the cause of all this talk of slavery in Washington? Missourians believed it was a conspiracy by the East to hamper the West's growing economic and political power.[26]

In December 1819, Scott again raised the question of Missouri statehood. By this time, Alabama had joined the Union as a slave state, creating an equal balance in the Senate and threatening, again, to defeat Missouri's efforts. At this time, however, another bill admitting Maine as a state was moving through committee, and members saw an opportunity for compromise. In January 1820, the Senate combined the bills while Jesse B. Thomas of Illinois managed to attach an amendment excluding slavery in the remaining Louisiana Territory north of latitude 36°30'. A conference committee then agreed to drop any further restrictions on slavery, and both chambers passed the measure. Finally, on March 6, 1820, after two years of deliberation, President Monroe signed the bill allowing Missouri to draft a state constitution.[27]

The news was met in St. Louis with joy and celebration. Candles lit the windows of homes; bonfires lit the night sky; bells rang, and cannons roared. Once the celebrations were through, the campaign for delegates to the state convention got underway. The singular issue was a question of whether, after a short grace period, Missouri should agree to Congress's recommendation and restrict the further emigration of enslaved people into the state.[28]

Edward's opposition to restriction was the most important attribute in his election to the convention. In April 1820, his name appeared in the *St. Louis Enquirer* alongside eight men deemed "the candidates opposed to the restriction of slavery." A month later, the same paper ran a public letter predicting the danger if restrictionists were elected. Signed MISSOURI, the contents of the letter and style of writing suggest it may have come from Edward's own pen. "I am sensible there is no danger [of restriction]," the author wrote, "if the advocates for the continuance of slavery are united in the convention; but if they *divide*, their adversaries will rise up to widen the breach . . . and thus enable them to obtain by stratagem a victory which they cannot even attempt in open day." Whether Edward wrote it, the sentiments of the letter were clearly shared by the voters. Not a single supporter of restriction was elected to the convention. The people had decided: There would be no further limitations on slavery in Missouri.[29]

On June 12, 1820, Edward joined thirty-nine delegates—including Benton, McNair, and David Barton—in the dining room of the Mansion House Hotel in St. Louis. The first day was largely occupied with preliminary measures, including the election of Barton as president of the convention and William Pettus as secretary. Following a pledge of allegiance to the Constitution of the United States, the convention officially got underway.[30]

The second day was more substantive, with the convention splitting into standing committees tasked with drafting rules for governing debate as well as framing the branches of the state government and drafting a bill of rights. It was here that Edward truly shined as a delegate. The second youngest member at the age of twenty-seven, he chaired the judiciary committee and the subcommittee on style, tasked with arranging and writing the final draft of the constitution. He also single-handedly wrote the constitution's preamble, though the specific language of that section of the charter was lackluster, being devoid of the linguistic eloquence that Edward so often exhibited in the courtroom. Lastly, and perhaps most important to his own governing philosophy, Edward played a pivotal role in inserting language into the constitution allowing for the charter of a state bank.[31]

Within a month, the constitution was finished, and, on July 17, the convention voted to approve the final draft by a margin of thirty-nine to one. The next day, among resolutions to archive and print the constitution,

Edward proposed that it be sent to the heads of the departments of the federal government, as well as the chief executives of the other states and territories. Two days later, on July 19, the delegates met one last time to sign the document. Barton was the first to sign. The other delegates lined up to do likewise—Edward signing on the top right side of the thirty-fifth page. Pettus signed last. After some final preliminaries—including the storing of the convention's furniture for use by the first state assembly—the convention adjourned.[32]

Most of the state constitution was relatively straightforward and un-controversial, consisting of—as was the custom—language lifted from other state constitutions including Alabama, Illinois, Indiana, Kentucky, and Louisiana. But one section proved troublesome. Section 25 of Article II barred the assembly from passing an emancipation law without the consent and compensation of the enslavers. It also prohibited the assembly from barring the emigration of enslavers and their chattel from other states. As a caveat to antislavery men, however, the provision did allow enslavers to emancipate enslaved people on their own, provided the newly freed person promptly left the state. Other states had similarly protected the property of enslavers, but none had gone so far as to expel freed Black people. It was this departure from custom that nearly derailed the Missouri constitution's final approval by Congress.[33]

The dramatic last act of Missouri statehood took place during the winter of 1821, as antislavery men in Washington, unhappy with Missouri's attempt to ban free Black settlement, attempted to bar the state from entry into the Union. Missourians in turn became incensed, interpreting this move as another ploy by Northerners to deny them their sovereignty. After a months-long impasse, Speaker Henry Clay proposed yet another compromise. Congress would grant its approval if Missouri promised, during its first legislative session, to drop the forced expulsion of free Black persons. As a measure of good faith, Congress preemptively passed the statehood bill, and Monroe signed it on August 10, 1821, welcoming Missouri as the twenty-fourth state.

Missourians brought up Clay's suggested compromise in the legislature's first session, but they never intended to keep their end of the bargain. By the time it went down to failure, Edward could exercise no control over the measure's fate. Were he even able to do so, there is no indication that he would have supported it. Adhering to the white supremacy that permeated his class as well as the predominant view among them that freed

Black people would breed unrest among enslaved people, he had agreed with the ban when it was proposed in the convention. As an enslaver, he also benefited from the protections offered by the state constitution. Later in life, he would have many profound things to say about slavery, but for now, the politics of the issue were simply too nascent to register with him personally or professionally.[34]

Moving to Missouri had been good for Edward Bates. He arrived in St. Louis at an exciting moment in the territory's history. Thanks to connections he made with friends of Frederick, he quickly rose from prospectless drifter in Virginia to accepted member of high society. Then, within a mere six years of his arrival, his neighbors elevated him to the state convention, where he managed to put his personal stamp on the constitution that would govern Missouri for the next forty-five years. And now, as voters prepared for the first time to elect their own state government, he would again be presented with opportunities to influence the course of events. Thanks to his work at the state convention, Edward Bates was beginning to move out of the shadow of his older brother and into his own light.

2.

Congressman

In 1821, any public office Edward Bates wanted could be his for the taking, and it was not long before he was presented with the first opportunity for professional advancement. Just two days after the state convention adjourned, the race for governor began as Colonel Alexander McNair and Territorial governor William Clark announced their candidacies.[1]

In many ways, McNair's rise to prominence mirrored Bates's. Born in 1795 into a strong Federalist family in Pennsylvania, McNair thrived in his adopted home of St. Louis. In 1806, Jefferson made him an adjutant in the territorial militia and a justice for the court of common pleas. In 1815, Madison elevated him to federal register of lands for the Missouri Territory. These offices, as well as his status as a capable land attorney, acquainted him with the influential citizens of the territory, and his popularity made him—again like Bates—a logical choice to attend the state convention.[2]

At the national level, thanks to the absence of an opposing political party, Monroe was unchallenged for reelection in 1820, but at the state level, partisan politics was very much alive. To contrast himself with Clark, whom McNair criticized as elitist for spending much of the campaign in absentia, McNair canvassed the state, speaking on issues that resonated with the average voter. It did not matter that Clark's reason for going to Virginia was to care for his dying wife; McNair had effectively painted Clark as elitist while reinventing himself as a man of the people. True, McNair too enjoyed proximity to the St. Louis gentry, leading Clark's surrogates to brand him a hypocrite, but in the end, it mattered little. When the voters went to the polls on August 26, 1820, McNair received 6,576 votes to Clark's 2,656.[3]

On September 18, the new governor and his lieutenant, William Ashley—himself a wealthy and well-known proprietor of the Rocky Mountain Fur Company—appeared before the state legislature and took their oaths of office. McNair then began making appointments to the vacant executive offices. The election was over, but McNair had trouble ridding himself of charges against his character made by the Clark camp. Indeed, an early act of the new governor's seemed only to reinforce the accusation of hypocrisy. During the campaign, he had railed against Missouri's independent judiciary, calling it an elite tribunal. When the time came to make appointments, however, he promoted Edward Bates—the architect of that branch—to the office of attorney general. If nothing else, the appointment confirmed that McNair was not above exploiting his own ties to elite power brokers if it would legitimize his political status.[4]

Bates's and McNair's professional careers followed similar trajectories, but they diverged in their governing philosophies. Bates was more conservative, and his inability to agree with McNair on policy prematurely ended his stint as attorney general. The effects of the Panic of 1819 hit the West just as the new government took office. What began as a panic over an oversupply of cotton on the international market soon forced small banks to suspend specie payments and drove down consumer demand for other manufactured goods. In response, McNair called a special session of the general assembly and urged it to pass legislation authorizing the government to print paper notes to be used as legal tender within the state. He also backed a bill allowing debtors who owned land additional time to pay their debts. McNair's actions, however, troubled the new attorney general who, like his brothers and his late father, was a Jeffersonian at heart. A strict constructionist reading of the state constitution led him to conclude that the government had no legal authority to issue paper bank notes. Because McNair was adamant on pursuing this policy—despite Bates's objection—Bates could not in good conscience continue to support the administration. He therefore resigned his office, and McNair replaced Bates with his old mentor, Rufus Easton.[5]

Bates's prompt resignation did not hamper his political prospects. The next August, his neighbors sent him back to the capital as a member of the House of Representatives. On November 19, 1822, he took his seat in the assembly, now located in the village of St. Charles, while it awaited the construction of a new capital in central Missouri. It was a modest setting, to be sure. The legislative and executive branches occupied the second story of a red brick building on Main Street. A thin wall separated the spacious room into the two chambers of the assembly while the governor conducted business from a small office just off the Senate. The capital's simplicity aside, Bates took his new job seriously. House leaders assigned him to the judiciary committee—a wise choice given his familiarity with that article of the constitution—as well as Ways and Means. In these capacities, he continued to serve as a leading foil to the governor's reform measures. He voted against bills requiring a popular vote for confirming judges and fixing their maximum salaries. He also continued the fight against the type of financial relief efforts that had compelled his resignation the previous year, declaring that the paper currency then in circulation provided no benefit to the people and only further depressed the public credit. While he lost the battle over the alterations to the judicial branch, Bates won the fight over paper notes.[6]

Bates had been elected to oppose McNair's governmental reforms, but he did support some modest alterations to the existing system. These efforts, however, were always driven by his conservative belief in honest governance. One measure to which he lent his support prohibited federally appointed officers from serving simultaneously in private positions within the state. Another required a referendum for amendments made to the constitution by the general assembly.[7]

As the session adjourned in December, Bates's legislative career was off to a successful start, in contrast to his short time as attorney general. His family life mirrored his public one. Sometime after moving his mother, sister, and their enslaved people, from Virginia to Missouri in 1817, Bates met Julia Coalter. Her father, David Coalter, had brought his wife and nine children from South Carolina to Missouri, where they settled in Dardenne

Prairie on a large tract of land not far from Frederick Bates's estate. It was at Coalter's farm that Edward and Julia became acquainted in 1823, and after briefly courting her older sister Caroline, Edward realized his feelings for the younger sibling.[8]

As John F. Darby later described her, Julia was, "when young, a most beautiful woman." A portrait done around this time reveals an oval-shaped face framed by dark hair curled and pinned up in the fashion of the day. She had large dark eyes, a sharp Roman nose, thin lips, and a rounded chin. A contemporary portrait of Edward does not exist, but a lithograph produced thirty years later hints at how he might have appeared at this time. The image shows a pair of deep-set black eyes framed by thick eyebrows and a high forehead. Although by the time this lithograph was produced he had begun to gray around the temples, there nonetheless remains traces of the dark thick mane of his youth. The couple was attractive, if somewhat ordinary looking. Julia's charming personality, however, made up for any lack in her physical appearance. "Modest, gentle, and retiring," Darby continued, "she was calculated to impart happiness around the domestic circle."[9]

On May 15, 1823, Edward proudly wrote to Frederick: "I am to be married on the last Thursday in this month (a fortnight from today), and hope you & my good sister will grace the occasion with your presence. It is not the intention to make any display on the occasion, but as the family connexion is pretty large, and I have invited several of my personal friends, of course there will be a considerable crowd. You will not only gratify me but comply with the wishes of the family by attending." It is uncertain whether Frederick made it to his brother's union—he was not among the witnesses who signed the marriage record—but Edward and Julia were blessed by the attendance at their nuptials on May 29 of other prominent figures including Joshua Barton and federal judge James H. Peck.[10]

Edward's marriage to Julia changed his career plans. Instead of running for reelection, he chose to start a private practice with Joshua Barton. That partnership was cut short, however, by Barton's death in yet another duel. On June 25, 1823, the *Missouri Republican* had published a pseudonymously written letter accusing William C. Rector, surveyor-general of Illinois, of corruption and nepotism. Rector's brother, Thomas, demanded the *Republican*'s editor divulge the author of the slanderous piece. When he learned that Barton was the culprit, Thomas Rector defended William's honor by challenging Barton to a duel. On June 30, they met on Bloody Island—the new name for the sandbar in the middle of the Mississippi—where Rector's bullet tore through Barton's chest.[11]

The Barton-Rector duel unnerved the St. Louis elite. Not only was Barton a highly influential person—having served as Missouri's first secretary of state and, later, as the U.S. attorney for St. Louis—but his brother David was then a serving as U.S. senator. Perhaps no one took his death harder than Bates. John F. Darby later recalled that it was he who took possession of Barton's body and saw him buried in St. Charles. "Bates used to say," Darby wrote, "that [Barton] had the finest legal mind and was the most accomplished lawyer he had ever known."[12]

Julia helped to soften the blow. Later that year, she gave birth to a son, whom she and Bates named Joshua Barton Bates but called Barton for short. Over the next decade, she gave birth to an additional five children: Holmes in June 1826, Nancy in December 1827, Fanny in April 1829, Maria in February 1831, and Julian in January 1833. Holmes, Fanny, and Maria each survived only one year, but more children would follow.[13]

New opportunities for career advancement also took Bates's mind off his friend's death. On June 30, 1824, Monroe appointed him District Attorney. "The transaction of this business," Edward wrote to Frederick, "I think will be worth to me several thousand dollars, and being of a public nature, calculated to attract the attention of the public & the Government, I feel particularly anxious to be enabled to do the business in such a manner as may be creditable both to myself and those whom I represent." In the meantime, he wrote, "I am too busy in court affairs to indulge at present in any political speculations."[14]

Frederick, on the other hand, did have time for politics and was by then bidding for the governor's office. In 1824, McNair declined to run for reelection. The campaign was spirited, with the older established families that—only a decade earlier—had opposed Frederick now supporting him, and the newcomers to the state lining up behind Ashley. In true conservative fashion, Frederick did not actively campaign, prescribing to the notion that to stump for the job made one appear hungry for power. Instead, it was up to the candidate's supporters to convince others to vote for their man. To that end, Edward proved a most loyal surrogate, writing several articles in the local papers tying Ashley to McNair, and both men to the corrupt William C. Rector—the man who had killed Edward's law partner. The tactic worked. On election day, Frederick won by 6,165 votes to Ashley's 4,631.[15]

Edward was elated by his brother's victory. "We were in daily expectation of seeing you in our City," he wrote Frederick from St. Louis on August 24, "& congratulating you on your easy & honorable election. Many of the good folks desire me to salute you *Excellent*." What was more, he scoffed at the notion made by some of Frederick's opponents that the new governor's victory was more a vote for Edward than Frederick. "[Ashley] & his most ardent supporters," Edward wrote, "will have it that you have not been so easily elected over him by the spontaneous wishes of the people, nor on your own solid popularity; but for sooth, that I, even I, E. B. *the great!* Did wickedly & maliciously write & compose devers [*sic*] wise, artful & cunning epistles and did most secretly & with great diligence & labor scatter & disperse them throughout the land, whereby the hearts of the people were suddenly turned & corrupted . . ."[16]

Edward was further pleased when Frederick named his friend, Hamilton Rowan Gamble, secretary of state. Of all of Edward's associates, none so mirrored his own rise to prominence as Gamble. Born in Virginia, he passed the bar and started practicing law the same year as Edward. He also quickly earned renown as a land attorney and, before long, began courting Caroline Coalter, Julia's sister and Edward's first love interest. They were married in 1827. Of Gamble's promotion to secretary of state, Edward wrote, "I think him *fit* for the office, and under present circumstances, I know the office to be particularly well *fitted* for him." The esteem that Edward felt for his future brother-in-law, and which Gamble returned wholeheartedly, would last the rest of their lives.[17]

At noon on November 17, 1824, Frederick Bates took the oath of office as Missouri's second elected governor. He then gave an inaugural address devoid of rhetorical flourishes that simply vowed to provide equal justice to all men. This lackluster opening speech was a harbinger of his term in office. The only exceptions were his surprising veto in January 1825 of a bill that would have outlawed dueling and his refusal to greet the aging Marquis de Lafayette upon his visit to Missouri later that summer.[18]

The veto of the anti-dueling bill was surprising in that Frederick and Edward had lost a brother—Tarleton—to dueling. Joshua Barton's recent death was likewise still a fresh wound to Edward. Frederick's refusal to sign the bill, however, had more to do with his skepticism of the government's role in molding human behavior than any personal hatred for the practice. The second controversy—involving General Lafayette's visit—was more politically damaging. As the fiftieth anniversary of American independence neared, the famous French general made one last visit to the United States, touring the east coast before traveling west. Lafayette was scheduled to arrive in St. Louis in early 1825. He was greeted warmly at each stop, but the conservative strict constructionist simplicities of the Missouri assembly kept it from appropriating funds for his entertainment. In turn, Frederick took the assembly's lack of funding as a directive to refrain from sending any representative to the festivities. The city of St. Louis and its most prominent citizens eventually appropriated funds to entertain Lafayette, but while his visit was remembered for generations, so too was the fact that the state government had snubbed the American hero.[19]

Aside from these controversies, Frederick's governorship was a time of steadiness. It was also short-lived. On August 25, 1825, after taking to his bed with pneumonia, Frederick died suddenly at Thornhill, his mansion in Bonhomme Township. As had Joshua Barton's death a year earlier, the loss of Frederick deeply affected Edward. Thirty-four years later, he still thought affectionately of his older brother. "[Frederick] was a man naturally of good parts," he recalled, "far above mediocrity, and by lifelong practice, methodical and exact in business. A constant and observant reader, well versed in the English classics; not ignorant of French literature; and a good historian of all times. He was no public speaker, having never practiced, but his powers of conversation were somewhat remarkable— fluent always, somewhat brilliant, and generally, at once, attractive and instructive. He was a very ready writer, using some diversity of style, but generally clear, terse and pungent."[20]

The loss may also explain why, in 1826, Edward, now responsible for carrying on the family name, once more ventured into politics. That summer, he challenged John Scott for the position of Missouri's at-large representative to the U.S. Congress. Until then, Bates had been a well-known figure in both St. Louis and St. Charles, but his name was less familiar than his late brother's in the rest of the state. To rectify that, on June 4, he introduced himself statewide through a public letter carried in several state newspapers.

Emphasizing his Jeffersonian roots, Bates wrote, "From my childhood, I was educated in the republican party, and imbibed most of my ideals of general politics from what I believe to have been the doctrines of that party at the time of the accession of Mr. Jefferson to the presidency." Nonetheless, he believed the Republicans had been so altered over the twenty-five years since Jefferson's victory that now "there remains nothing of what was once a great question of principle, but a disgraceful contest about men."[21]

Bates was alluding to the gradual decline of virtuous government and the rise of the professional politician. Honest government was the ultimate shibboleth of Jeffersonianism. The idea was a central tenet of Jefferson's governing philosophy, in which he argued that a public servant should prioritize the interests of the people over his own. Jefferson personally expressed this lofty goal best in his first inaugural address, urging Americans to "arrange themselves under the will of the law, and unite in common efforts for the common good."[22]

Bates was a true believer in virtuous government and harkened to the idea in his comparison of his political record with that of his opponent, Scott. Andrew Jackson had won the popular vote in Missouri in 1824, but a rumor persisted that, to secure a patronage post for his brother, Scott had voted for John Quincy Adams when the House settled the election in February 1825. Even though he personally supported Adams, Bates believed that, by ignoring the popular vote, Scott had violated the will of his constituents. "If I distinctly know the wishes of the state," Bates promised, "I will give the vote accordingly, without regard to my own personal predilections."[23]

Bates also assured voters that, if he were elected, he would not simply be a mindless follower of the Adams administration. "I belong to no party," he asserted: "The expectation of finding any set of men, or any one man, with whom we can agree in all things is idle and extravagant. It is a hope against nature, and contrary to all experience. We have to decide not who is always in the right, but who is least often in the wrong."[24]

In the end, changes in politics meant that, unlike Frederick—who strictly relied on surrogates—Edward was forced to engage in what he saw as the odious practice of lauding his own accomplishments. Even so, he reinforced his distinct conservative ideology in his vehement opposition to base populism—that is, to the tendency of Jacksonian politicians to play to the fear and suspicions of lower-class voters as a means of juxtaposing themselves with upper-class politicians currently holding public office. His congressional record and his public character, he believed, stood as exemplars of his immaculate conduct as a public servant. Given the evidence, whether he would make a good public servant was ultimately for the voters to decide. To that end, on August 10, they chose him over Scott in a landslide.[25]

By 1827, when Bates arrived to take his seat, Washington, D.C., was fast becoming the epicenter of power in America, but it had a long way to go before looking the part. Its two most identifiable features were the newly reconstructed President's Mansion to the west and the Capitol building to the east. Between these graceful structures was a network of dirt roads that turned to seas of mud in the rain, and a cluster of ragtag boardinghouses, churches, taverns, hotels, and government offices. Still, the Capitol was impressive. The House chamber, with its marble columns, gold-fringed red drapes, and cast-steel overhead dome, was a sight unlike anything Bates had seen in his thirty-four years.[26]

The Twentieth Congress came to order on December 3, 1827. Given his work arguing land cases in Missouri courts, Bates was a natural choice to serve on the Committee on Private Land Claims. From there, he was true to his word to be a virtuous representative of his constituents. For instance, he worked on a popular program to make it easier for Missourians to buy public lands for the building of schools and other public venues. When the will of his constituents was less clear, however, he did not hesitate to act on his own intuition. One such case was the issue of slavery. Aside from the brief attention it got during the Missouri statehood debates, the issue had garnered little attention in Bates's home state. Likewise, he did not at that time exhibit any serious emotions about slavery's existence one way or the other. Thus, when offered the opportunity to serve on the House Committee on the American Colonization Society, he did so more out of his own curiosity than any pressure from the voters.[27]

Established in 1817, the society sought to address the conflicting status of the United States as a slave republic predicated on the idea of liberty and equality. During the American Revolution, northern states outlawed the institution. The Constitutional Convention even mandated the closing of the international slave trade after a period of twenty years following ratification of the Constitution. Still, slavery had become lucrative in the cotton-growing states. The result was the establishment of a new domestic trade that relocated most enslaved people to the Deep South, where slavery formed not only the basis of the economy but the social system as well.

At the same time, uprisings of enslaved people on the island of San Domingue in the 1790s and in Virginia in 1800 convinced many Americans that maintaining slavery in their midst could lead to revolution and bloodshed. In that vein, the Colonization Society sought to promote voluntary emancipation connected with compulsory deportation of freed Black people from the United States. In 1822, the society established the independent colony of Liberia on the west coast of Africa, then began publishing pamphlets and newspaper advertisements beseeching white Americans to take advantage of the new settlement to disenthrall themselves of this practice.[28]

In joining the Colonization Society, Bates was making a clear statement. He already owned nine enslaved people—five males and four females—possibly inherited from Frederick or purchased before his death. Still, while Missouri allowed slavery within its borders, it never became the destination that the cotton-growing states did. Bates saw the writing on the wall. Within a short time, he adopted the society's principles of voluntary emancipation and colonization as his own and, in the years to come, vowed to gradually emancipate his enslaved servants as his income made his family more self-sufficient. Within a few months, he was elected vice president of the Colonization Society's St. Louis chapter. As a leading figure in state politics, Bates believed that lending his name to such an important issue would gain it, and himself, much attention. It would be another thirty years, however, before those hopes were fully realized.[29]

Despite Bates's promise to his constituents to be a virtuous representative of their interests, he had nonetheless become a reliable supporter of John Quincy Adams and Henry Clay's policies—specifically what Clay called the "American System," which championed the federal subsidization of bridges, canals, and roads and sought to empower the Second Bank of the United States to issue private loans to Americans. Not only did Bates admire Clay's agenda, but like many of his contemporaries, he was enchanted by the man himself. "When I look upon his manly and bold countenance and meet his frank and eloquent eye," he wrote Julia, "I feel an emotion little short of enthusiasm in his cause. . . . He is a great man—one of Nature's nobles." Such sentiments, however, did not win him many fans at home. As the time for reelection drew near, he found himself out of favor with Missouri voters.[30]

Following the 1826 congressional election, Jacksonian populism swept the state. While Bates stayed true to his principles of honest and virtuous government, it was not enough to stave off a challenge from the highly popular secretary of state, Spencer Pettis. A protégé of Thomas Hart Benton, Pettis staked out positions in the campaign on banking, currency, and tariffs that aligned well with both the senator's agenda and that of Jackson himself. In the contentious presidential rematch of 1828, Missouri overwhelmingly gave its electoral votes to the general, ensuring that Pettis would be the new congressman come March.[31]

Even in the face of mounting political pressure, Bates stayed true to his principles, making him the conservative in the House race in 1828. And though they cost him his job, he refused to reject those values for the sake of political advancement. What was more, and unbeknownst to him, those ideals were soon needed in his home state, where in the coming months a power vacuum among the Anti-Jacksonians gave him an opportunity to infuse his ideals into the development of a new two-party system.

3.
Party Leader

On February 17, 1829, just days before he would leave Washington, D.C., Bates wrote to his friend and brother-in-law Hamilton Gamble, laying out his plans upon returning home. He was determined "to make money, if it can be had in our profession. Devoting all my serious efforts to the law and only attending to my domestic concerns as a recreation & thoughtful labor." Still, Bates could not help worrying at the state of political affairs—especially with the government in the hands of what he called "vandals who are tearing down all that is valuable in the fabric of our constitution." He was discouraged by the obstruction of Jacksonian congressmen to further internal improvement projects during the closing days of the session, and indignant at their refusal to consider any appointments to federal offices made by the outgoing President Adams. As to President-elect Jackson, Bates had heard—accurately, it proved—that he was busily entertaining "a flood of sycophants, office hunters, & toad eaters" who hoped to make a full sweep of pro-Adams officeholders and install themselves in their stead. The promise of what Bates saw as corruption in the name of populism was more than he could bear. Indeed, he would be glad not to witness it firsthand.[1]

Returning to Missouri, Bates set about relocating his family to his farm in Dardenne Prairie and resuming his law practice in St. Louis. To his surprise, before he made much headway, his neighbors implored him to again stand for public office. Dr. Hardage Lane was campaigning in the district for a seat in the state assembly on the old populist promise of making all state judicial offices elective. Hardage also hoped to be a deciding vote in the assembly against sending David Barton—himself an Anti-Jacksonian—back to the U.S. Senate. Because Bates had helped design Missouri's independent judiciary a decade earlier and had fended off similar reform measures under Governor McNair, he was convinced to run for office; in the fall of 1830, he defeated Lane for the seat.[2]

Once more, Bates set out for the state capital, now located at Jefferson City, a small village situated on a bluff overlooking the Missouri River near the center of the state. As he took his seat, he could not help but note the contrasts between the federal capitol's gleaming white marble harkening to the splendor of ancient antiquity and the drafty, six-room brick building that served as both the meeting place for Missouri's assembly as well as the official residence of its governor. Still, Bates treated his new assignment with the same level of respect and seriousness he had given to his previous one at the national level.[3]

Senate leaders once again assigned Bates to the judiciary committee. As he had during his last stint in the assembly a decade earlier, he was instrumental in slowing, if not stopping, the attempt to popularize the state government. In these efforts, however, he again exercised a certain amount of pragmatism, accepting that, in some instances, reforms were necessary. In one instance, he introduced legislation to expand the number of judges on the state supreme court and extend the length of its term. He also proposed increasing the number of circuit courts across the state. His sensible reforms also extended to his other committee assignments, including the committee on education, where he helped incorporate the Missouri Library Association.[4]

Despite his accomplishments, Bates now grappled with a new phenomenon: serving as a member of the minority party. By winning the election, Bates blocked his opponent from deciding David Barton's fate in the assembly, but it was clear once he took office that the Anti-Jacksonians' twenty-seven votes would not offset the Jacksonians' forty-five in the Senate and save Barton's seat. Bates and his fellow partisans hoped to do better in 1832, when Thomas Hart Benton would be up for reelection, but despite their fervent efforts to organize Benton's opponents behind one candidacy, Benton's return to Washington was never in danger.[5]

The Jacksonian successes in the Missouri senate races highlighted the damage Jackson's victory had done to the old Republican Party in Missouri. Over the next few years, desperate pro-Adams men searched for a leader who could communicate their policy positions eloquently enough to make themselves relevant once more with the electorate. By the middle of the decade, Bates—with his championing of nationalist economics and his opposition to populism—effectively became that leader and worked to form what would soon become known as the Missouri Whig Party.[6]

Not until 1833 did Jackson's opponents refer to themselves at the national level as Whigs. In Missouri, they took even longer to adopt that designation. In the meantime, they answered to Anti-Jacksonians, National Republicans, and sometimes simply "the opposition." They were nonetheless identified by common characteristics. They sometimes campaigned for public office but avoided stumping, limiting their efforts to writing essays in the local papers. They insisted that the federal government was a unifying force with the power to promote commercial and industrial expansion through public works and tariffs. They counted among their members a high number of lawyers, merchants, physicians, and shop owners, but in a country largely agricultural, they also courted farmers. Yet despite their promotion of agriculture as a virtuous calling, Whig farmers were usually large property owners who speculated in real estate rather than toiled in the day-to-day grind of subsistence farming.[7]

In contrast, Jacksonians harkened to the concerns of average citizens. In the wake of the Panic of 1819, they condemned wealth and privilege. They also waged a war against banks that, they noted, had weathered the late depression while the average citizen suffered immeasurably. This, they argued, proved that the deck was stacked against the lower classes. Give them the reins of government, they promised, and they would destroy this system of cronyism.[8]

Bates felt firsthand the brunt of the Jacksonians' anti-elitism. During his brief term in Washington, he promoted the subsidization of the construction of a canal linking the Mississippi River to Lake Michigan. His efforts expanded Missouri's access to new and expanding markets but were lost on voters who were taken in by Pettis's criticism of Bates's elitism. Bates was a lawyer; he had supported banking interests in the state constitutional convention; he enjoyed status as the brother of a former governor of the state; and he was well connected with influential people in St. Louis and St. Charles. Bates also had publicly stated his belief that a lawmaker reserved the right, when necessary, to act independently of the voters if he knew better than them the effects of the laws on which he voted. This put him in league with Adams who, in his first message to Congress, suggested that the members avoid being "palsied by the will of our constituents."[9]

Pettis's victory in 1828 proved that Jacksonians had a head start on party organization in Missouri, but, in the following years, Anti-Jacksonians found their voice. Still, as they began to flesh out a coherent policy agenda, Jacksonians countered with a foolproof plan to defeat them—identity politics. Beginning to call themselves Democrats, the Jacksonians claimed that their party was defined simply by allegiance to the seventh president. Jackson was the savior of the country in the War of 1812, and his crusade against the Second Bank of the United States made him a powerful symbol of American populism. His popularity was such that the Anti-Jacksonians simply had no one of similar stature with which to compete.[10]

The congressional election of 1831 was an early indicator of trouble for Anti-Jacksonians. A recent schism in Democratic ranks between those who favored nullification, led by Vice President John C. Calhoun, and those who favored national supremacy, led by Jackson, convinced some Anti-Jacksonians that an opportunity existed to win back Bates's old House seat. To that end, Bates and his friends courted Abiel Leonard, a highly respected attorney from Howard County, to run and put their energy into winning over the Calhounites. Leonard, however, doubted their success, predicting that Jackson's popularity would carry the state and that Pettis would ride his coattails to victory. He therefore declined to run, leaving the Anti-Jacksonians to instead nominate ex-senator Barton. Just as Leonard feared, Democrats successfully painted Barton as a pro-bank elite and vanquished him by an even greater margin than Pettis had defeated Bates in 1828.[11]

In a surprising turn of events, Anti-Jacksonians soon had another chance to win the seat. During the late election, Jackson's war against the Second Bank of the United States boiled over at the local level into a violent feud between Pettis and Thomas Biddle—a major in the U.S. Army stationed at Jefferson Barracks and brother of the bank's president, Nicholas Biddle. During the campaign, both men publicly insulted each other in the local press. With his blood boiling, Biddle escalated the conflict by barging into Pettis's sick room at the City Hotel and assaulting the congressman with a cowhide. A duel was unavoidable, and on August 26—just after the election—they rowed out to Bloody Island and shot each other dead.[12]

St. Louisans were shocked by the senseless violence, but they could not afford to pause long to reflect. Pettis had to be replaced before the next session of Congress began. Democrats William Ashley and Robert W. Wells put their names forward, while Bates and the Anti-Jacksonians, learning the lessons of their recent defeat, backed the lesser of two evils rather than run a candidate of their own. They endorsed Ashley, an affluent member of the St. Louis business community. Meanwhile, Benton, seeing Ashley's candidacy as a dubious plot to divide Democrats, urged his supporters to vote for Wells. In the end, the strategy worked: Ashley won by a narrow margin.[13]

The lesson was clear. Throughout the remainder of the 1830s, Anti-Jacksonians concluded that their best hope at electoral success lay in serving as a moderating influence among Democrats. In 1833, they backed Dr. John Bull, a pro-bank Democrat in the same mold as Ashley, who squeaked out a victory over anti-bank Democrat George Strother for a newly apportioned congressional seat. Still, the anti-bank Democrats remained a formidable force in the state. They defeated Bull's bid for reelection, and when Ashley, citing ill health, declined another congressional term in 1836, they also won back his seat. Meanwhile, in the gubernatorial elections of 1832 and 1836, anti-bank Democrats Daniel Dunklin and Lilburn Boggs kept a tight hold on the governor's mansion. Missouri's senate seats likewise remained firmly in their grip.[14]

In October 1839, Anti-Jacksonians in the state assembly, believing that the absence of a formal political party might be responsible for their electoral woes, officially organized the Missouri Whig Party. At their first convention, held in Jefferson City, they nominated candidates for governor and lieutenant governor, congressmen, and presidential electors. Unlike earlier years, where they had supported moderate Democrats, each Whig candidate now stood firmly on an established platform opposing the hard-money, anti-bank policies of Benton and President Martin Van Buren. Yet while William Henry Harrison's presidential candidacy injected excitement into the national election, Whigs continued their losing streak in Missouri. Van Buren lost the White House, but he won Missouri by over seven thousand votes. The Democratic gubernatorial candidate, Thomas

Reynolds, did even better, defeating Whig candidate John Bullock Clark by seventy-four hundred votes. Missourians also returned a Democratic majority to the state house. Democrats, furthermore, would enjoy a monopoly on the governor's mansion for the next twenty years.[15]

The campaigns of the 1830s provided a valuable lesson to Bates and his Whig colleagues. The popularity of Jackson—even though he was no longer in office—kept his party in good favor in Missouri. The Whigs would spend the next two decades vigorously expounding their principles and seeking converts to their cause, but while the cult of Jackson remained strong, the Whigs would always be in the minority.[16]

By 1840, Bates no longer held a government office. After trading the Missouri senate for the house in 1832, he sensed the winds of political change in his own district and declined to run for another term. His absence from public office did not end his political career, however. As a private citizen and prominent attorney, he continued to support and lead the fledgling party—albeit from the wings rather than center stage.[17]

In many ways, the emergence of St. Louis as a modern metropolis mirrored Bates's rise in political influence. After a slump during the Panic of 1819, the 1820s saw a boom in commerce as, following Mexican independence in 1821, St. Louis became a jumping-off point on the Santa Fe Trail. In 1831, Congress designated the city a port of entry for foreign goods. By 1841, with nearly two thousand steamboat landings a year, St. Louis was second only to New Orleans in river traffic.[18]

Merchants still bartered in the old fur trade, but now visitors to the city also enjoyed access to booksellers, banks, brokerage and insurance firms, dry goods shops, butcher shops, jewelers, and wholesale warehouses. Goods from the southwest, such as woven wool, silver, horses, and mules were soon being exchanged for eastern commodities including cotton, linens, silks, and manufactured tools.[19]

As the commercial district grew, so too did the city's residential and government districts. The new circuit court was completed in the 1820s; the new city hall was finished in the next decade. Hotels, boardinghouses, and brothels also popped up along the levy, and by the middle of the next decade, more commercial and private lots were developed all the way to Jefferson Barracks, ten miles to the south.[20]

Bates and his family benefited personally and professionally from this rapid expansion. In 1846, as a means of cutting down costs and time traveling between Dardenne Prairie and his law offices in St. Louis, they moved to a new home six blocks from the commercial center. The house was a three-story brownstone, the upper windows of which provided a magnificent vista of the city and the river beyond. As described by Bates, the place carried about it "every sign of being healthy as well as pleasant."[21]

The city's booming commercial activity, which Bates could observe from the comforts of his own study, also provided an opportunity for him and his colleagues to highlight the effects of Whiggish policies. The source of their attention was the old dueling grounds at Bloody Island, which, during the 1830s, had grown from the collection of silt, making it an impediment to the bustling traffic on the St. Louis wharf. In 1834, realizing that the state lacked the necessary funds to mitigate the problem, Bates and his colleagues in the assembly had requested that Congress intervene. Two years later, Congress appropriated $65,000 and deployed the Army Corps of Engineers under the management of Virginian Robert E. Lee to build a series of wing dams reinforcing Bloody Island's western shore and deepening the river in front of the wharf. Within a decade, St. Louis was saved. The channel on the island's eastern side dried up, while the western waterway remained deep enough for large steamboats to pass the whole year round.[22]

For Whigs, the Bloody Island improvement project was a shining example of the American system's potential. However, the Panic of 1837 and the electoral successes of Democrats in the 1840s put a damper on any future projects. In 1846, Congress passed the Rivers and Harbors Act, allowing for the appropriation of funds to improve other rivers, but President James K. Polk vetoed it on the grounds that the bill was an unconstitutional extension of federal power. Polk's action provoked frustration within the northern wing of his own party, as well as among the Whigs who hoped to capitalize on it in the presidential election of 1848.[23]

In response to the veto, Bates's fellow St. Louisan, William Hall—a Democrat, but one who recognized the importance of river improvements—called for a convention in support of internal improvements to meet in Chicago on July 5, 1847. Eventually, thanks to Hall's efforts and a little help from the national Whig newspapers, over ten thousand people—including Bates—attended. Boarding a steamboat from St. Louis to Peru, Illinois, Bates then took a stagecoach overland to Chicago, sitting up with the driver much of the way to inspect construction of the Illinois and Michigan Canal. The canal had taken years to get started, but it too gave credence to the power of the American system and put Chicago on the map.[24]

On July 5, the convention came to order beneath a large circular tent. Here, Bates and forty-four of his fellow Missourians joined some of the nation's foremost advocates for the American system. Among them were New York newsmen Horace Greeley and Thurlow Weed, Indiana newsman Schuyler Colfax, and, among the Illinois delegation, the newly elected Whig congressman from Sangamon County, Abraham Lincoln. Bates himself was at the center of activity. Due largely to his reputation as a founding father of the Missouri Whig Party, as well as his status as a pillar of the community in the country's second largest river city, the convention elected him as its president.[25]

On the first day, spectators heard speeches from several national figures, but nothing stirred the crowd like Bates's opening address. Not expecting this honor, he had not prepared any notes and was forced to speak extemporaneously. As his friend William Van Ness Bay later recalled, "Mr. Bates was a natural orator, and gifted with all the graces of elocution. He had a sweet, musical voice, and words fell from his lips without any apparent labor. Whether in a deliberative or promiscuous body, at a dinner party or social gathering, he could make an interesting speech without a moment's preparation, and upon any subject that could be introduced." True to form, Bates's address entranced the spectators to such an extent that the reporters present failed to attend to their notepads. "The speech," Weed later wrote, "if ever published as delivered, will be pronounced one of the richest specimens of American eloquence." J. C. Edwards of O'Fallon, Missouri, later lamented, "No account that can now be given will do it justice." The minutes of the convention are equally unhelpful at divulging the content of the speech—they merely described Bates's remarks as "appropriate." In the end, although it had a profound impact on its audience, what was arguably the greatest oratorical achievement of Bates's life was lost to history.[26]

The convention was a rare moment in American politics. Northern Democrats joined Whigs in pledging their support for improvements and affirming to the rest of the nation the benefits of such projects. Among supportive Democrats were former president Van Buren, Governor Silas Wright of New York, and Bates's own adversary, Thomas Hart Benton. On the second day of the convention, letters from these men, as well as Henry Clay, were read aloud and received much acclaim. Benton's letter, particularly, intrigued Bates. Having been invited to attend, Benton regretted having to decline and asked that his absence not be construed as opposition to the constitutionality of internal improvements. Citing the booms presented by the Erie and Illinois canals in navigation and commerce, Benton wrote: "I never had a doubt of the constitutionality or expediency of bringing that navigation within the circle of internal improvement by the federal government, when the object to be improved should be one of general and national importance."[27]

Although Democrats and Whigs set aside their differences on this issue, under the surface varying degrees of separation remained. Pennsylvania Whig Andrew Stewart, for one, gave a rousing speech supporting the use of federal power in construction projects like those mentioned in Benton's letter. In response, David Dudley Field, a Democrat from New York, argued that the Erie and Illinois canals were not good examples of federal projects, because both were contained within a single state. The enumerated powers of the Constitution, he explained, limited federal subsidization only to those projects that were national in scope. Field's response aroused much consternation among the Whigs, but as Greeley later wrote, "For my part, I rejoiced that the wrong side of the question was so clearly set forth."[28]

Ultimately, the delegates agreed on fifteen resolutions to present to Polk and Congress. Because the revenue raised by the federal government through taxation belonged to the people, the convention asserted, those funds must be applied to the "common interests" of internal trade and navigation. In the past, the central government fulfilled its obligation by erecting lighthouses and constructing piers and breakwaters for Atlantic harbors. So far, however, it had failed to give the same attention to the Great Lakes and the major riverways of the West. If anyone raised sectional arguments against the central government's authority to do this, the document declared, that person "must be wanting in information of the extent of the commerce carried on upon those lakes and rivers, and of the amount of teeming population occupied or interested in that navigation." It was a strong assertion of the growing prominence of nationalism.[29]

Bates believed that the issues raised at the convention surpassed partisan politics. He was disheartened at first that the presence of more Whigs than Democrats would give the convention a political taint. But the fifteenth resolution helped to allay that concern: "We disavow all and every attempt to connect the cause of internal trade and 'commerce among the States' with the fortunes of any political party, but that we mean to place that cause upon such immutable principles of truth, justice, and constitutional duty as shall command the respect of all parties, and the deference of all candidates for public favor." It was a sentiment that Bates would embrace wholeheartedly in his public career over the coming decade.[30]

What most surprised Bates about the convention was the honor and prestige it had bestowed upon him. "The convention," he later wrote, "in its progress & in its results thus far, looks to me more full of public honor & private gratification than any passage of my life." Back in St. Louis a few days later, Bates again reflected: "I do believe that those three days at Chicago have given me a fairer reputation & a higher standing in the nation, than I could have hoped to attain by years of labor & anxiety in either house of Congress. With that I am more than content, and now return to my office & my family, with the resolution to *do* & *to enjoy* with increased energy & satisfaction." He could not have known at the time just how much his participation at the River and Harbor Convention would change the course of his public life.[31]

As Bates's political prospects were resurrected, his hometown continued to mirror his professional trajectory. On November 7, 1847, upon returning by steamboat from a trip to Jefferson City, he marveled at a new technological wonder. "On getting ashore," he later wrote, "I was struck by the unusual brilliancy of the lights along the streets . . . & in many of the stores & shops, and learned, on inquiring, that it was the first experiment of gas-light in the city." A month later came even more innovations. Thanks to the telegraph, on December 10, a mere four days after Polk gave his annual message to Congress, it was printed a thousand miles distant in the *Missouri Republican*. "And so," Bates reveled, "the electric communication between us and the eastern cities is completed." No longer a backwoods town on the distant frontier, St. Louis was now connected to the heartbeat of the nation. "Truly," he concluded, "man is created omnipotent over matter."[32]

The rapid growth, however, came with a price. New buildings were equipped with gas lighting, but on occasion leaks in the plumbing could produce devastating results. In June 1848, an explosion on Water Street leveled a warehouse and blasted out the glass windows of the surrounding buildings. The weather, Bates noted in his diary, had been stormy, leading some to speculate that lightning may have struck the building and ignited a leak in the basement.[33]

Buildings sprouting up around town had brick and marble facades, but the frames and shingled roofs were still made of wood, making them susceptible to fire. This fact was driven home two years later, when on the night of May 17, 1849, cinders falling from the smokestack of a passing steamer ignited a pile of mattresses stored on the upper deck of the paddle wheeler *White Cloud*. Within minutes, the steamer was ablaze. Strong winds then carried the embers to the neighboring steamboats as well as to the freight loaded on the pier. Before long, the nearby warehouses were ablaze, threatening the residential district mere streets away.[34]

As the fire spread, sirens from the steamboats and the clanging of bells from the volunteer fire engines and the churches made a cacophony of noise that robbed hundreds of residents of a peaceful night's sleep. Many of them later recalled standing about, watching as the fires consumed much of the downtown. One citizen, sitting on the upper balcony of her home several blocks away, recalled reading a newspaper by the glow of the flames. Fire companies descended on the riverfront but, because of the scarcity of hydrants, were unable to save the buildings on the north levee. A greater catastrophe was averted only by setting up barricades along several crossroads and even using explosives to demolish buildings directly in the fire's path. By morning, the Great St. Louis Fire had destroyed twenty-three steamers and barges and leveled fourteen city blocks. The city assessor eventually valued the destruction at over $6 million ($208 million today). Thousands were put out of work, hundreds became homeless, and several leading St. Louis businessmen saw their livelihoods destroyed.[35]

Bates fought hard to keep the fire from reaching his neighborhood. Afterward, he toured the devastation with his daughter, describing the scene as "a horrid sight!" It was indeed shocking. A daguerreotype made days later captured the loss. To the east, the foreground was a wasteland of charred rubble—the ruins of once proud warehouses and storefronts. In the distance, the steeple of the St. Louis cathedral stood resolute against the rubble, and just beyond could be seen the tops of homes saved by the hard work of the fire brigades.[36]

The city residents got little reprieve. While the fire raged, St. Louis was also on the cusp of a worse catastrophe. The 1840s had seen a significant population boom. In 1830, just over 14,000 people lived within the city. The next census, however, counted more than 36,000. By 1850, that number nearly tripled to 105,000. More people brought more commerce, but it also increased the spread of disease. To that end, in the last days of December 1848, the citizens learned ominous news from steamboats recently arrived from New Orleans: the Crescent City had fallen victim to the dreaded cholera. One of the worst killers of the nineteenth century, cholera was a swift killer caused by ingesting water contaminated by *Vibrio cholerae*—a pathogen found in human waste. The cause was unknown to medical science at the time, but the symptoms were easy enough to spot. Its onset was marked by acute diarrhea, spasmodic vomiting, and cyanosis—a blue tinting of the skin from a lack of oxygen in the capillaries. Severe dehydration led to circulatory collapse, and death could come within two or three hours. Some unfortunate victims, however, lingered in agony for days.[37]

The virus, it turned out, arrived with the news itself. On December 27, the steamer *Missouri* docked, carrying the bodies of two deckhands who had died suddenly from an illness resembling cholera. Several more of its passengers fell ill and died within days. At the same time, the steamer *Amaranth* docked with thirty confirmed cases onboard. By the end of January, ships carrying cholera were arriving daily—sometimes hourly.[38]

Cholera at first spread slowly among St. Louisans. With the onset of spring, however, its transmission quickened. On February 24, one St. Louis resident noted in his diary that the spring rains were making St. Louis "a very muddy place" The ground was so saturated, he continued, that wagons were sinking to their hubs and the cobblestones were coming loose. Indeed, that spring would prove to be one of the wettest on record, leading another resident to astutely observe the correlation between the current season and the spring of 1833, "when epidemic Cholera prevailed so extensively."[39]

As the rains continued to fall, Bates watched as cholera wracked his community. In late June, he noted that, on average, 60 to 80 persons were dying daily. "Hearses can be seen moving to the different graveyards, at every hour of the day, and even in the night," he wrote. As the days ticked away, the dying only increased. On July 1, he recorded 125 deaths in a single day and a weekly total of almost a thousand.[40]

On that same day, Bates noted that, "by order of the Committee of Health, fires were made all over the City—burning not only light combustibles, but coal, brimstone & tar—Our boys made a grand fire, the heavier materials of which are still (10 A.M.) slowly burning." The use of fire as a purgatory measure was odd for a city still recovering from the conflagration of a few months earlier, but the people had become desperate. The back pages of the *Missouri Republican* were filled with crack remedies such as "Dr. Martin's Compound Syrup of Wild Cherry," and "Dr. Martin's Universal Purgative Pills," alongside "anti-cholera bottled soda," while the *Republican*'s editorial page was pushing an alternative plan. "The great plague in London was stayed in its ravages and totally disappeared, by a remarkably destructive fire that occurred at the time," the editor noted. The same weapon could be wielded now in St. Louis with similar effect. Giving credence to the idea, the Committee of Public Health—charged with mitigating the effects of the epidemic—passed a resolution calling for the daily burning of "shavings, chips, or other dry and combustible materials . . . in the street or alley directly opposite [carpenters'] shops." Later, it ordered block inspectors to enforce the burning of coal, resinous tar, and sulfur in areas especially impacted by cholera.[41]

For all these efforts, though, the epidemic only worsened. By the second week of July, Bates tallied the number of dead at 145 a day. By then, the disease had come directly to Bates's doorstep. On July 8, Peter, a freed Black man in the family's employ, died after a few hours' illness. "We did all that could be done for him during the night," Bates wrote. "At daylight, I went for the physician, and on my return, about sunrise, found to my surprise that he was dead."[42]

By then, St. Louisans had found other ways to mitigate the spread of disease. Chouteau's Pond, located between 8th and 22nd Streets, soon became a focal point of their efforts. More than two miles long and averaging a quarter mile in breadth, it had become a cesspool by 1849—due in large part to the industries that dumped their refuse there. Medical experts still did not know the cause of cholera, but they correctly made a correlation between its spread and the filthy ponds in and around the city. Their theories incorrectly tied cholera's spread to the breathing in of noxious fog coming off these ponds—a process known as *miasma*—rather than from consuming the water itself, but by targeting these bodies of water, they nonetheless inadvertently stemmed the tide of the epidemic.[43]

Bates's home stood on the banks of Chouteau's Pond, and he had long been an advocate for its cleanup. Still, the pond notwithstanding, he and his neighbors continued to attribute their survival to the location of their homes just outside the city limits. To an extent, they were right. Bates's house was on open, high ground. At the time he and his family moved in, the city water pipes did not extend that far, forcing them to secure a supply of drinking water from an eighty-foot well. He also installed cisterns around the house to draw rainwater into it. Thus, while the city residents were drinking groundwater teeming with pathogens, the Bateses' drinking water was relatively clean.[44]

By August, the worst was over. Besides its burn mandates and its efforts to clean up the city's cesspools, the Committee of Public Health also deputized men to collect all "filth and impurities" off the streets and apply lime and other disinfecting agents. Meanwhile, then-mayor James Barry issued ordinance number 2215, giving the committee full unilateral authority to enforce these regulations until the epidemic subsided. A person who did not comply might be levied a fine to pay for the cleanup. Such sanitation methods as these were made permanent in the next decade. Whigs saw an opportunity from the destruction of the Great Fire and the epidemic to again press for public works. Mayor Luther M. Kennett, for one, was swept into office on the promise that he would invest in making St. Louis safe from future tragedies. Within a decade, the river district was rebuilt with wider streets, and the wharf was extended further inland, putting more space between the steamboats and the warehouses. Kennett also expanded the number of fire hydrants and connected them to a new, complex sewer system. So effective were these measures that, in 1866, when cholera again swept the country, thanks to lessons learned in 1849, St. Louisans withstood a similar catastrophe. The later epidemic killed over 3,500 people—1.8 percent of population in the 1860 census. It was a moderate, but substantial drop from the 4,300—nearly 12 percent of the population in 1840—killed twenty years earlier.[45]

As the 1840s ended, Bates—nearing his sixtieth birthday—reflected upon the sights he had seen over the previous twenty years. When he arrived in St. Louis, it was a small French village of only three or four main streets running parallel to the raging Mississippi. Now, it was a thriving port, rivaling New Orleans. Despite setbacks such as the Great Fire and the 1849 cholera epidemic, the city had flourished and grown. And the new amenities about to be installed gave promise of the city's continued expansion in the coming years.

Bates also reflected on the mix of tragedy and happiness in his own family. He was saddened by the mental decline of his sister Sarah and the death of his mother, Caroline, in 1845. Furthermore, of the fourteen children born since his and Julia's marriage twenty-two years earlier, six had died before reaching adulthood. He was nevertheless uplifted by his surviving children, the eldest of whom—Barton, Nancy, and Fleming—were beginning to venture out on their own. Barton, at twenty-six, had recently embarked on a legal career. Nancy, three years younger and unmarried, had become an equal partner with her mother in maintaining the household. And, in 1848, Bates petitioned Congressman T. Butler King of Georgia, chairman of the Committee on Naval Affairs, to appoint fourteen-year-old Fleming to a midshipman's position in the U.S. Navy. Then, in March 1849, Barton married Caroline Matilda Hatcher and settled in St. Charles County, where, in February 1850, their first child, Onward, was born.[46]

In a similar vein, the family grew in their religious education. In July 1846, thirteen-year-old Julian experienced what Bates described as "a crisis of faith," the result of a sermon given by the parish minister of the Second Presbyterian Church. A pensive boy, he began reading the Bible and any religious tracts he could lay his hands on. "The spirit of God has touched his heart," Bates wrote of his son. In February 1849, Julian, Edward, Julia, and Barton all transferred from the Second Presbyterian Church to the new Central Church to ensure that the rest of the family would receive a stronger instruction in the faith. Bates had long been a faithful man; he now beamed with pride to see his children take after him and their mother.[47]

It had indeed been a decade full of surprises, with perhaps none greater than Bates's resurrected political career. Based on his newfound fame coming out of the River and Harbor Convention, he was poised to influence the future direction of his beloved Whig Party. While he continued to resist the temptation to run for office, events were already in motion that would remold the Whigs and, in the process, cast Bates adrift in search of a new party from which to make his stand on one of the most important issues of the century.

4.
Conservative Reformer

During the 1840s, Bates crystallized his positions on the two most divisive issues of the nineteenth century: slavery and war. Slavery's existence within the American republic had long been a sticking point, but the Mexican-American War brought it to the fore of American politics and, in the process, challenged Bates's previous position on the matter. By the end of the decade, Bates's understanding of this odious practice, as well as his position as a willing enslaver of others, had fundamentally changed, setting him up to be a leading antislavery voice in the next decade.

Texas was at the root of much of the trouble surrounding slavery's extension. Following their independence from Mexico in 1836, Texans began lobbying the United States for annexation. The Van Buren administration chose instead to focus what political capital it had on shoring up the economy after the Panic of 1837. In contrast, President John Tyler—who took office upon the death of Van Buren's successor, William Henry Harrison—had a strong desire to see the Lone Star Republic brought into the Union and worked behind the scenes to accomplish that end. After a long debate in Congress and several setbacks, including growing tensions with Mexico over a disputed region of territory near the Rio Grande River,

Tyler achieved annexation in March 1846 through a controversial joint resolution of Congress, just days before he was set to leave office.[1]

James K. Polk, Tyler's successor, next took up the matter of Texas statehood. To those critics who condemned Democrats' boasting during the late campaign that America would take the territories of Oregon and Texas by force if necessary, the new president—specifically referencing Texas—now argued that his agenda was not aggressive but peaceful. Only let the United States have what was, by right, theirs, he maintained, and there would be no cause for war.[2]

Polk settled the Oregon question with Great Britain without a fight, agreeing to split America and Canada along the forty-ninth parallel. Texas, however, was a different matter. On June 23, 1845, the Texas congress accepted the joint resolution of annexation and set elections for a constitutional convention. By the end of summer, Texans had a state constitution, which they approved by referendum on October 13. Finally, on December 29, Polk signed a bill accepting Texas as the twenty-eighth state. In all, Texas's territorial phase lasted just over nine months.[3]

Polk fulfilled his dual promises of Oregon and Texas acquisition, but the repercussions of such hasty maneuverings soon caught up with him. The border dispute between Texas and Mexico, it turned out, had not been settled. After Mexico rejected Polk's offer to purchase the disputed territory, the president ordered General Zachary Taylor's garrison of U.S. troops into the region. Then in May 1846, after a detachment of Mexican cavalry killed eleven soldiers near Matamoros, Polk requested that Congress declare war on Mexico. The vote was 174 to 14 in the House and 40 to 2 in the Senate.[4]

Like many Whigs, Bates opposed aggressive territorial acquisition. He was surprised, however, to find that some members of Polk's own party, especially Bates's old nemesis, Thomas Hart Benton, agreed. On May 14, 1847, in the St. Louis courthouse, Benton condemned the hasty annexation of Texas and asserted that less passionate management of the border dispute could have resolved the matter peacefully. In a rare moment of solidarity, Bates later wrote: "[Benton] evidently does not like the conduct of the war, nor does he seem to expect any great good from any series of victories. Is he not right there?"[5]

Bates joined national Whigs in questioning the legitimacy of Polk's war. Had not the presence of Taylor's troops in the disputed region instigated the attack by Mexico? If so, he reasoned, then what, short of hunger for fertile lands in the Southwest, could have compelled Polk to make such an order? "War is naturally & essentially barbarous & brutal," Bates wrote in his diary. "It is in every instance, an appeal from Reason to brute force. And when that appeal is once made, then the strongest nation, like the strongest tiger, wounds & mangles, & kills its adversary." The United States, he argued, naturally had a right to defend itself. But, short of attack, "all our institutions are averse to war. The founders of them taught us a solitary dread of the military powers." An army, he warned, "just in proportion to its good discipline & efficiency, is at once an example & instrument of arbitrary power." Polk, he believed, was guilty of just such a power grab.[6]

At first, the war was popular. As such, congressional Whigs from swing districts were compelled to cast votes to pay for provisions and other necessities that made them appear supportive of the conflict. As American boys began dying in the deserts of Mexico, however, people back home listened more attentively to Whig arguments of arbitrary power and inept management, and, in the midterm elections of 1846, they awarded Whigs a slim majority in the House of Representatives. Their solidarity with moderate Democrats like Benton, who also questioned the administration's reasoning for war, made them a formidable force. On May 22, 1847, Bates attended a party at the Planter's House Hotel in St. Louis where Benton used the opportunity to unveil a plan to force a vote in the Senate aimed at restoring peace with Mexico. Such an act, he reasoned, would end Polk's dreams of aggressive territorial expansion.[7]

Bates once again found himself in agreement with Benton, but before Congress could convene and Benton execute his plan, the U.S. Army captured Mexico City in September 1847. The next February, Polk's plenipotentiary, Nicholas Trist, signed the Treaty of Guadalupe Hidalgo, bringing the conflict to an end and ceding to the United States all Mexican lands north of the Rio Grande. In the Senate, support for ratification of the treaty was divided along party lines. Whigs wanted to end the war without any territorial acquisition while Southern Democrats rejected the treaty and demanded more territory. Northern Democrats became the final arbiter, convincing the Whigs to accept the treaty as it stood. On March 10, 1848, by a vote of thirty-eight to fourteen, the Senate approved it without further amendments.[8]

Bates saw the treaty in tragic terms, referring to it in his diary as "*conquering a peace*, with a vengeance." Were he a senator, he wrote, he could never sanction it. By not consulting with Congress before sending Taylor into the disputed territory and then lying that Mexico had started the conflict, Polk had illegally started "a wicked war of vanity & lust." Indeed, he wrote, the most naïve child could see "that the object was not peace, but plunder and conquest." Beyond Polk's erosion of the constitutional separation of powers, however, Bates thought the greatest crime was the complicity of both political parties in the conflict. He expected the Democrats to be corrupt and base, but he could not so easily forgive the Whigs. When the war began, they had made no attempt to stop it. What was needed, then, was new blood in politics. "A new man," he hoped, "with equal mind & general information, will come to the great subject with a fresher patriotism and a mind far less likely to be soiled & based by party schemes & electioneering calculations."[9]

Bates's concerns over expanded presidential power went together with his fear that the war had opened a Pandora's box surrounding the issue of slavery. The Missouri Compromise had tabled the issue for decades, but starting with the election of 1848, slavery became the most contentious political question of the day. Nationally, the intraparty competition over economics had outweighed any ideological or moral concerns about slavery. Both camps also looked upon the abolition movement with scorn. Still, as an advancing wave of religious fervor spread across the country, pro- and antislavery advocates engaged in a war of words over the institution's place in a modern democracy.[10]

By the mid-1830s, the national parties began to espouse clear differences of opinion on slavery. Democrats' control of the national government largely accounted for its inaction. Northern Democrats thought slavery ran counter to majoritarian democratic foundations, while their Southern cohorts believed that enslaving Black people was both the natural order of things and a rite of passage for white men. Both groups acknowledged, however, that slavery was sanctioned by state laws and therefore beyond the reach of the federal government. Whigs were equally divided. Northerners openly attacked the institution, while Southerners and border statesmen like Bates saw slavery as morally wrong but agreed with their Democratic opponents that to enslave people was both legal and an individual choice.[11]

Missourians could only avoid political and social discord over slavery for so long. On April 28, 1836, after a biracial steamboat worker named Francis McIntosh murdered two white policemen in St. Louis, a frenzied crowd retaliated by dragging McIntosh to a vacant lot and burning him alive. When the affair was brought before Judge Luke E. Lawless's bench in the St. Louis Circuit Court, Lawless blamed the whole affair on the abolitionist presses for stoking the anger of pro-slavery St. Louisans ahead of the incident.[12]

Lawless's condemnation of abolitionists invoked the memory of an event that occurred six years earlier in Southampton County, Virginia. In August 1831, enslaved people under the leadership of Nat Turner slaughtered sixty white men, women, and children before a white militia captured Turner and brought him to justice. In the aftermath, politicians demonized abolitionists for giving Turner the idea in the first place. It did not take much of a stretch of the imagination to see McIntosh's violent act as an extension of Turner's.[13]

Following Lawless's indictment, abolitionist Elijah Parish Lovejoy and his paper, the *St. Louis Observer*, became the target of pro-slavery St. Louisans. In July 1836, they ransacked his office and threw his printing press into the Mississippi. Lovejoy ordered a second press and moved the paper, and his family, across the river to Alton, Illinois. Over the next year, he became more virulent in his opposition to slavery while pro-slavery men from St. Louis became more determined to silence him. On the night of November 7, 1837, when another pro-slavery mob arrived from St. Louis to ransack Lovejoy's press, they ended up killing Lovejoy in the process.[14]

Lovejoy's death fanned the flames of discord over slavery nationwide. In December 1837, the abolitionist orator Wendell Phillips delivered a rousing speech at Boston's Faneuil Hall denouncing pro-slavery attempts to undermine abolitionists' rights. Other antislavery advocates, while appalled at the violence, were more tempered in their response. Abraham Lincoln, for instance, used Lovejoy's death as the background for a speech to the Young Men's Lyceum in Springfield, Illinois, where he condemned mob violence without ever mentioning Lovejoy by name. Lincoln refused to overtly defend abolitionists. Still, he warned, this issue, if not faced head-on, threatened to tear the country apart.[15]

Bates did not personally witness McIntosh or Lovejoy's deaths, but he and Lovejoy had gravitated among the same social circles. Likewise, as an attorney, Bates had conducted business many times before the bench of Judge Lawless—with whom he had nearly fought a duel a decade earlier. Moreover, as a member of the conservative antislavery colonization society, he sympathized with the tempered assessments of slavery made by those like Lincoln in the wake of Lovejoy's death. And while he never mentioned Lovejoy or McIntosh by name in public or private correspondence, it is clear from Bates's actions following their deaths that these men had a profound impact on him.

Bates had profited from enslaving Black people. Yet he disliked the practice and sought to limit its hold over the country's social and economic well-being. This, after all, was the impetus behind joining the American Colonization Society a decade earlier. Still, he spurned those abolitionists who questioned the morals of enslavers. He and his conservative antislavery colleagues instead concentrated their efforts on the legal definitions of liberty and personhood. The enslavement of others was legal under the Missouri state constitution, but an 1807 territorial law and an 1824 state supreme court decision afforded the right to sue for freedom to enslaved people who felt themselves wrongfully held captive. If state law sanctioned slavery, Bates theorized, it might also be a weapon against it. Starting in the late 1820s, he and several prominent St. Louis attorneys began bringing freedom suits before the local courts.[16]

Suing for one's freedom was not an easy process. Of the more than three hundred cases that were brought in the Missouri court system, only half resulted in a person's freedom. But if the plaintiff could prove that they met one of three criteria, it was possible—even in a slave state—to win one's liberty. The enslaved person had to have been taken by their captor into a free territory or state, freed in a will or by purchase, or born to a Black woman of free status.[17]

Bates advocated for enslaved persons in many freedom suits, but his most famous case occurred in 1842 when he defended Lucy Ann Berry. Lucy was born to a free Black woman named Polly, who had herself been kidnapped by a slave trader at a young age. Polly successfully sued for her freedom on the grounds of having originally been born with free status, and in September 1842, she employed Bates to free her daughter.

After detailing Polly's capture and sale into slavery, Bates spoke of the issues in this case in personal terms. "I am a slave-holder myself," he admitted. "But, thanks to the Almighty God, I am above the base principle of holding any a slave that has as good right to her freedom as this girl has been proven to have . . . no free woman can give birth to a slave child, as it is in direct violation of the laws of God and man!" The jury agreed. Because her mother was born with free status, Lucy too was free.

Aside from benefiting from his abilities as an orator, Bates's case, as was true of many of the freedom suits, had been heard by a sympathetic judge, Bryan Mullanphy. A wealthy and eccentric Democrat, Mullanphy had a deep and abiding respect for the law and was known for his charity and benevolence toward the poor and downtrodden. According to Lucy, when the defendant protested against the jury's verdict, Bates rose from his seat and retorted, "Is it not enough that this girl has been deprived of her liberty for a year and a half, that you must still pursue her after a fair and impartial trial before a jury, in which it was clearly proven and decided that she had every right to freedom?" Mullanphy shared Bates's indignation: "I agree with Judge Bates," he ruled, "and the girl may go!"[18]

Despite his efforts on behalf of freepersons like Lucy, Bates had reservations against exerting greater pressure on slavery itself. Personally, his actions regarding enslaved people were in line with his contemporaries, who exhibited no personal qualms with treating Black people unequally. At times, Bates hired out his enslaved servants to his neighbors. At others, he profited from their sale. When he liquidated his mother's Virginia estate in 1817, for instance, he sold several of her enslaved servants to traders. Later in his life, he sold three Black children belonging to Nancy, an enslaved woman in his household, as a punishment for their mother running away and leaving them behind. "Poor foolish thing," he wrote of Nancy. "She will never be as well off as she was in our house. We determined at once to be no longer plagued with [her children] and so, sent the three to Gurle & Garrett to be sold."[19]

Bates's angry sale of Nancy's children belied his work in the freedom suits and the American Colonization Society, but perhaps ruing his retaliatory treatment, he worked gradually toward freeing the other men and women he had enslaved. In 1848, the same year that he sold Nancy's children, Bates agreed to free Adam White, nearly twenty-one, if he would promise to serve the family for five additional years. He wrote similar contracts for two other people he had enslaved. Within twelve years, Bates had emancipated all the people he had enslaved.

Bates's effort to emancipate his enslaved people came with one important caveat. At the time of Adam's manumission, racial tensions in the border states—on display in such a terrible way in the McIntosh and Lovejoy affairs a decade earlier—were still dangerously high. Thus, as was befitting a prominent member of the American Colonization Society, Bates mandated that Adam immigrate to Africa. Emancipation without a contingency plan to safely alleviate the racial pressures it wrought, Bates wrote, was both disadvantageous to the former slave and an "evil to the community." He felt it was better for freed people to go to the colony of

Liberia. As Bates concluded his contract with Adam, "In the providence of God, [the colony of Liberia] is likely to become the instrument of spreading the enjoyment of civil liberty and the knowledge of Gospel truth among millions of men, otherwise doomed to be enslaved people and pagans."[20]

The contrasting cases of Nancy and Adam reveal several key factors influencing Bates's stance on emancipation. He showed no remorse about selling Nancy's children, but most of the time, he was prudent and rational about the enslaved people in his household. Much of that rationale was predicated upon a strict reading of the law. And, not infrequently, he weighed the matter of racial tensions raging in his home state as well as a case-by-case assessment of his family's and his enslaved servants' individual needs in deciding upon their emancipation.[21]

One thing was certain: Bates disallowed any personal moral scruples to influence his public stance on slavery. For a time, this put him in the mainstream of antislavery opinion in the border states. In the end, however, events outside of his control made it harder for Bates to maintain a purely legal interpretation. The crisis began with the presidential election of 1848, wherein national concerns over economics that had preoccupied the political parties in earlier decades were replaced with sectional ones.[22]

Bates approached the election as an opportunity to enhance his role as a Whig Party leader. On February 8, 1848, he gave a speech favoring Zachary Taylor's candidacy for president and urging unity between his party and the "Americans," a faction of Whigs then raising concerns over increasing waves of immigration from Europe. Bates shared the Americans' anxieties that immigrants would transfer the violence of the revolutions in the Old World to the New. Nonetheless, he was certain that the Americans could not carry an election on their own and that splitting the Whig vote would mean a Democratic victory. It was important to Bates, then, that the Whigs unite behind one candidate. When the state party nominated Taylor at their convention in April, he was pleased to conclude that "I believe the good work is done."[23]

To his surprise, Bates now found his own name thrust into the campaign. When they met in convention, in a surprising act, Missouri Whigs nominated him for vice president. Viewing the Whigs' act as a mere courtesy to a leading member of their party, Bates acknowledged that Missouri lacked the influence to carry his nomination to the national convention later that summer. Indeed, when the convention met in June, it nominated Taylor on the fourth ballot but, because the general hailed from a Southern state, chose a Northerner for vice president. Millard Fillmore of New York was in, and Bates was out.[24]

Bates's electoral prospects did not end there, however. This contest added dimensions beyond the binary choices of Taylor and the Democrat Lewis Cass. For the first time since the days of Jackson and Calhoun, Democrats split their vote. Northerners embraced Cass's plan for "squatter sovereignty"—later more commonly called "popular sovereignty"—which proposed that slavery's extension into new territories be determined by those who lived there rather than by the federal government. Southern Democrats, on the other hand, condemned the idea on the grounds that the Constitution's property clause protected slavery everywhere in the United States. Some Northern Democrats then broke away and, with antislavery Whigs and some Northern abolitionists, formed the Free-Soil Party later that August. As a means of beating Cass at his own game, Free-Soilers proposed that public land grants in the West be given to people who opposed the extension of slavery, thus creating antislavery societies that would stop the institution's spread. Here, the delegates again floated Bates's name for vice president. However, to ensure Bates's antislavery bona fides, George Stone of Albany wrote to him requesting his views on slavery's extension into the territories.[25]

Bates liked the Free-Soilers because they did not wish to agitate the slave question in places where it was already settled. "If Congress be the governing power of the nation," he wrote, "then it has power to establish what government & laws it pleases over acquired territory, however acquired. It can prohibit the introduction of slavery as well as the introduction of ardent spirits (which it has often done)." Furthermore, he believed that Southerners who opposed this philosophy did so on a perverted reading of the Constitution.[26]

Free-Soilers were pleased by Bates's opinion but in the end chose to nominate the old Democratic warhorse Martin Van Buren for president and Charles Francis Adams for vice president. Taylor then won the presidency in November with 163 electoral votes, having carried states both North and South, while Cass gave a respectable finish with 127 electoral votes. The Free-Soilers failed to carry a single state, as most Americans, including Bates, stuck with their favored parties. Still, while the third party did not determine the outcome of the election, it did serve notice that slavery would be an unavoidable issue in future contests.[27]

The election was over, but Bates's political prospects continued to improve. On the last day of the year, he reflected on the whirlwind of events over the previous twelve months, waxing philosophically on the promises offered by the incoming Taylor administration. Of the Democrats, he wrote, "God has confounded their cunning, and caught them in their own snares." In contrast, with Taylor's election, "the lovers of truth, justice & internal comfort & prosperity may rest in confident hope that he will administer the government in a spirit of peace & moderation."[28]

Before long, rumors began to circulate that the president-elect might ask Bates to join the cabinet. To that end, the *Missouri Republican*, the *St. Louis New Era*, and the *Albany Evening Journal* endorsed him as an ideal choice. Bates's humble Christian sensibilities, however, began to tug at his ego. "I am made a lion in spite of my teeth," he admitted. The character created by persons favorable to his nomination was, he feared, so inflated as to be wholly unrecognizable in comparison with the original. Besides, as he had already concluded, Missouri had no political weight in the national Whig Party. As such, he doubted that Taylor would choose him, and he instructed his friends to withdraw their solicitations for such an offer from the new president. Nonetheless, while desiring no office himself, and unsure that he could afford to leave his private practice even if an offer were made, he chose to wait and see whether one would be forthcoming before declining outright.[29]

In February 1849, Bates revisited his position. By then, the Whigs in the Missouri legislature had submitted a petition to Taylor requesting that Bates be named attorney general. "I must needs consider the project in its various bearings," he wrote, "& calculate the advantages & disadvantages, so as to have my mind settled, whether to accept or refuse it, in case the offer should be made." Still, he could not bring himself to imagine that Taylor would extend an invitation. His friends, however, did not share his misgivings. Two weeks later, Bates took to his diary to complain that acquaintances, believing him to be soon installed in Washington, D.C., had begun lobbying him for jobs. One asked for a clerkship in the office of the attorney general; another wanted to be recommended as postmaster of Wheeling, Virginia; and yet another requested assistance in preventing the removal of a lighthouse keeper on the Chesapeake. Bates ultimately brushed them off, writing that "in a few days, they will find that I am [a private citizen], & then I shall be relieved of all this trouble."[30]

In the end, Taylor went with Reverdy Johnson of Maryland for attorney general. Bates had not made the cut but did not seem disappointed. Reflecting on the new administration, he wrote, "My name has been often mentioned in connexion with the atty genl's office. But, I really never coveted the place, high as the honor may seem."[31]

Bates was not going to Washington in 1849, but there was no doubt that he had made an impact in political circles. His comportment at the River & Harbor Convention had cemented his status as a leading voice of Whig ideals, and his eloquent defense of Black men and women in the Missouri courts—despite being a slaveholder himself—had likewise made him a bulwark of conservative antislavery reform. Furthermore, the Polk administration's aggressive desire for territorial acquisition and the resultant war with Mexico solidified his position on questions of executive power and the constitutionality of slavery's expansion into the territories. His positions on these matters would become ever more important in the next decade. Originally enjoying a position largely on the sidelines of political affairs, Bates was suddenly thrust front and center of events in the 1850s. The most important phase of his public career was about to begin just as the country was tearing itself apart.

5.

Winter of Discontent

In late 1849, the ravages of the late cholera epidemic convinced Bates to again relocate his family. On June 9 he purchased a plot of land four miles west of St. Louis for $1,000. Construction on a new house began later that summer. Originally called Green Acre, the property was eventually renamed Grape Hill. It was an impressive home of red brick, with thirteen rooms laid out over two-and-a-half stories. It was surrounded by several outlying structures—possibly slave quarters and a stable—and situated among a beautiful array of sycamore and oak trees, a peach orchard, gooseberry bushes, and grape vines (from which the estate derived its name).

On July 3, 1851, at 10:30 A.M., while Bates sat at his desk in his upstairs study, he felt a tremor run through the house. It was preceded by what he later described as a "rumbling sound" that was "distinctly visible & audible." It was the type of small earthquake common along the New Madrid fault line but could easily have been a portent of things to come. Although the second two-party system survived the turmoil of the 1840s, the cohesion it generated between Northerners and Southerners began to unravel in the next decade, and this shifting of allegiances from party to section soon opened a chasm that threatened to swallow the country whole.[1]

The tumult began during the early months of the Mexican-American War. On August 8, 1846, Pennsylvania Democratic congressman David Wilmot attached to a $2 million appropriations bill an amendment that intended to outlaw slavery in any territory purchased or acquired by the United States in connection with the ongoing conflict. The measure was a response to Southern Democrats, who denied that they were planning to extend slavery into the fertile lands of the southwest. Wilmot's measure passed the House—every Northern Whig and all but four Northern Democrats voted for it—but it failed in the Senate, where the South was stronger. In February 1847, Wilmot reintroduced the measure, again with similar results. The next year, Wilmot tried once more, this time attaching it to the passage of the Treaty of Guadalupe Hidalgo, but again it failed to obtain the requisite majority.[2]

Even though Congress failed to pass the proviso, what had started as an attempt to get Polk's supporters on record defending the extension of slavery became a full-blown political issue in the next presidential election. And while American voters North and South managed to coalesce behind Taylor and Fillmore, the Wilmot Proviso and the subsequent drama around slavery in the 1848 campaign opened a Pandora's box that divided the geographic sections according to their stances on this one issue.[3]

Two years later, California statehood exacerbated the tensions. Due to a sudden spike in population from the discovery of gold, Taylor attempted to bypass the territorial process and admit California and New Mexico as sovereign states. Because of a Mexican ban on slavery, though, both territories would likely become free states. Seemingly overnight, disagreements over slavery between North and South resurfaced. Northerners supported California and New Mexico's immediate admission, while Southerners objected over the sectional imbalance the new states would create in the Senate. It was the Missouri controversy all over again.

New Mexico statehood failed but California had drafted a state constitution outlawing slavery and joined the Union as the thirty-first state in the fall of 1849. The issue breathed life into a Southern unity movement begun by the aging senator John C. Calhoun earlier that year. By the spring of 1850, Calhoun's disciples in the South called for secession unless they were granted permanent equality with the North in the US Senate. The growing animosity between the sections was palpable. Fistfights broke out on the floor of Congress, and one senator even pulled a revolver on another.[4]

For the last time, Henry Clay—along with Calhoun and Daniel Webster—attempted to deescalate the situation. Their outlook toward success, however, was mixed. In January, Clay gave a speech proposing a half-a-loaf plan that appealed to some but satisfied none. The North would get California statehood along with a statute outlawing the slave trade in the District of Columbia. The South would get the establishment of popular sovereignty in the rest of the territories acquired from Mexico, as well as passage of a new, stronger fugitive slave law. Calhoun, however, was skeptical of the plan. In March, he wrote a speech—delivered, due to his failing health, by his friend James Mason of Virginia—denouncing the compromise and declaring that the future of the Union was in danger. Webster, for his part, denounced the secessionists, upheld the perpetuity of the Union, and endorsed the full adoption of Clay's compromise.[5]

Watching from St. Louis, on March 15, Bates wrote of Calhoun: "Poor man, he will soon find himself abandoned, and in a meagre minority, even in the South." Calhoun, however, did not live long enough to test Bates's theory. When he died on March 30, one of the most prominent Southern voices against the compromise was silenced. Then, in July, Taylor, who opposed the compromise in favor of immediate statehood for California without concessions to the South, also died. The new president, Fillmore, was more favorable to the compromise, and when in June Clay presented the measures to Congress as an omnibus bill, he hoped that both sides would be happy with those carrots that benefited their individual sections. Instead, the Senate rejected the bill, reviving it later that fall only after Illinois senator Stephen Douglas broke it into smaller bills and then assembled coalitions in favor of each provision. In August, Fillmore signed them into law.[6]

In Missouri, the shifting political alliances over the compromise were the first indication to Bates that something was amiss. The state Democratic Party experienced a schism between secessionist firebrands, led by state senator Claiborne Fox Jackson, and pro-union pragmatists, led by Thomas Hart Benton. In 1848, Jackson offered a series of resolutions asserting that Congress had no authority to limit slavery in the territories and pressured Missouri's senators and congressmen to vote against any such measure. Benton, in return, vocally opposed his party's seeming adhesion to slavery, setting up a fight between the two factions that played out as Benton sought reelection to a sixth term in 1850.[7]

Unlike the Democrats, Missouri Whigs largely supported the compromise. "For my part, I have no country but the *United States*," Bates wrote in his diary that November: "I acknowledge no nationality but the states *united*. The Federal Constitution & laws are as much *our* constitution & laws—and that by our own consent & adoption are the Constitution & laws of Missouri; and are of higher authority, for they are the 'Supreme law of the land, any thing in the constitution and laws of any particularly state to the contrary notwithstanding—and the judges in every state shall be bound thereby.'" Even so, as secession fever gripped the South, Bates lamented, "that allegiance is due to the state and not to the Union." It was essential, then, that the Jackson resolutions not tie the hands of Missouri's congressional delegation. The upcoming senatorial contest would thus become the venue through which to test the Whigs' unionism.[8]

Anti-Benton Democrats lobbied hard for Whig support. What could be more enticing, they argued, than to finally defeat Benton? Conversely, Benton Democrats played to the Whigs' unionist sensibilities. A vote for the Anti-Benton candidate, they urged, was a vote for the Jackson Resolutions and disunion. Bates, however, had reservations about siding with either camp. To do so, he wrote, "we must unavoidably abandon our own true principles & good men and support the bad doctrine of our adversaries, and their little leaders, whom we despise, and for no higher consideration than revenge against an old enemy. And that is a feeling unworthy the Whig Party & the patriots & statesmen who compose it." By refusing to endorse either Democratic faction, he believed, Missouri might finally elect its first Whig senator.[9]

The Whigs pulled off a critical victory that August, winning three of Missouri's five congressional districts and picking up an additional twenty-nine seats in the state legislature. With 41 percent of the state house and 36 percent of the senate, they would now be the deciding factor in the New Year in choosing the next U.S. senator. Benton would be running for reelection, but Henry S. Geyer, a pro-slavery attorney from St. Louis who was uncommitted to the compromise and had served one term as Speaker of the Missouri House, surprisingly emerged as a strong Whig opponent.[10]

Geyer's chances, at first, seemed remote. His noncommittal attitude toward the compromise attracted him to Anti-Benton Democrats but made him anathema to Bentonites and moderate Whigs. Likewise, no one could deny the formidable candidacy of the incumbent, Benton. "His partisans are firm, & united in unhesitating allegiance to their chief," Bates observed. "The anti's, on the contrary, have no leader, & no distinctive principle but hatred to Benton, and that they hold with fear and trembling. The probability is that enough of them will go back to their old master to reelect him."[11]

Geyer nearly derailed his candidacy by publishing an article in the *Missouri Republican* in September that denied the legitimacy of the Jackson Resolutions by supporting Congress's ability to restrict slavery in the territories. Then, in late December and early January, as Anti-Bentonites in the assembly denied him a majority, Geyer wrote two more letters published in the *Missouri Intelligencer* reversing his earlier position by arguing that, when voting on important measures, a United States senator was obliged to follow orders from his state legislature, regardless of his own personal feelings on the matter. Despite Geyer's contradictory political statements, the enticement of defeating Benton was great enough to compel Anti-Bentonites, on the fortieth ballot, to give Geyer a slim victory. "GEYER IS ELECTED, and no mistake," wrote a correspondent for the *Palmyra Weekly Whig*. "That is glory enough for one Missouri Legislature."[12]

The Missouri Democratic split injected energy into the Missouri Whig Party at a time when the Whigs were losing steam elsewhere. This fact may account for Bates's sober response to Geyer's victory. Personally, he liked Geyer. They had worked together in the state convention thirty years earlier, as well as the state assembly in the early 1830s. More recently, they had served as co-counsels for the defense in a sensational murder trial. He was also pleased that the Whigs had remained united and not fallen back on their usual tactic of picking the lesser of two Democrats. On the other hand, Bates feared that his old friend had given up too much to win his seat. Geyer's waffling on the Jackson Resolutions, Bates reasoned, made him "a most unlucky senator" because it undermined his support with antislavery Whigs.[13]

Bates was most disappointed with Geyer's stated opinion on whether a senator should sacrifice his constitutional scruples to the will of his constituents, which ran counter to the principles that Bates had espoused all his life. Geyer would do well, he thought, to remember that as late as 1847, the Missouri legislature had given instructions to Benton to defend extending slavery into Oregon, California, and New Mexico. Since the general assembly had yet to rescind those instructions, if Geyer really believed what he wrote in his latter two epistles, then he would be forced to defend the Jackson Resolutions, thus contradicting his own stated opinion on slavery in his earlier article in the *Missouri Republican*. "Alas, poor Geyer!" Bates wrote a few days before the election, "I'd give my best horse to have that silly letter unwritten."[14]

While Benton's adversaries cheered his downfall, Bates could not shake the feeling that the victory was a pyrrhic one. On the national scene, despite some gains in congressional representation from Ohio, Illinois, and Michigan, Whigs lost senatorial contests in Delaware, Florida, New Jersey, and Pennsylvania, as well as the governorships of North Carolina and Maryland. What was more, Northern Whigs' determination to make war on the fugitive slave act and popular sovereignty alienated their Southern counterparts and severely undermined the party's legitimacy in the eyes of voters.[15]

In Missouri, the Whig ascendancy was short lived. During the next session, the assembly failed to repeal the Jackson Resolutions, and Geyer publicly gave way on the matter. Legislators in Jefferson City were discernibly angry. Each faction had come to believe that Geyer would defend its position. Thanks to his recent waffling, many now began calling for his resignation. "I think Mr. G must have fallen asleep with his heart bent on a seat in the Senate," Bates wrote in his diary, "and his mind intensely occupied with schemes to win the Black Democrats and dreamed all about this supposed opinion of his." Still, Bates could not find it in himself to abandon his old friend. When Geyer came to him for advice, Bates counseled him to stay the course and remain above the fray. The Whigs, he assured Geyer, "would give him a fair & honest support." Geyer took that advice, likely saving his office. Privately, though, Bates believed Geyer's fate was sealed. "If Mr. G had steadily pursued the good policy . . . & had nothing to do with either faction," he concluded, "he would have been elected easily, & the party would have remained in unity & honor. His departure from sound principle & good old policy has wrought this mischief. Verily, 'the way of the transgressor is hard.'"[16]

Politics was becoming something of a no-win situation for the Whigs, but Bates could at least retreat into the tranquility of his domestic life. By 1851, he was feeling every bit of his fifty-seven years. On April 29, for instance, he recorded in his diary that Julia had been seriously ill for the second time in eight weeks, and he had been down for two weeks with influenza. Still, he found replenishment in both his new gardens as well as the blessings of his children. In March, after Bates amicably dissolved his partnership with Hamilton Gamble, who needed rest on account of ill health, he entered business with Barton. A few months later, Barton and his family, who had been living with Bates and Julia since their wedding in 1849, moved into their own home. Meanwhile, Julian would soon leave home for Kanawha to study medicine.[17]

Bates also continued to find happiness in his marriage. On May 29, he was a guest at the wedding of his friend Charles Gibson to Virginia Gamble. As he watched the happy couple recite their vows, he could not help but reflect on his own wedding on that same day twenty-eight years earlier. "I cannot wish my young friends greater blessings," he wrote, "than that they may live together as I & my wife have done & are doing." Almost three decades later, Julia was still the center of his world, and he credited her for the family's happiness. In July, when two of the household servants— Patrick and Mary Maher, both immigrants from Ireland—suddenly left on account of Patrick's unwillingness to take orders from Julia, Bates recorded that "no one shall stay on my place who does not know that my wife is Mistress & Queen, & her word the law of the household."[18]

Julia was equally devoted to him. When Bates returned home from court one afternoon in November, he found that Julia and the children had relocated his furniture from the study on the south side of the house to an attic room on the north side, presumably allowing better air flow and light. Overwhelmed by this display of love and devotion, he wrote in his diary, "How happy is my lot! Blessed with a wife & children who spontaneously do all they can to make me comfortable, anticipating my wishes, even in the little matters of personal convenience, as if their happiness wholly depended on mine."[19]

Bates's family took his mind off political matters, but he could never entirely escape them. The threat of disunion was now penetrating avenues of life beyond simple politics. When the general assembly of the Presbyterian Church met in St. Louis in May, Bates was surprised to learn from the assembly's star speaker, Dr. Aaron Whitney Leland of South Carolina— one of the Presbytery's leading theologians—that the reverend feared slavery would force a schism within the church. Bates could not believe that the issue was that serious. Seeing the fate of the church as mirroring that of the country, he consoled Leland "that the *Union* is indispensable, & *Secession* so obviously absurd that it never could be carried out into a fact."[20]

Doubling down on his denial a few weeks later, Bates pasted into his diary a May 31 article from the *St. Louis Intelligencer* in which a correspondent in South Carolina attested that the largest enslavers in the state were unequivocally opposed to secession. "This is but another proof of the correctness of my opinion long entertained," Bates observed, "viz: that slavery is not the real question. The question is only a struggle among politicians for sectional supremacy, and slavery is drawn into the contest only because it is a very exciting topic, a topic about which sensible people are more easily led to play the fool, than on any other subject."[21]

The Whigs, Bates theorized, might provide a solution to the sectional problem. South Carolina would be the test case. The recent election of Robert Barnwell Rhett to finish out Calhoun's term had produced serious fissures in the Southern phalanx. Rhett was ardently pro-secession, but his efforts to create a Southern Unity Party were frustrated when the rest of the South rejected his call for disunion. Although this did not stop South Carolina from electing Rhett to the Senate, Bates hoped that the secessionists would soon come to their senses. "After this," he concluded in his diary, "there will be a Union Party there, very soon, and after a little while, it will be found to consist mainly of Whigs. Mark that prediction."[22]

If Southern Whigs failed to live up to Bates's expectations, perhaps the North and South could yet be held in check by the West. Bates first played with the idea in a speech at New Haven, Connecticut, in the summer of 1850. In November, he returned to it in a letter to the Western Convention in Evansville, Indiana. The influx of immigrants from the Eastern United States, he argued, made the Valley of the Mississippi—what he deemed the West—a mediating force in sectional politics. "The feelings and passions of the Western People," he wrote, "like their interests, are not local and sectional . . . mixing with every variety of man, they soon wear off all feelings and prejudices that are merely local."[23]

Bates's theory was driven by his own observations about the population boom then occurring in St. Louis. On April 29, 1851—the thirty-seventh anniversary of his arrival in the city—he marveled that he "found this place, a French village of about 2,000 people. Now it is a great city of about 10,000 inhabitants!" Of the new residents, however, most were "mixed up of all the varieties of Europe, though the Germans & Irish predominate . . ." Therein lay a problem. In Bates's mind, the West could not check North and South so long as its people were culturally divided. The presence of European immigrants in St. Louis was not a new phenomenon, but the earlier generations had willingly assimilated into the community. This new generation, however, chose to remain autonomous and supported radical ideas that conflicted with the established political and social order. The Germans clamored for free labor, which appealed to moderate antislavery men, but their refusal to adopt mainstream views on matters such as temperance and Protestantism compelled a backlash from the established ruling class. These nativists, as they were sometimes called, soon began a concerted effort to villainize the Germans and thereby curb their influence in the community.[24]

Bates was troubled by the rift between his German and nativist neighbors. On the one hand, he agreed with the Germans' antislavery, free-labor principles. On the other, he was a member of the Missouri Temperance Society, which opposed the opening of German beer gardens around town. He was also a member of the Presbyterian church, which worried at the growing influence of Catholicism. Finally, as a member of the Freemasons— having joined the Grand Lodge of Missouri in 1821—he shared the fraternity's sympathy with nativist fears of radicalism. Of greatest concern, however, was the fact that the presence of German radicals was compelling Bates's beloved Whig Party to again ally with Anti-Benton Democrats—as it had done in the election of Geyer—to promote xenophobic policies such as outlawing all foreign languages in public schools and curtailing hours of operation for taverns.[25]

Bates hoped that the social tensions would pass, but by the end of 1851, he was losing his patience. In his eyes, the Germans deserved most of the blame for rousing the passions of the people in support of the revolutions in Europe. This was an age when men were foolishly embarking on unauthorized military expeditions—called filibusters—to liberate South American countries. Just the previous September, several Americans were executed in Cuba for their role in a failed coup. With the way the Germans were agitating the people, he wondered, what was to stop a similar occurrence from happening in Europe?[26]

On January 23, 1852, St. Louis was rocked by another earthquake. If the quake the previous summer was a portent of a widening tear in America's social fabric, this second foretold of even greater turmoil to come, for in the coming months, the rift between the Germans and the nativists took a violent turn. On March 27, a German mob crashed an assembly of Whigs and Anti-Benton Democrats—meant to promote nativist candidates in the upcoming elections—at the St. Louis courthouse. A few days later, nativists retaliated by attacking a German rally near Laclede Market. Several prominent Germans drew pistols and threatened to open fire, but the city police intervened on the side of the nativists. Then, on Election Day in August, a nativist mob attacked the polling place of the First Ward—the epicenter of German political activity—smashing the ballot box and dumping the contents into the street. They also plundered the nearby German taverns and, when a few Germans tried to fight back, shot at them with revolvers. Again, the city police did nothing to quell the violence, while a fire brigade turned their hoses on bystanders who tried to help the wounded Germans.[27]

In the end, nativists claimed a victory in Mayor Luther Kennett's re-election, but the cost of their antics from that spring and summer was far greater than the reward. Germans and other foreigners unified behind Thomas Hart Benton, whose surprise comeback wrestled from the Whigs an important seat in the U.S. House of Representatives. Likewise, the Whig unity that resulted in Geyer's election two years earlier had finally given way to more infighting over the nativist influences in their party and, in the end, cost them the gubernatorial election.[28]

The one consolation for the Whigs was that, at the state party convention that spring, they had finally taken a strong stand against the Jackson Resolutions and expressed unequivocal support for the Compromise of 1850. They also once more recommended Bates for the vice presidency when the national convention met in June. That place on the ticket eventually went to William Graham of North Carolina, but Bates was nonetheless flattered by his party's faith in him, and he used the opportunity to express his thoughts on the most important issues of the day. In a letter read before the state convention, Bates defended the Compromise of 1850 in the strongest of terms, condemning as "dangerous" any politician who spoke against it. He also offered his clearest expression yet on the matter of slavery's extension into the territories: "Congress has the power to legislate over the Territories which we conquer or buy, in regard to the subject of slavery, as well as all other subjects which concern the prosperity and social relations of the inhabitants of the acquired provinces."[29]

Despite such strong statements, in the end, the Whigs' newfound authority amounted to very little. The editor of the *Missouri Republican* described the Whigs' loss in the state contests that fall as "a perfect Waterloo defeat to us." Particularly stinging was the outcome in the presidential election. At the national convention, Missouri Whigs supported Fillmore, but the nomination ultimately went to General Winfield Scott, who had been ambiguous on the Compromise of 1850. The disappointment among the Missouri delegation was palpable. Bates himself privately described Filmore as, "the best President we have had in 40 years, writing in his own character, more of baldness & firmness, forbearance & energy, cool prudence & prompt action, than any President since Washington." Only after Scott won the nomination did Bates and the Missouri Whigs give him lukewarm support. No one was surprised, in the end, when Democrat Franklin Pierce took the state's electoral votes and the White House.[30]

The election of 1852 was the beginning of the end of the national Whig Party. That reality, however, was not universally apparent across the country. In some states, Whigs held on longer than others. Missouri was one of these. Over the coming years, Bates seemed always to be waiting in the wings—a potential savior for the foundering organization. As early as September 14, 1852, the *Missouri Glascow Times* pondered Bates's availability for the U.S. Senate in 1854. David Rice Atchison was up for reelection, but the fiery pro-slavery Democrat had made himself notorious as a foil for Thomas Hart Benton, whom Atchison helped to defeat for reelection in 1850. Atchison also exacerbated the slavery frenzy when he advocated for opening the territory northwest of his home state to slavery. To align the national Democratic Party with Southern interests, Atchison recruited prominent senators Robert M. T. Hunter and James Mason of Virginia and Andrew Butler of South Carolina to his cause. They got their wish when, in November 1853, Congress passed the Kansas-Nebraska Act, formally repealing the Missouri Compromise line. This latter act made Atchison—not to mention Geyer, who voted for it—a pariah in Missouri's antislavery circles.[31]

The notoriety of Missouri's two senators gave Whigs another chance to claim a senate seat. Many saw Bates as their man. Unlike Atchison, his long-standing bona fides as a conservative antislavery man were by now well-known. Furthermore, his governing philosophy stood in stark contrast to Geyer's, which more resembled that of a Democrat than a Whig. Despite these attributes, the main obstacle to Bates's potential candidacy was more a matter of geography than philosophy. St. Louis already claimed one senator and was unlikely to get another. Then there was the fact that, in February 1855, Bates refused the job in a public letter released to the press. At sixty-one, he was content with private life. Likewise, he was concerned by rumors that the state Whig Party was breaking apart over whether to support Geyer's reelection in the coming year. "If our chosen Representatives allow themselves to be divided into cliques and sections," he admonished his compatriots, "individuals may win in temporary triumph, but the party will be dangerously wounded." He would not allow himself to be the cause of his party's destruction.[32]

Moderate Whigs were despondent, and in the end, neither party settled on an acceptable replacement for Atchison. Unlike with Geyer, they refused to consider anything but an ideologically pure candidate. As such, when Atchison vacated the seat the next year, it remained unfilled for two years. The same phenomenon occurred in Indiana and Pennsylvania, ominously suggesting a growing inability of pro- and anti-Nebraska men to form governing coalitions. In Missouri, the Whig Party splintered into irrelevancy, never again putting forward a serious candidate for state or federal office. Some Whigs, like Bates, resisted leaving the party, even in the face of overwhelming evidence of its decline. But as they continued to search for a unifying candidate, national matters only hastened the political realignment occurring in the North.[33]

The Kansas-Nebraska Act threatened to turn the American West into a realm wholly controlled by pro-slavery oligarchs. Unable to stomach that possibility, Northern Democrats, fearful of the Southern interests that controlled their party, and Northern Whigs, resigned to the death of their organization, joined together in 1854 to create the Republican Party. In 1855, they joyfully observed as anti-Nebraska men won several important senatorial contests, including those in Iowa, Illinois, New Hampshire, New York, and Wisconsin. None of the men elected in these contests was Republican, but they nonetheless strengthened the Republican movement by solidifying anti-Nebraska forces and officially moving to the new party during the coming congressional session.[34]

The next year, 1856, Republicans were strong enough in the Northern states to put forward their first presidential candidate, John C. Frémont. Frémont was famous for mapping the West as well as for marrying Thomas Hart Benton's daughter, Jessie—a partnership that lent him considerable legitimacy among antislavery Democrats. Nominated on an anti-Nebraska platform that denied the extension of slavery into the territories, Frémont were clearly the strongest foil to the Democrats, who attempted to win back their Northern compatriots by nominating Pennsylvanian James Buchanan. In Missouri, however, the fledgling party was not yet strong enough to be a contender in state elections. This was partially due to men like Bates who held out hope that the Whigs might yet survive.[35]

After 1852, Bates privately worried that any ambitions he might hold for future public office were sunk. His legal career continued to boom—he was elected judge of the St. Louis Land Court in 1853—but his precious Whig Party continued to stagnate. Bates's own ambitions were nearly snuffed out when in September 1856, to reunify Northern and Southern Whigs, he agreed to serve as chairman of what would be the last National Whig Party Convention in Baltimore.

From the start, the convention was a pitiful affair. Anti-Know-Nothing Whigs, rather than Fillmore's friends, arranged it. Only later did Fillmore—who by then heartily embraced Know-Nothingism—urge his old-guard Whig allies to attend, and then only as a means of ensuring that no other man *but* Fillmore was nominated. Bates was one of these delegates. With only 144 attendees, the meeting was also one of the smallest political conventions ever assembled. Several states did not even send delegates; nearly half the men present came from New York.[36]

Convention chairmen traditionally made an address on the first day, which would be carried in most of the national newspapers, and with so many Whigs abandoning ship for the Republican standard, Bates hoped to win some of them back. In a rare moment of levity, he used self-deprecating humor to contrast the differences between the young and untried Republicans and the seasoned Whigs: "We have been called old line Whigs. I am not exactly sure that is the correct appellation. For my own part they call me an old fogy—that I am not even a line, that is true. I am a dot, a full stop, a period, whenever you propose to me to abandon the opinions of my fathers, and adopt new fangled inventions of the present day." To rousing applause, he then called the Whigs the "bodyguard of the Constitution" and praised them for being "as much good service to your country when in the minority as in the majority."[37]

Bates's goal was to show the Whigs as a political organization still relevant to the times. Instead, his attempt at humor only highlighted the old-fashioned views of the party as well as the middle age of the delegates themselves. One newspaper observed that, though those assembled were intelligent, respectable men of good standing, not one of them was in touch with reality. They had no more hope of electing Fillmore, the reporter asserted, than Orthodox Christians had of bringing about the Millennium.[38]

Despite his flat attempt at humor, Bates was more eloquent in his defense of conservatism and his strong condemnation of disunion. Whigs had withstood "the downward tendency of things," he told the convention, and had served as "a warning voice in time of danger, inviting those who have been entrusted with the government of the country to consider the origin of this power, and to whom they must trust for support." To stem the tide of disunion, Bates pressed his fellow countrymen to reflect upon their common ancestral roots. His father had fought at Yorktown; no doubt others in the assembly had similar family histories. Their common past was, he believed, the key to uniting Americans beyond political affiliation. Four years before Abraham Lincoln would speak to the "mystic chords of memory, stretching from every battlefield and patriot grave to every living heart and hearthstone," Bates proclaimed that, if the government failed to harken to the people's common past, it would be unworthy of "the veneration which I was taught as a child to bear towards it."[39]

Bates ended with a shocking admission: the Whigs were too weak to elect a candidate of their own. They must therefore choose from one of the three existing presidential contenders—Democrat James Buchanan, Republican John C. Frémont, or Nativist Millard Fillmore. Although he disagreed with Fillmore's embrace of nativism, Bates believed the former president the most acceptable candidate. Democrats, he believed, had tied themselves to slavery while the Republicans were too radical to win national support among moderate antislavery voters. Fillmore, on the other hand, had a proven record of checking the influence of the slave power.[40]

By lending their support to Fillmore, Bates and his colleagues hoped to unite Northern and Western antislavery men. Their efforts, however, were fruitless. By the time the convention met, Fillmore's loss was almost foreordained. In November, only slightly more than 21 percent of the electorate cast their ballots for him. His sole victory in the electoral college was in the state of Maryland. Many Northern antislavery Whigs instead voted for Frémont, giving him 33 percent of the popular vote and 114 electoral votes. The Democrat, Buchanan, won the popular vote by 12 percent over Frémont, as well as the electoral college by 60 votes.[41]

On January 12, 1857, the long debate over who would fill Missouri's vacant Senate seat finally ended when Democrats, now enjoying a strong majority in the assembly, elected James S. Green over Benton, who had suffered a second blow to his political career the previous year when Frank Blair Jr. defeated him for reelection to the House of Representatives. After nearly a decade of infighting and dealmaking, the Missouri Democratic Party was once more the supreme power in the state.[42]

Democrats also maintained their hold on national power, but it was clear from the late election that Republicans were a force to be reckoned with. Over the next three years, Bates privately lamented to friends and family the irrelevancy of his once beloved Whig Party, to which his colleagues often responded by encouraging him to lend his influence to the new Republican Party. While other prominent Whigs such as William Seward and Lincoln had made the switch, however, Bates simply could not. The late election clearly showed, he responded, that his ideas were old fashioned and unlikely to attract an audience large enough to influence the outcome of elections. "How strange a thing it would be," he wrote to Indiana journalist and politician Schuyler Colfax in 1858, "for any party to sink its hopes of success on a man who was not even numbered in its ranks, nor bound by its creed." Still, Bates's friends were not so easily swayed, and in the coming months they—as well as national events—would compel Bates to reconsider his own self-assessment.[43]

6.
Candidate

Bates's self-imposed exile after 1856 came at an inauspicious time. The new president—James Buchanan—was a Northerner and a Democrat, but no one expected him to take a stand against slave interests in his party. Without bold leadership from the top, slavery would only exacerbate divisions North and South during the next four years. As pro- and antislavery radicals grew more violent, the country desperately needed a voice of moderation to quell the sectional tensions.

The violence began two years earlier during the debates over Kansas-Nebraska. Antislavery men prepared to immigrate to the Kansas Territory to neuter any attempts by slaveholders to use popular sovereignty to extend slavery there. Meanwhile, pro-slavery men already in the territory formed militias to protect their interests. Ruffians from Bates's home state made matters worse when they crossed the border and cast fraudulent votes in the November election, making sure that the nonvoting representative from Kansas was a pro-slavery man. In March 1855, they employed the same tactic to ensure the election of a pro-slavery territorial legislature.[1]

The pro-slavery government set up shop in Lecompton, but antislavery men in Lawrence refused to accept it as legitimate and formed their own government in Topeka. From there, matters only worsened. In Washington, President Franklin Pierce condemned Topeka, and in May 1856, pro-slavery men sacked the town of Lawrence. John Brown and his band of radical abolitionists responded by brutally murdering five pro-slavery men along the banks of the Pottawatomie Creek. Nearly two years after Congress opened Kansas to popular sovereignty, the region was embroiled in civil war.[2]

The turmoil ground on through 1856. Then on March 6, 1857, the Supreme Court exacerbated the problem by delivering a thundering seven-to-two decision on slavery in the Dred Scott case. Two days earlier, Buchanan anticipated in his inaugural address that the court would use the case to settle the twin issues of popular sovereignty and the extension of slavery for all time. The decision when delivered, however, completely dashed those hopes.[3]

Bates and his fellow St. Louisans were intimately familiar with the case, which had first been tried in the St. Louis circuit court in 1846. Dr. John Emerson, a surgeon in the U.S. Army stationed out of Jefferson Barracks, had taken his slave, Dred Scott, to live in the free state of Illinois and the territory of Minnesota. After returning to Missouri, and upon Emerson's death, Dred and his wife, Harriet, believed they were no longer enslaved people and sued for their freedom. The circuit court sided with the Scotts, but in a two-to-one ruling—with Hamilton Gamble the lone dissenter— the State Supreme Court reversed the lower court's decision and returned them to bondage.[4]

Scott's lawyers next appealed in the federal courts. In 1854, the lower court upheld the Missouri Supreme Court's ruling, but the plaintiffs took their case directly to the Supreme Court, where arguments were heard in 1856 and the decision was held over until after the inauguration. Speaking for the majority, Chief Justice Roger B. Taney ruled that, despite having lived for a time in a free territory, the Scotts were indeed still enslaved people. Moreover, a Black man "had no rights which the white man was bound to respect." In this one act, the court had nationalized slavery, overturned decades of legal precedent involving individual rights for Black freedmen, and rendered moot the experiment in popular sovereignty then playing out in Kansas.[5]

Bates's reaction to the Dred Scott decision was complicated. He had defended dozens of Black men and women in freedom suits and publicly stated many times his belief that Congress had the power to halt slavery's spread into the territories, but those earlier cases had not depended on the citizenship of the defendant. Because citizenship was understood, at this time, as the prerogative of white men only, Bates—like many of his fellow conservatives—found himself agreeing with Taney's assertion that Dred Scott was not a citizen. Still, Bates felt that the question of Scott's citizenship was beyond the scope of the case, and he predicated his opposition on these grounds.[6]

If Buchanan and Taney thought the Dred Scott decision would quell the violence over slavery, they were sorely mistaken. Shortly after the court released its ruling, the Lecompton government drafted a state constitution protecting slavery and barring freed Black people from emigrating to Kansas. When, in January 1858, the acting territorial governor called a referendum on the Lecompton constitution, it failed by huge margins— 10,000 opposed; 162 in favor. It was a major blow to pro-slavery forces throughout the country. Unwilling to risk losing the South by recognizing the vote, Buchanan chose to see chicanery in the lower number of favorable votes and instead attempted to ram the Lecompton constitution through Congress. With this act, the concept of popular sovereignty, upon which Northern Democrats had staked their political hopes, fast became a joke.[7]

Buchanan's Northern partisans were outraged at his obtuseness and, although the Lecompton constitution passed the Senate, were able to kill it in the House. In August 1858, Congress forced Kansas to hold a second referendum, which—this time—soundly rejected Lecompton by 11,300 to 1,788. Congress and the president were now at an impasse on further consideration of Kansas's statehood. In the Senate, Stephen Douglas, angered that the Kansas debacle had made a mockery of popular sovereignty, now challenged the president for the mantle of party leader. The Kansas question would remain in limbo for the foreseeable future, while the question of slavery continued to divide the Democratic Party between North and South, and the country with it.[8]

The Democratic schism presented yet another serious threat to national unity. The Whigs had collapsed a few years earlier, and the Republicans had little support in the South. Without a national party, fear existed that Americans might begin to identify with sectional factions and adopt separatist ideas. To avoid such a tragedy, in February 1859, a group of New York Whigs, sickened by the way that slavery had divided the country, passed a resolution calling on their compatriots to refrain from further agitating the issue. Hoping that their party could rise from the ashes and remembering Bates's fervent support of the Union at the national convention in 1856, they petitioned Bates for his advice on the most important issues of the day. In a long response published in the *New York Tribune*, Bates commended the Whigs' promotion of nonagitation on the slavery issue—which he called "a pestilent question, the agitation of which has never done good to any party, section, or class. . . ." National politics, he argued, suffered from this old debate, which was constantly raised in order to sweep "some unfit men into office, and keep some fit men out." If officials simply stopped harping on the matter, he hypothesized, it would recede from the public mind. The American people could then focus on more important matters, such as disrupting attempts by expansionists to aggressively take more land from Mexico and Spain, constructing a transcontinental railroad, and passing a homestead bill.[9]

Bates's public letter marked his return from political exile and immediately made him a contender for high office. Antislavery men, however, were split over his ideas. Abolitionists were unimpressed; conservative antislavery men, who wanted emancipation but at a gradual pace, were more sympathetic. In the end, Bates cared little for his essay's reception. After all, he wrote, "my opinions are of no importance to anybody but me, and there is good reason to fear that some of them are so antiquated and out of fashion as to make it very improbable that they will ever again be put to the test of actual practice." In that, he was wrong.[10]

One prominent person enticed by Bates's public letter was *New York Tribune* editor Horace Greeley, who, although vehemently antislavery, was skeptical whether Senator William H. Seward, current frontrunner of the Republican Party, could get elected. Greeley also had a personal vendetta against the New York senator, believing that Seward and his political manager, Thurlow Weed, had never properly rewarded him for his support in earlier state elections. What was needed, Greeley thought, was a man who could unite moderates in both the North and the Border States. While Bates's ideas on slavery, he wrote, "do not in all respects accord with our own convictions, we hail them as embodying the soundest, the clearest, the most forcible expressions yet put forth of the genuine Conservative sentiment of our country." Greeley thought that most conservatives would agree. He therefore took it upon himself to begin building a Bates-for-president movement. Before long, he had recruited prominent newspaper editors Samuel Bowles of the *Massachusetts Republican* and John D.

Defrees of the *Indianapolis State Journal*. Others, while not directly endorsing Bates's candidacy, nonetheless gave his public letter glowing reviews. F. Y. Carlile of the *Evansville Daily Journal*, for instance, called it "one of the most concise, as well as comprehensive expressions of a decided opinion, we have yet seen."[11]

Some well-respected politicians also took notice. Seven days after his letter's publication, Bates received an invitation to a private dinner at the home of Missouri Republican congressman Frank Blair Jr. Also attending were Missouri Supreme Court justice John C. Richardson, a staunch Unionist who shared Bates's distaste for radicals; George Gibson, Bates's former law student and member of the Missouri Whig Party; and Republican congressman Schuyler Colfax who had come to St. Louis to meet Bates in person.

Aside from perhaps Senator Benton—who died in 1858—and Benton's son-in-law John C. Frémont, there were few men in St. Louis other than Blair with deeper connections to national politics. His father, Francis Blair Sr., was a leading figure in politics and had been a close advisor to Andrew Jackson. Through his editorship of the *Washington Globe*, Blair Sr. had been one of the leading voices against the theory of states' rights. Frank Jr.'s brother Montgomery was also a national figure, having argued before the Supreme Court in defense of Dred Scott. In Missouri, the Blairs supported Benton in his crusade against the pro-Southern forces. When they realized that the Democrats were hopelessly co-opted by slave interests, they abandoned that party and helped found the Republican Party in April 1854. In 1856, they helped draft the new party's platform and orchestrated Frémont's campaign as the first Republican presidential nominee. In March 1857, as the Supreme Court fanned the flames of civil war, Frank Jr. entered the U.S. House of Representatives as Missouri's sole Republican congressman. Now in April 1859, by inviting Bates to dine with him, Frank was making a statement that, in the upcoming presidential contest, his family intended to again play the part of Republican kingmaker.[12]

Colfax, the other guest of honor that night, also experienced a meteoric rise to prominence. He was elected to Congress in 1854 as a Whig but ran for reelection two years later as a Republican. The next year, as the Kansas controversy erupted into fistfights and shouting matches on the House floor, and as Senator Charles Sumner was being caned by a South Carolina congressman in the Senate chamber, Colfax became a leading voice within the Republican caucus. In March 1858, he delivered a caustic denunciation of the Lecompton government. The speech was later published, broadening Colfax's appeal within the new party.[13]

Signs boded well for Republicans in 1860. The recent introductions of Minnesota and Oregon into the Union, with their aggregate of seven electoral votes, made it increasingly likely that, if Republicans made a sweep of every Northern state, they would take the White House. That would mean wrestling away from the Democrats Pennsylvania, Indiana, and Illinois—states crucial to Buchanan's victory in 1856 but which were now in play due to the political fallout over slavery. Thus, it was essential that the nominee of the Republican Party not only support the restriction of slavery and the perpetuity of the Union but also appeal to a diverse swath of voters. Toward that end, Blair and Colfax were eager to speak with Bates. This was more than a social gathering; it was the vetting of a presidential candidate by high-ranking members of a new political organization.

Seward had long been a leading voice of the antislavery movement—famously proclaiming in 1850 that providence, even more than the Constitution, dictated slavery's restriction—but his nomination was far from certain. In 1858, he had committed a serious blunder when he described the rising sectional discord as an "irrepressible conflict" that would end in the nation becoming all slave or all free. Although, in hindsight, he was correct in his assessment, Seward's provocative language made him sound to his contemporaries like a warmonger.[14]

Ohio governor Salmon P. Chase was Seward's strongest rival. Over the previous two decades, he had built a strong coalition of antislavery Democrat and Whig voters that he then led into the Republican Party. As such, he believed himself—not Seward—to be the party's natural standard-bearer. Conservatives, though, were skeptical. Many disliked Chase because of his leadership in 1844 of the Liberty Party, an organization that, by running a third-party candidate in New York, had denied Henry Clay the presidency. Furthermore, because Chase had at different times vacillated between the Democratic and Liberty Parties, they saw him as governed more by political expediency than by morals.[15]

The level of disapproval exhibited by various factions toward Seward and Chase suggested to the Blairs that room existed for an alternative candidate. Bates, in their opinion, was a true conservative. He might be just the man to break through the Seward-Chase phalanx. Bates had not, before this time, intended to take on the Republican frontrunners. At the time he wrote his public letter to the New York Whigs, he swore that it was not meant as a "candidate's letter." By the time of his meeting with Blair and Colfax a week later, however, his vanity had been stoked. Whether or not Bates considered himself a presidential candidate before the meeting, afterward—given the amount of space he devoted to presidential matters in his diary—he was fully invested. After a decade watching from behind the scenes as the sectional and political divisions brought the nation to the brink of destruction, Bates took center stage in the battle over the country's future.[16]

Bates was hopeful of his chances of winning the nomination. True, some Republicans expressed reservations over his brief flirtation with the American Party in 1856. Radical abolitionists, particularly, found nothing in his candidacy appealing. But with the Blairs in his corner, he thought, winning over conservatives in the border states would be relatively easy. The campaign would thus hinge upon moderate Northerners. Surrogates like Colfax and Greeley were crucial to that end. As for strategy, defeating Chase and Seward would depend upon stressing the unpalatable nature of their candidacies. Bates could then position himself as the best alternative.

By the summer of 1859, Bates's friends were well into their work. First, they needed to reconcile his views on slavery with the general opinion of the Republican base. Colfax feared that moderates would reject his nonagitation stance. The 1856 party platform earnestly opposed slavery's expansion into the territories, Colfax argued. The nominee in 1860 must not appear soft on that issue. Furthermore, Bates's suggestion that Americans turn a blind eye to slavery for the sake of national unity sounded like something Democratic senator Stephen Douglas—the quintessential Republican bogeyman—might say. In fact, some conservative Northerners were already courting the senator—albeit, in the end, unsuccessfully—to run as a Republican in the coming election. The first thing Bates must do, Colfax urged, was clarify his opposition to slavery.[17]

Colfax made a compelling case, but Bates still initially refused his advice. A thorough rereading of his previous speeches, he argued, would reaffirm his antislavery views. To that end, he offered Colfax extracts from two letters—one to Governor John H. Means of South Carolina in 1854, and another to Congressman Luther M. Kennett in 1856—in which he expressed his distaste for slavery but pressed for nonagitation. Bates firmly believed slavery was on the fast track to extinction. Even if not, free states would outnumber slave states before long. The South, if it hoped to compete economically, would have to embrace reform. It never occurred to

Bates that a rebellious South might choose instead to break away from the North and then seek to create new slave states by annexing more territory in the Gulf of Mexico. Still, Colfax would not relent and eventually wore Bates down, convincing him to work harder to appease Republicans. Bates thus allowed Colfax to share his letters with several newspapers. "Of course, I have no objection," Bates recorded in his diary on July 27: "my letter, tho' not written for publication, is not secret."[18]

Over the rest of the summer, a sense of optimism permeated Bates's diary entries. Shortly after his sixty-sixth birthday in September, his close friend James McPheeters shared with him an amusing anecdote. McPheeters had recently attended a Sunday school meeting where the superintendent quizzed his pupils on their knowledge of current events. "Well children," the teacher asked, "can you tell me who is President of the United States?" "Yes, yes," the pupils responded: "Buchanan!" "Now children, can you tell me who will be the next President?" the teacher asked. As McPheeters retold it: "There was a dead pause for a few seconds, when a bright faced little boy on a back seat, cried out—'Yes sir, I can tell you. Mr. Bates! Pa says he ought to be, and I reckon the People will do right.'"[19]

That same month, Illinois attorney Orville Hickman Browning visited Bates while passing through St. Louis. Browning had been born in slave-holding Kentucky and became involved in Whig politics when he moved to Illinois. After the Whigs' demise, he was a member to the convention that formed the Illinois state Republican Party. His would undoubtedly be a strong voice at the upcoming national convention in Chicago. At the time, he was uncommitted to any candidate, but after spending the day with Bates, he wrote in his diary that he found Bates to be "a man of more force and vigor of intellect than I had supposed him to be. He will be, to me, a most acceptable candidate for the Presidency, and I doubt not altogether the best man that the Republicans can support."[20]

News continued to be favorable through the autumn—especially after the radical abolitionist John Brown's failed attempt to seize the arsenal at Harpers Ferry, Virginia, and mount a servile insurrection. Bates described Brown as "a madman," and his plan as a blending of "wickedness . . . wild extravagance and utter futility." As dangerous as the abolitionist was, however, his actions played the dual function of exposing the folly of electing an extreme antislavery man and laying bare the threat the slave power posed to national unity. As the national presses reported on Brown's trial, Southern editorials conjured images of rabid abolitionists fomenting bloody civil war against the slave owners if Republicans should carry the next election. "Fear is a mean passion in itself," Bates wrote in his diary, "and produces a brood of other mean passions. . . ." Such was the natural reaction, he felt, of a people forced to reconcile with the egregious injustice of slavery, which they had allowed to perpetuate. On the other hand, wisdom and prudence dictated that national leaders avoid playing into such fears. Hence, on December 1—the day before Brown was scheduled to hang—Bates concluded: "I think now, that the probabilities of my nomination are strengthening every day. In the present state of public feeling, the Republican party (even if they desired it, which I think they do not) will hardly venture to nominate Mr. Seward."[21]

Despite Bates's increasing prospects, some obstacles remained. In Missouri, many antislavery men, unable—after John Brown—to reconcile with the Republican Party's abolitionist base, refused to embrace the organization. Instead, a fusion group of Whigs and Know-Nothings styled themselves as "the opposition party" and attempted to nominate Bates as their candidate on a third-party ticket. The attempt was, however, an embarrassment for Bates. If he could not hold together the antislavery men in his own state, how could he hope to do so nationally? As he explained to Colfax on December 13, he had only agreed to stand for the Republican nomination on the grounds that it was the best vehicle to unite under one banner conservative Know-Nothings and Whigs. "*With* that understanding," he explained, "the thing is safe; *Without* it, we shall have a scene of . . . violence never before equaled."[22]

Party unity in Missouri was crucial. To that end, Charles Gibson left immediately for Jefferson City to address the "opposition" convention while other surrogates stepped in to assist. On December 17, Abiel Leonard wrote to Bates of a meeting he had with state senator Robert Wilson—himself a delegate to the opposition convention—in which Leonard warned Wilson of the dangers of a split party. The admonition seemed to stick, for Wilson promised to persuade others at the convention to stay with the Republicans. On the tail of this letter came news from Judge William T. Woods—a Whig from St. Louis with some influence over voters in Missouri's western districts—pledging his support for Bates and the Republicans. Then two days later, Gibson reported triumphantly the majority of the opposition had agreed to support Bates on the Republican ticket and postponed their convention until February to give Bates's surrogates time to convince the remaining stragglers. "The nomination," Bates wrote optimistically in his diary, "is a great point gained. . . ."[23]

Bates's growing popularity in the other border states was crucial to his strategy at the National Convention. From North Carolina, Governor William A. Graham sent news that support there for Bates appeared strong, while Congressman Henry Winter Davis of Baltimore promised Frank Blair that he would deliver Maryland's Republicans for Bates if Missouri Republicans nominated him first. A few weeks later, Missouri Republicans did just that, and the "opposition" convention then voted overwhelmingly to support the Republican ticket. Yet, at every turn, Bates's friends encountered opposition questioning Bates's Republican bona fides. Indianan J. W. Gordon spoke for many when he wondered at Bates's switch from the Whigs to the Republicans. Was it not, he asked, because Bates was unelectable under any other banner? Greeley published his response in the pages of the *Tribune*. Bates, he wrote, had held Republican values for over forty years: "He has asserted and vindicated them in every stage, from the establishment of the Missouri Compromise to the present day; and he has done this while living in a Slave State, and in disregard of the menaces which frown upon him. Who has done more?" This statement rang particularly true given the fact that Bates had, in the last decade, freed his remaining enslaved people. For the first time in his life, Bates could claim to be completely devoid of the institution that now threatened the country.[24]

Greeley's testimonial again made a difference. By early 1860, Bates had won the endorsements of several more newspapers, including the *Boston Advertiser*, the *Baltimore Clipper*, and the *Baltimore Patriot*. In February 1860, a letter to the editor of the *New York Times* eloquently expressed the opinion of many Northern conservatives who believed the fate of the Republican Party hinged on nominating a moderate candidate. A Bates presidency, the author further theorized, "would be at once a rebuke and a chastisement of [the Democratic Party] which now, for the first time, has erected the idol of Slavery, and calls upon its devotees to fall down and worship it, as a beneficent . . . institution, to be extended and perpetuated forever."[25]

It all came down to three days in May. As delegations from the western states traveled east to the Republican national convention in Chicago, they stopped to pay Bates a visit and reassure him that, while Seward was their first choice, should the New Yorker be unable to gain the nomination on the first ballot, Bates would certainly be nominated on the second. Once in Chicago, the delegates poured into a massive wooden structure nicknamed "the Wigwam" and immersed themselves in the arduous process of jockeying for their candidates. Since the mid-1830s, these conventions had been an essential part of the American political process and were known for the national enthusiasm they generated. This gathering, though, like the election that followed, proved one of the most important in U.S. history.[26]

Delegations were met in Chicago by a carnival atmosphere that included nightly serenades, fluttering banners, and martial music. The warm reception, one *New York Times* reporter posited, was undoubtedly coordinated to produce a spirit of bonhomie among men tasked with picking a nominee. They arrived with orders from their state conventions to steadfastly support a specific candidate, the reporter noted, but once balloting began, if a nominee was not chosen on the first ballot, the momentousness of the occasion and the need to find the most "available" candidate might sway some to reconsider their loyalties. Seward was still the frontrunner, but recent news out of Charleston, where the National Democratic Party had split over the nomination of Stephen Douglas, made some Republicans anxious. Recognizing the increasing likelihood of their victory in November, they more earnestly questioned the New Yorker's strength in the general election. Even this late in the game, the *Times* reported, anything was possible. The Bates men were counting on it.[27]

The first day, Wednesday, May 16, set the tone for the rest of the convention. Over one thousand people jammed into the Wigwam while others crowded around the doors and windows to watch the selection of David Wilmot—the author of the antislavery Wilmot Proviso—as temporary chairman. The choice affirmed the antislavery principles of the Republicans and, because Wilmot was a Democrat, also signified the universality of the party's ideals. In his opening speech, and to spirited applause, Wilmot harkened to the ideals of the founding generation, proclaiming that the Republican Party's mission was "to restore the Constitution to its original meaning: to give it its true interpretation; to read that instrument as our fathers read it." In that vein, the party denounced the slave interests. "This republic," he proclaimed, "was established for the purpose of securing the guarantees of liberty, or justice and of righteousness to the people and to their posterity. That was the great object with which the revolution was fought: these were the purposes for which the Union and the Constitution was formed." Then, to even greater applause, he declared, "Slavery is sectional. Liberty national."[28]

Even now, the shadow of John Brown loomed over the proceedings. Not only did Wilmot speak for conservatives who held a natural skepticism of government, he also spoke for many—like Bates and the Blairs—who were descended from families that had long supported Jefferson's party. Surely a political party that praised Jefferson as one of its patriarchs was not a party of radical abolitionists bent on using the power of the government to stifle the sovereignty of the states.[29]

The second day, May 17, was spent drafting the party platform. Before a nominee could be chosen, the party needed a formal declaration of its political agenda. The presidential nominee would then be expected to defend those principles and—if elected—transform them into policy. To that end, several prominent conservatives, including Francis Blair Sr. and Horace Greeley, made sure to get assigned to the drafting committee and wove the ideals of free labor and honest government into the document.[30]

On the third day, the party began the work of choosing a nominee. The moment that Bates had waited for finally arrived. To rousing applause, New Yorker William Evarts started off by nominating William H. Seward. Norman B. Judd of Illinois then proposed Abraham Lincoln; Ohioan David K. Cartter named Salmon P. Chase; and, lastly, Frank Blair Jr. put forward Bates's candidacy. Other names in the mix included William Dayton, the party's vice presidential candidate in 1856, and Senator Simon Cameron of Pennsylvania. Once all the nominations were made, Massachusetts governor John Andrew moved that the convention begin voting.[31]

The first ballot went much as expected. Out of 465 votes, with 233 needed to win, Seward was in first place with 173.5 votes; Lincoln came in second with 102; Simon Cameron was in third with 50.5; and Salmon Chase followed in fourth with 49. Bates trailed Chase with 48. The one surprise came in the form of dissension in the Maryland delegation, whom Henry Winter Davis had promised to deliver for Bates. When called to cast their ballots, one of their members requested that its delegates vote as a unit, and announced their eleven votes for Bates. This would have landed Bates in fourth place, edging out Chase by two votes, but another Maryland delegate objected because, while the state convention had indeed considered a resolution to cast its votes *in toto* for Bates, that resolution had been defeated, and Maryland's delegates were therefore free to vote as they pleased. After a brief debate, the party leaders let the Marylanders vote individually and, in the process, irreparably damaged Bates's candidacy.[32]

After the first vote, the convention immediately proceeded to the second, where Bates's numbers dwindled to 35 as those delegations originally promised to support him on the second ballot realized the weakness of his candidacy. Most of Bates's first-ballot votes went to Lincoln, whose numbers increased from 102 to 181. Seward's numbers also increased to 184.5, but the momentum was clearly behind Lincoln, who enjoyed a gain of 79 votes on the second ballot while Seward won only an additional 11.[33]

The third vote put Lincoln within striking distance of the nomination. Seward's numbers dropped only slightly from 184 to 180, but Bates's plummeted from 35 to 22, and Chase's dropped from 42.5 to 24.5. On the other hand, Lincoln gained 50.5 votes over his second ballot total, and a net gain since the first ballot of 129.5. The nomination was made official when Ohio moved an additional four Chase votes to Lincoln, putting him over the top with 235.5.[34]

Bates learned of the outcome at Chicago when he read the May 19 headline of the *Missouri Democrat*: "LINCOLN NOMINATED ON THIRD BALLOT." While Missouri had remained steadfast for its favorite son to the very end, only Connecticut had done likewise. All the other delegations that had pledged support for him had instead sprinted to Lincoln. Once the landslide to Lincoln began, his nomination was simply unstoppable.[35]

Bates's loss was a bitter pill. Until recently, Lincoln had been relatively unknown outside of Illinois. Like Bates, he had served one term in Congress—during the Mexican-American War—where his contemporaries laughingly referred to him as "Spotty Lincoln" for his speech on the floor of the House of Representatives in 1848 calling upon President Polk to point out on a map "the spot" where American blood had been spilled by Mexican troops. Lincoln's national acclaim had only come after his failed attempt in 1858 to deny Senator Stephen A. Douglas a third term. Lincoln had done a masterful job of expressing the Republican antislavery position in that contest, but Bates never considered him a serious opponent. Indeed, most of the other frontrunners had spent the better part of a year drumming up support for their candidacies. Lincoln, in contrast, seemed late to the game; so late, in fact, that a compilation of biographies of potential presidential candidates published in early 1860 did not even mention him.[36]

Bates feared that Lincoln's dark-horse candidacy threatened to jeopardize the unity of the Republican ranks. Having openly debated Douglass in 1858, Lincoln's views on slavery were a matter of public record and ran counter to Bates's theory that nonagitation was the best means of uniting the country. As such, Republicans had committed a "fatal blunder" by nominating Lincoln over a more conciliatory candidate. "They have . . . weakened [their party] in the free states," Bates predicted, "and destroyed its hopeful beginnings in the border slave states."[37]

The stark contrasts between Bates and Lincoln—both in terms of their background and philosophies—led naturally to the question of what went wrong with Bates's candidacy. Leading up to the convention, Bates's chances of beating Seward seemed strong. The main problem, it turned out, was the large number of German immigrants present at the convention who saw Bates's previous flirtation with the antiforeign American Party as anathema to Republican values. It did not matter that he had denounced the nativists in private; he had supported Fillmore in 1856, forever tying his name to the nativists' cause. Two leading Germans in particular, Carl Schurz of Wisconsin and Gustave Koerner of Illinois, sealed Bates's fate at the convention by speaking out against him at a German political rally held in between the first and second day, and by getting themselves elected to the platform committee, where they weaved in language denouncing nativism that effectively made Bates's nomination impossible.[38]

The German Republicans had deemed Bates unacceptable, but it remained an open question as to why they moved to Lincoln instead of Seward. Schurz—originally a pro-Seward man—posited two reasons. Lincoln's published speeches were less bombastic than Seward's, and Seward's managers at the convention were more in the open about promising patronage positions to those who voted for their man, tainting the Seward camp with corruption. In an age when the presidency was still an office that was supposed to *seek the man*, Seward's tactics looked too much like a power grab.

By this point in American politics, it was virtually impossible for a presidential candidate to be devoid of at least some ambition. The days of the country bestowing the office on the occupant, as it had supposedly done to George Washington in 1789, were long gone. The development of professional politics in the second quarter of the nineteenth century had seen to that. Indeed, Lincoln himself was no less ambitious than the other candidates. Furthermore, his *House Divided* speech was little more than

Seward's *Irrepressible Conflict* address couched in fairer language, and the Lincoln camp was as active as Seward's at recruiting voters at Chicago. Indeed, on the third day, Lincoln's campaign manager, David Davis, had successfully packed the galleries of the Wigwam with spectators directed to shout as loud as possible for Lincoln once his name was placed in nomination, giving the illusion that the Illinoisan was being nominated by acclamation. In short, Davis's plan was so masterfully choreographed and executed as to outsmart Lincoln's rivals.[39]

Davis's presence at the convention, as well as Seward's man Weed, also made a tremendous difference in comparison with Bates, who left much of the organization of his candidacy to surrogates without ever selecting one specific man to lead them. Blair, Colfax, and Greeley were prominent voices in the Bates-for-president movement, to be sure, but no single person coordinated the floor vote at Chicago.

Bates had much time for reflection in the weeks following the convention. Cast adrift by the dissolution of the Whig Party, he had nonetheless remained confident that Whiggism could yet survive in the guise of Republicanism. The results at Chicago quashed those hopes. With the failure of his candidacy, he now lamented, "I have no future. I may hereafter . . . occasionally make a speech or write an essay, but I shall not engage so deeply in any political question as to be seriously disturbed by the result." Then, in a moment of finality, he declared, "My political life has closed."[40]

To friends who fought hard for his candidacy, Bates opened his heart a little more. In a letter to Colfax, he wrote: "I was surprised, I own, but not at all mortified at the result at Chicago." He was thankful to have been considered for high office, but he now convinced himself that he never really wanted the nomination. He could not help, however, offering a projection for the general election in November. "Can you carry [Lincoln's candidacy] in [Indiana]?" he asked Colfax: "I hope so, but doubt it, if Douglas be the opposing candidate." Indiana and the other swing states would never cast their electoral votes for John C. Breckinridge, he believed, but neither were they friendly to Lincoln.[41]

Lincoln's surrogates were equally worried about that outcome. However, they saw Bates as the man best suited to do something about it. Shortly after the convention, Orville H. Browning—to shore up Whig support for Lincoln—reached out to Bates expressing Lincoln's respect for the old Whig and reassuring him of Lincoln's steadfast support for both the Union and the restriction of slavery in the territories. Because Bates's own views so closely aligned with Lincoln's, Browning suggested, might Bates consider making a public statement of support for the Republicans? After some initial reluctance, Bates conceded that such an endorsement would go far toward keeping the party unified. Furthermore, given his personal disdain for the Democrats, and his lack of faith in the Constitutional Union Party, Bates conceded that the Republican ticket was the only viable choice. Thus, on June 23, he wrote a public letter, published in the *New York Times* and picked up by other nationally syndicated papers, praising Lincoln and endorsing his candidacy.[42]

"It ought not to have been doubted that I would give Mr. Lincoln's nomination a cordial and hearty support," Bates wrote. Many conservative Republicans had honored him by considering him a candidate for the nomination, and he personally shared the party's opinion that the national government had the power to regulate slavery in the territories. Then there was the nominee himself. In a somewhat exaggerated statement, Bates wrote, "I have known Mr. Lincoln for more than twenty years and, therefore, have a right to speak of him with some confidence." In truth, the two likely met at the 1847 River and Harbor Convention. Nonetheless, Bates's next statement was accurate enough: "As an individual, [Lincoln] has earned a high reputation for truth, courage, candor, morals and amiability: so that, as a man, he is most trustworthy." More importantly, Lincoln was a good Whig. "All his old political antecedents are, in my judgment, exactly right," Bates concluded, "being square up to the old Whig standard. And as to his views about 'the pestilent negro question,' I am not aware that he has gone one step beyond the doctrine publicly and habitually avowed by the great lights of the Whig Party, Clay, Webster, and their followers. . . ."[43]

It is uncertain whether Bates's letter convinced any straggling Whigs to cast their vote for Lincoln, but the results of the general election were all Bates could have hoped for. In October 1860, Ohio, Pennsylvania, and Indiana returned safe majorities for the Republicans and thus ensured their electoral votes for Lincoln. On October 13, Bates wrote in his diary: "Now the election of Lincoln is as certain as any future, human event. . . . The Democratic party, as organized and managed since Polk's accession to the Presidency, in 1845, is *destroyed* by Lincoln's election." Furthermore, he predicted of the Republican Party, "if it be but moderately wise" in bestowing patronage posts, refusing to further annex southern territories, implementing a liberal protectionist tariff, and investing in public works projects, would "become the permanent, governing party."[44]

On November 6, Lincoln's election was assured. Out of 303 electoral votes, Lincoln won 180, sweeping every Northern state, as well as California and Oregon. Breckinridge came in second with 72 votes, having swept the lower South as well as Maryland and Delaware. John Bell—the nominee of the Constitutional Union Party—won 39 votes from Tennessee, Kentucky, and Virginia; and, lastly, Stephen Douglas came in fourth with 12 votes from Missouri and New Jersey. Not one slaveholding state voted for Lincoln. Still, conservative Republicans found some solace in the fact that Missouri, Tennessee, Kentucky, and Virginia—with their votes for Bell and Douglas—had soundly rejected disunion. Thus, there was reason to hope that Lincoln could find support in the upper South if the lower South followed through on its threat to secede.[45]

Bates was personally bolstered by Lincoln's victory. Many conservative Republicans assumed that, once elected, "Honest Abe" would preside over an honest government. To that end, with the country divided and threats of secession from the South, Lincoln wanted to bring into his cabinet as many groups—ideologically and geographically—as possible. On election night, he scribbled out on the back of a scrap of paper a list of potential cabinet members that included William H. Seward, William L. Dayton, Norman B. Judd, Salmon P. Chase, Montgomery Blair, Gideon Welles, and Bates himself.[46]

On December 13, Bates received a telegram from the president-elect requesting an earnest conversation at the earliest possible moment. Bates packed a bag that night and boarded a train for Springfield the next morning. There, Lincoln's young secretary, John G. Nicolay, caught a glimpse of him sitting down to breakfast in one of the city's hotels, and jotted down his impressions. "His hair is grey," Nicolay wrote, "and his beard quite white, and his face shows all the marks of age quite strongly." Still, something of the eloquent and commanding attorney of years past remained. Later that day, Nicolay was privy to Bates's discussion with Lincoln, where Bates "spoke his thoughts in clear, concise language, indicated a very comprehensive and definite intellectual grasp of ideas, and a great facility in their expression."[47]

Later that morning, the two former political rivals met in Lincoln's office at the Illinois statehouse, where they talked over several important matters. Even as they spoke, in South Carolina, a convention of delegates angry at the outcome of the late election was debating whether to take the state out of the Union. Bates believed the secessionists "absolutely demented," but he held no illusions that they would prevail and drag the other cotton-producing states "into the pit" with them. Hence, Lincoln explained, the importance of his summons. The president-elect needed strong-willed, prudent men in his administration. He confessed that he had already offered the State Department to Seward earlier that month, but Seward had yet to accept. If he should decline, Lincoln assured Bates that the post would be his. Otherwise, he hoped Bates would accept the offer to become the next U.S. attorney general.[48]

Bates was somewhat apprehensive about Seward joining the cabinet. It might send the wrong message to conservatives that Lincoln had compromised his principles for the sake of political expediency. Regarding his own place in the administration, Bates explained to Lincoln that his offer was not wholly unexpected and that, initially, Bates intended to decline on the grounds of age—he was now sixty-seven—as well as the low salary of a public officer. The tranquility of a less busy lifestyle, compared to the constant entertaining of Washington society, was also an enticement. However, Bates had made that conclusion back in October, when peace prevailed. Now, he later wrote, "I am not at liberty to consult my own interests and wishes, and must subordinate them to my convictions of public duty. . . ."[49]

Glad to have Bates on board, Lincoln then issued his first orders. Between now and the inauguration, he wanted Bates to familiarize himself with the Constitution and the laws regarding secession and be ready to give an opinion on the matter. Bates acquiesced and stated upfront his belief that Lincoln could maintain the Union by force. As Nicolay later described, Bates professed himself to be "a man of peace, and will defer fighting as long as possible; but that if forced to do so against his will, he has made it a rule *never to fire blank cartridges.*"[50]

Bates was emboldened by Lincoln's resolve to preserve the Union. In a January 31 letter to Missouri conservative James S. Rollins, he more eloquently expressed his reasons for joining the new administration. By then, Seward had accepted the State Department, and Rollins—himself recently elected to Congress as a Constitutional Unionist—pressured Bates on why he joined an administration that seemed to be anything but conservative. Bates replied that the national crisis outweighed any political or philosophical differences he might have with Seward. By then, five Southern states had seceded; Texas would leave the next day. With the hope for reconciliation between the Union and the disaffected states growing smaller by the day, there was simply no room for squabbling. "I go into [this] service willingly," he wrote, "putting to hazard all that I have and all that I am, in a strenuous effort to preserve the Union." Come March 1861, Bates would occupy a unique position from which to infuse his conservative values into the first Republican administration.[51]

The Republican Convention of 1860 marked the last time Bates entered the public arena as a candidate for elective office. His defeat for the nomination, however, was not due to any lack of professional qualifications. Rather, he was ultimately defeated because of a fatal decision to support the nativist presidential ticket in 1856. Likewise, the Republican Party proved too publicly antislavery to accept Bates's proposal of nonagitation. With his middle-of-the-road approach, Lincoln represented a new generation of political leader that could unite moderate, conservative, and radical antislavery men alike. Bates had misjudged his own chances at the nomination, discovering that he was too conservative to win the prize. Nonetheless, because of his steadfast loyalty to the Union and his status as a genuine antislavery border statesman, Lincoln wisely invited him into the cabinet. While Bates initially thought that his political career was over, his acceptance of the attorney generalship marked the start of the most important chapter of his life.

As late as the 1850s, Edward Bates, *above*, still maintained the deep-set eyes and thick mane of his youth. From *DeBow's Review* (1855), Missouri Historical Society Photographs and Prints Collection.

Bates's friend, John F. Darby, described Julia Bates, *left*, in her youth as "a most beautiful woman." Missouri Historical Society Photographs and Prints Collection.

Edward Bates's older brother, Frederick, was one of the most influential citizens in the Missouri Territory and a role model to his younger brother. Missouri Historical Society Objects Collection.

Edward Bates's brother-in-law, Hamilton R. Gamble, was a capable attorney, associate judge of the Missouri Supreme Court, and governor of Missouri during the Civil War. Missouri Historical Society Photographs and Prints Collection.

Edward and Julia Bates's oldest son, Joshua Barton Bates, followed in his father's footsteps as an attorney. His uncle, Hamilton R. Gamble, later named him to the Missouri Supreme Court. Missouri Historical Society Photographs and Prints Collection.

Senator Thomas Hart Benton was a worthy political opponent who later found himself on the same ideological side as Bates in the fight over slavery. Library of Congress Daguerreotype Collection.

Senator Charles Daniel Drake was Bates's most formidable political adversary during the Civil War and Reconstruction. Library of Congress Prints and Photographs Division.

The Great St. Louis Fire of 1849 ravaged the St. Louis commercial district, leaving much of it in rubble. In a few years, a new, safer city would rise from the ashes. Missouri Historical Society Photographs and Prints Collection.

By the time this photo was taken, somewhere between 1861 and 1865, Edward Bates had begun to show the stress of his office. Library of Congress Prints and Photographs Division.

In December 1860, President-
elect Abraham Lincoln asked
Edward Bates to serve in his
administration as attorney
general. Library of Congress
Prints and Photographs Division.

Bates was concerned at Lincoln's
decision to include New York
senator William Seward in his
administration as secretary of
state. Library of Congress Prints
and Photographs Division.

Bates was equally unsure of Lincoln's inclusion of Ohio governor Salmon P. Chase in his administration as secretary of the treasury. Library of Congress Prints and Photographs Division.

Joining Bates in the Lincoln administration as postmaster general was fellow conservative Montgomery Blair. Library of Congress Prints and Photographs Division.

Another conservative in Lincoln's administration was Secretary of the Navy Gideon Welles. Library of Congress Prints and Photographs Division.

Initially, Bates got along well with Secretary of War Edwin Stanton. Their relationship soured as the Civil War progressed. Library of Congress Prints and Photographs Division.

Francis Bicknell Carpenter's painting, *First Reading of the Emancipation Proclamation of Abraham Lincoln,* was later rendered into this engraving by A. H. Ritchie. The original painting is in the possession of the U.S. Senate. Library of Congress Prints and Photographs Division.

This bronze statue of Edward Bates, located in Forest Park in St. Louis, Missouri, was dedicated concurrently with the opening of the new park in 1876. In the 1930s, it was moved from the southeast end of the park to its current location on the western side. Author's Personal Collection.

7.
The Union Dissolved;
The Union Defended

In late December, Bates's friend and former St. Louis mayor, William Carr Lane, wrote to express his concern that the country was quickly approaching the point of disaster. "A few more onward steps," he warned, "will bring us to the awful plunge, into disunion, anarchy, and civil war, with all their attendant horrors." If such an outcome occurred, he continued, the Lincoln administration would bear the blame for keeping the South in the Union by force. "Coercion, my friend," Lane wrote, "is utterly impossible." It was far better, he concluded, to let the South go, and Missouri with it.[1]

Bates did not share his friend's futility. As he wrote former Virginia governor Wyndham Robertson in November: "I can hardly realize the thought that any considerable number of men should attempt by force to destroy the government. . . . It is incredible that sane men should incur the guilt of treason." Should such a thing happen, Bates posited, the government possessed the tools to uphold the law. "Every other government, under the sun," he wrote Robertson, "is armed with force to repress evil & punish crime; and, for the highest good of society, persons are appointed for the very purpose of applying all the sanctions of the law, from the highest to the lowest, from the gallows to the rod."[2]

The secession crisis, Bates believed, was the work of a minority of disaffected Southerners. The proper response was to show restraint. Referencing Southern loyalists, Bates wrote to Robertson: "I would appeal to them by every motive that binds us to a common Country . . . to put down the mischief-makers, quietly and beforehand, and not allow to be forced upon the general government, the painful but inexorable duty to put them down by any & all means provided by the law."[3]

Lincoln, in contrast, made it clear that he would act on the matter. As he traveled eastward to his inauguration, he said as much to thousands of spectators across the North. At Philadelphia, for instance, Lincoln expressed to a crowd in front of Independence Hall the overwhelming emotion he felt at standing in the very place where the Union had been born. Now, with the black clouds of civil war looming, Lincoln's resolve to preserve the nation had only grown more resolute. "If this country cannot be saved without giving up that principle," he exclaimed, "I would rather be assassinated on this spot than surrender it."[4]

Lincoln's steadfast unionism pleased Bates, but news from Congress of a compromise with the South made him increasingly anxious. Despite the Republican Party's emphatic support for restricting slavery from the territories, Kentucky senator John J. Crittenden hoped that the very real threat of disunion would compel like-minded conservatives to abandon this principle. As a means of stopping the spread of secession and possibly bringing back those states already gone, Crittenden and his cohorts proposed a series of amendments to the constitution that would bar the government from intervening in the matter of slavery in the states where it already existed, compensate slave owners for runaway enslaved people, and reinstate the Missouri Compromise line.[5]

Bates had no personal connection to the ongoing discussions in Washington, but, as a representative of the incoming administration, he was nonetheless solicited by his neighbors in St. Louis for a formal response. He avoided replying directly—believing that the president-elect should speak for the new administration—but instead hurried off a note to Lincoln detailing his thoughts on the matter. Southerners, he felt, were negotiating in good faith, but even so he believed the amendments to bar the government from interfering in slavery and extend the Missouri Compromise line were nonstarters. Even if they passed Congress, they would never get the requisite three-fourths of the states to ratify them. The Union could never be saved by this means. Yet, if a silver lining existed to these proposals, Bates wrote, it was that the debates in the state legislatures would provide time for loyal Southerners to mobilize and take back their states without much interference on the part of the federal government.[6]

As concerned as Bates was by the compromise measures, events closer to home were just as troubling. In August, Missourians elected Democrat Claiborne Fox Jackson—author of the Jackson Resolutions—as governor. That fall, however, they voted for Stephen Douglas for president, suggesting support for popular sovereignty and the preservation of the Union. Jackson nonetheless took an ardently pro-Southern stance once he assumed office in January. Misrepresenting the Republicans as a cadre of radical abolitionists, he rejected the notion that they sought only to limit slavery's extension into the territories. Because Missouri's commerce—not to mention its people—was inextricably linked with the South, Jackson reasoned, the state risked being shut off from Southern markets if it sided with the North. He therefore called for a state convention to decide on Missouri's place in the Union.[7]

The state legislature set February 18 as the date for electing delegates to the convention and secessionists in St. Louis immediately put forward a list of candidates and preemptively formed a pro-Southern militia— named the "Minute Men"—to begin drilling for the defense of the state. In response, unionists in the city created their own list of candidates and formed their own militia, called the "Home Guard." If civil war came to Missouri, these two sides would inevitably be among the first to come to blows.[8]

Bates could not attend the convention himself—he would be too busy in Washington—but he did have a personal stake in the choice of delegates. After all, Hamilton Gamble was running for election to the convention as a unionist. He was content in his certainty that the unionists would carry the majority, but he also surmised that the real drama would likely be the struggle by the two militias to control the federal arsenal on the outskirts of town.[9]

The arsenal had the largest cache of weapons west of the Mississippi and was under the command of Major William H. Bell, a subordinate of Jackson's who refused to grant the Home Guard access to the arsenal grounds. He was supported in this by Brigadier General Daniel M. Frost of the Missouri State Militia—a third paramilitary force independent of the two St. Louis militias—who was also a Jackson supporter. After receiving pressure from pro-Union Missourians like Frank Blair Jr., President Buchanan ultimately sent a paltry forty U.S. soldiers to the city. They arrived on January 11 and were soon stationed on the arsenal grounds. Meanwhile, Blair worked to bolster the federal ranks by recruiting an additional two militias made up of German radicals and lobbying Washington to send more men. St. Louis, it was clear, was fast becoming a powder keg.[10]

Bates personally stayed out of these affairs but kept Lincoln apprised of them. "The Arsenal at St. Louis, is I fear in a dangerous condition" he wrote on January 30: "It ought to be guarded by a garrison strong enough to handle the evil disposed from making any attack upon it. Whereas I hear that the force stationed there is so small as to rather invite attack than repel it." Realizing that there was virtually nothing that Lincoln could do until he assumed office on March 4, Bates hoped that if the president-elect at least joined his voice with those unionists already pressuring the Buchanan administration, it might at least compel the president to act.[11]

No evidence exists that Lincoln pressured Buchanan one way or the other, but the president seemed to come to his senses regarding the direness of the situation in St. Louis. In the last week of January and the first of February, he sent federal soldiers from Jefferson Barracks under the command of Captain Thomas Sweeny and from Fort Riley, Kansas, under Captain Nathaniel Lyon to reinforce those already stationed at the arsenal. Meanwhile, Buchanan relieved Major Bell from command and replaced him with Brevet Major Peter V. Hagner.[12]

More good news came on March 4 when a decided majority of the delegates to the state convention in Jefferson City expressed their unconditional support for the Union and voted to relocate to the Mercantile Library in the pro-Union stronghold of St. Louis. While former Missouri governor Sterling Price—himself questionable on loyalty to the Union—was named chairman of the convention, the true power was in the hands of Gamble, who dominated the proceedings and convinced a strong majority of delegates that secession was too rash a move.[13]

By that time, Bates was no longer able to serve as an eyewitness to these events. On February 5, Lincoln's secretary, John G. Nicolay, sent a cable informing him of the president-elect's plan to depart for Washington on the eleventh of that month and that Lincoln would like very much for his attorney general to join him on the trip. Bates was forced to take a later train, however, in order to finish putting his affairs in order, which included payment of several outstanding loans and settling his portion of his late sister Sarah's estate. It was not until February 25, accompanied by son Richard, that he departed St. Louis for the nation's capital.[14]

Three days later, he arrived in Washington, D.C., and checked into the National Hotel on Pennsylvania Avenue. He then immediately launched into a flurry of activity: attending to office seekers, dignitaries, and well-wishers. Indeed, on Bates's first night in the city, Congressman Elbridge Gerry Spaulding invited him to dinner, where Bates found himself in the company of not only Lincoln but also William Seward, Salmon P. Chase, Gideon Welles, and Charles Francis Adams—soon to be minister to Great Britain.[15]

During his inaugural tour of the Northern states, Lincoln had remained noncommittal on the compromise measures floated in Washington. It was now clear to Bates that Lincoln was no more committed to a plan of action in private than he was in public. Lincoln's inaugural address on March 4 thus became his clearest statement on the great questions before the new administration. No state, he said, could lawfully leave the Union, and any acts of violence against federal authority would be met by his administration with a proportional response. All the South had to do to avoid such a calamity was put down their arms and return their elected officials to Washington. The "momentous issue of civil war" was in their hands, not his.[16]

Bates's only mention of the inauguration was to note that no attempt was made to disrupt the proceedings. He made no comment—privately or otherwise—of his thoughts on the content of the inaugural address. However, given his previous statements to Lincoln professing faith in the existence of a Southern counterinsurgency, he was likely pleased at the unprovocative nature of the speech.[17]

The next day, Lincoln submitted his nominations for cabinet officers to the U.S. Senate. Joining Bates were Seward at the State Department; Chase at Treasury; Gideon Welles of Connecticut at the Navy Department; former Pennsylvania senator Simon Cameron at the War Department; former U.S. congressman from Indiana Caleb Smith at the Interior Department; and Montgomery Blair of Maryland as postmaster general. As political rivals for the Republican presidential nomination, Seward and Chase were perhaps best known. Behind them, though, were the equally formidable personalities of Welles and Blair. Possessing a full white beard and ill-fitting wig, Welles resembled the jovial Father Christmas but was, in practice, a shrewd Yankee politico. Like Bates, he was raised in a fervently Jeffersonian family but had taken a different path in politics. In the mid-1830s, he joined the Democrats and became a close associate of Van Buren. He served in the Navy Department under Polk but abandoned the party in 1848 to support the Free-Soilers. Support for that antislavery ticket naturally brought him into Republican circles after 1854, and his strong support of Lincoln in 1860 made him a natural choice to return to the Navy Department in the new administration.[18]

Blair, too, had deep Jacksonian roots. The first son of Francis Preston Blair, and the older brother of Frank Blair Jr., he got his education in Democratic politics from his father as well as Andrew Jackson himself. After he graduated from West Point in 1835, he saw action in the Second Seminole War and earned a law degree from Transylvania University before opening practice in St. Louis, where he floated in the same social circles as Bates. In 1852, he moved to Maryland, and in 1856—despite being a member of a slaveholding family—his antislavery principles led him to defend Dred Scott before the Supreme Court. If Bates represented the old-line Whig element of the new Republican coalition, Blair and Welles represented the old Democratic faction.[19]

The office into which Bates now stepped had enjoyed a unique evolution since it was created by the Judiciary Act of 1789. Edmund Randolph, the first U.S. attorney general under George Washington, once described it as "a sort of mongrel between State and U.S.; called an officer of some rank under the latter, and yet thrust out to get a livelihood in the former." Randolph headed no department and brought in a salary of $1,500—too meager to support himself and his family. As such, he kept a side practice to supplement his government income; a precedent that subsequent attorneys general followed until the early 1850s. Furthermore, while attorneys general did not traditionally reside in the nation's capital, they were, as chief legal advisor to the president, nonetheless expected to be available and were occasionally summoned as needed to cabinet meetings. As such, the office was occupied by men who either hailed from geographic regions within a few days' travel of Washington or were wealthy enough to rent quarters in nearby cities.[20]

As the federal government increased over time, subsequent presidents from Madison to Polk sought to reform the office of attorney general, putting it on par with the other cabinet positions. Congress was slow to act, however, only increasing the attorney general's salary in the late 1840s so that the occupant no longer had to rely on side work to make ends meet. Still, by 1861, the attorney general made $8,000 a year (approximately $241,088 in 2021 dollars), enjoyed equal status with the rest of the cabinet, and resided full-time in Washington. It was into this newly expanded office that Bates entered as the twenty-sixth U.S. attorney general, ready to offer legal counsel to President Lincoln in the greatest constitutional crisis to ever face the country.[21]

Lincoln had thrown down the proverbial gauntlet to the seceded states, and before long they tested the mettle of his new administration. No new states joined the Confederacy in the days immediately following Lincoln's speech, but neither did any of those already seceded rejoin the Union. Rather, in South Carolina, war became imminent. Awaiting Lincoln on March 5 were letters from acting secretary of war Joseph Holt, General-in-Chief Winfield Scott, and Major Robert Anderson, commander of Fort Sumter in Charleston Harbor. The letters held bad news. Fort Sumter constituted the last Union presence in South Carolina. Buchanan tried to reinforce it earlier in the year, but that endeavor was aborted when Confederate batteries fired on the *Star of the West*, the ship carrying the soldiers. Since then, no effort had been made to aid the beleaguered garrison. Now, Anderson was reporting that he and his men had only enough supplies to last a few weeks.[22]

Lincoln did not immediately present the matter to his cabinet. Instead, their first gathering on March 6 was, as Bates described it, "intended, I suppose to be formal and introductory only—in fact, uninteresting." It was not until three days later that the President mentioned Fort Sumter. When he did, Bates was shocked at the pitiful state of Anderson's garrison as well as disheartened to learn that General Scott and Anderson both recommended evacuation on the grounds that it would take a force of twenty thousand men and "a bloody battle, to relieve it."[23]

Lincoln—like his attorney general—was not inclined to accept this assessment. In the days that followed, he sought advice from numerous sources on the best course of action. Aside from his regular cabinet and General Scott, other voices sought by Lincoln included Army chief engineer general Joseph Gilbert Totten, Commodore Silas H. Stringham of the U.S. Navy, and Assistant Secretary of the Navy Gustavus Fox. A division of opinion split the two branches of the military, with the army stressing the infeasibility of any expedition to Fort Sumter, and the navy arguing that an expedition of light draft vehicles could easily run the Confederate batteries with minimal risk.[24]

Personally, Bates was bolstered by the navy's assessment, but he understood that there was more at stake than simply successful completion of a mission. Sending an expedition to Fort Sumter, he feared, might provoke a war. The bigger question was whether Fort Sumter was worth the price. Charleston was of little consequence militarily, he thought. Fort Pickens, another fort then being harassed by Confederates in Pensacola Bay, was a far better prize. Therefore, Bates wrote Lincoln: "I am willing to evacuate Fort Sumter rather than be an active party in the beginning of a civil war."[25]

Seward, Welles, and Cameron echoed Bates. Aiding Fort Sumter, Welles thought, did nothing to lift the "dignity, strength or character of the government." Seward, on the other hand, feared that any news of an expedition would reach Charleston before the ships did and might provoke the Confederates into a preemptive attack. When the fight came, Cameron added, the federal government would find that it had wasted so much time vacillating on the matter that Confederate batteries there were now nearly impregnable. Surrender was only a matter of time, and "the sooner it be done, the better."[26]

Chase and Blair were the only cabinet members to support holding Fort Sumter. It was a matter of principle, wrote Chase. The federal government had a clear right to defend its property. Blair agreed but—fearing that too strong a display of federal power might hinder Southern loyalists—urged caution. Any action, he wrote, "should be done with as little blood-shed as possible" and must be accomplished to create such an "outburst of patriotic feeling" that it would "initiate a reactionary movement throughout the South which would speedily overwhelm the traitors."[27]

The prospects for a Southern counterrevolution were on the minds of many in the cabinet. The governments of the Southern states, they believed—not the people themselves—were responsible for secession. Most Southerners, deep in their hearts, were still loyal to the Union and would, if supported by the administration, eventually band together and overthrow the hotheads. Perhaps referring to events in Arkansas, North Carolina, Missouri, Virginia, and Tennessee—all of which rejected initial calls for secession—Bates told Lincoln: "A reaction has already begun, and, if encouraged by wise, moderate and firm measures on the part of this government, I persuade myself that the nation will be restored to its integrity without the effusion of blood." The meeting adjourned without a decision, but one thing was certain. Overtures of peace would continue, but if Confederate forces surrounding Forts Sumter and Pickens fired on the American flag, the federal government would be forced to respond in kind.[28]

Lincoln personally sympathized with Chase and Blair, but he agreed to wait for the time being. Then, seemingly out of nowhere, General Winfield Scott changed his mind and proposed abandoning all Union forts in the South as a means of de-escalating tensions. On March 29, Lincoln called an emergency cabinet session to consider Scott's new idea. As the men began to argue, Bates sought to bring order to the proceedings by suggesting that each minister submit his opinion in writing. Soon it became evident that Scott's suggestion had sparked a change in the cabinet, though not in the way he had hoped. Almost all the men now favored defending Fort Sumter. For himself, Bates added only that he felt that the time had come to make a final decision on the matter, one way or another.[29]

Rejecting Scott's proposal, Lincoln now decided unequivocally to reprovision Sumter. To ensure protection of the provisioning force, the president also authorized an accompanying naval expedition with orders that it remain anchored off the coast of South Carolina. On April 8, the ships sailed from New York. Simultaneously, Lincoln dispatched his close friend and associate, Ward Hill Lamon, as special envoy to South Carolina. Lamon's orders were to speak with Governor Francis Pickens and reassure him that the expedition, which would arrive on April 11 or 12, was a peaceful one. "If Maj. Anderson hold out till then [sic]," Bates wrote in his diary on April 8, "one of two things will happen—either the fort will be well provisioned, the Southrons forbearing to assail the boats, or a fierce contest will ensue, the result of which cannot be foreseen—the fort may be demolished or the City burned—In either case, there will be much slaughter."[30]

These last-ditch efforts to avoid war ended in failure. When Governor Pickens notified Confederate president Jefferson Davis of the Union naval expedition, Davis in turn ordered Brigadier General P. G. T. Beauregard, commander of Confederate forces surrounding Fort Sumter, to demand Robert Anderson's surrender. Anderson refused, and at 4 A.M. on the morning of April 12, with the Union ships helplessly tossed about in a gale off the South Carolina coast, Beauregard opened fire. After a bombardment lasting thirty-three hours, Anderson surrendered on April 13 and evacuated Fort Sumter the next day.[31]

No administration since Washington's had been pressed with solving such dire issues. For Bates, the stresses took their toll. On March 22, at the height of public speculation over which way Lincoln would go, Bates wrote to his grandson, Onward, that he suffered from a bout of influenza that confined him to bed for two days. The weather in Washington had been dreary, but he hoped that if the following day proved fair, he might be able to attend a cabinet meeting. In a tender moment, after explaining the importance of cabinet councils to the affairs of the nation, Bates wrote: "And so my dear child, you can see that it is a great matter, because the fortunes & the lives of thousands of people may depend upon what we do." Then, he added: "No man ought to be there who does not fear God & love his country—and I wish all my pious friends to pray for me, that I may be able to give honest & wise advice, for the good of the country."[32]

8.
Constitutional Scruples

In March 1861, as the cabinet debated what to do with Fort Sumter, Bates wrote to Barton in St. Louis that "the work for office is overwhelming & I find that more official appointments pass through *my mill* than I was aware of. . . ." Indeed, in his first month in office, Bates found himself hounded daily by office seekers, making recommendations for territorial judgeships and federal marshals, and reviewing petitions for clemency such as that from a delegation of Chickasaw Natives requesting that Lincoln stay the execution of tribesmen Reyburn Porter and Billy Jimmy for the murder of two white men (the president indefinitely delayed their sentencing on April 2).[1]

Lincoln also tasked Bates with more complicated legal matters. On March 18, for instance, he requested Bates's opinions on whether he could create a bureau of militia within the War Department and whether he could legally collect duties in the seceded states by posting naval vessels offshore and forcing all incoming ships to offload their goods. Although Bates never answered the latter question—the outbreak of war and subsequent blockade of Southern ports made that issue moot—he denied that the president had the power to create a militia bureau. Still, he wished to make an important distinction. The proposed bureau would have been a separate entity within the War Department, with its own administrator appointed by the president. Such an entity required an act of Congress. However, Bates noted, the Constitution conferred upon the president direct management of the state militias during war. If the South fired on Sumter, Lincoln wouldn't need Congress to take control of the militias.[2]

Bates worked on his opinion during the last weeks of March and the first week of April, presenting it to Lincoln on April 18—four days after the evacuation of Fort Sumter. By then, Lincoln had already nationalized the state militias on April 15, calling for seventy-five thousand volunteers to suppress the rebellion in the South. Nonetheless, questions persisted. Exactly how would he use this force? Where would he send it? And what would be its objective?[3]

By waging a civil war, Lincoln ran the risk of violating the very constitution he had sworn to uphold. The Declaration of Independence, with its language about the duty of the people to alter or abolish a government that threatened their natural rights, seemed to legitimize rebellion, but the Constitution did not. Aside from a brief mention in Article I, Section 9, which dealt with the suspension of habeas corpus, the Constitution made no reference at all to rebellion. Because the Constitution failed to define rebellion as an act of war, Lincoln technically lacked the power to intervene in the South.[4]

Bates, for one, believed that a state of war—he did not use the word *rebellion*—existed. Nonetheless, he continued to place his faith in the supposed existence of loyal Southerners, whom he hoped would settle the dispute without the need for federal troops. "I am for 'enforcing the laws' with no object but to reinstate the authority of the Government and restore the integrity of the nation," he wrote on April 15. "And with that object in view I think it would be wise and humane, on our part so to conduct the war as to give the least occasion for social and servile war, in the extreme Southern States, and to disturb as little as possible the accustomed occupations of the people."[5]

Lincoln concurred with Bates in his hope for a unionist counterrebellion, promising in his inaugural address that, should war come, it would be conducted in such a way as to avoid a military invasion of the states to give Southern loyalists as much time as possible to take back control of their states. "There will be no attempt to force obnoxious strangers among the people," he proclaimed. Indeed, if his and his advisors' suspicions were correct, such a policy would be unnecessary.[6]

In their hope for a loyal Southern counterrebellion, the administration underestimated the zeal of the Southern people. There were few Southern unionists after 1860. Southern conservatives preferred to wait and see what Lincoln would do. Some even suggested waiting to secede until the congressional elections of 1862 or the presidential election of 1864. But regardless of when the moment came, these men were as supportive of secession as their radical cohorts. As the state conventions voted overwhelmingly for secession in the winter of 1861, the conservatives generally went along with the majority. If the true intentions of the Southern conservatives were not well known to Lincoln and his advisors in March 1861, their actions in the second wave of secession after the fall of Fort Sumter—in which Virginia, Arkansas, North Carolina, and Tennessee joined the Confederacy—offered a valuable lesson.[7]

The cabinet continued to provide a means for Southerners to handle the mess themselves, but Lincoln's April 15 call for volunteers ensured that, if no counterrevolution manifested, he would be ready to enforce the laws with the use of the military. Bates fully supported his chief in that aim. Indeed, in a memorandum he submitted at the April 15 cabinet meeting, Bates proposed a nine-point strategy for prosecuting the war that included fortifying Washington, D.C., stopping the federal mail in the Southern states, employing the navy to close the Atlantic and gulf ports and patrol the Chesapeake Bay, building and maintaining a river flotilla to control the Mississippi River and guard St. Louis, and occupying strategic locations such as Harpers Ferry.[8]

Within days, Lincoln acted on several of Bates's proposals. In anticipation of Virginia's secession, on April 15, General Scott ordered all soldiers in the capital to report for duty "till reinforcements arrive" and had personally seen to the defense of the armory at Harpers Ferry. A few days later, on April 19, Lincoln proclaimed a naval blockade stretching from the coastline of South Carolina to Texas. Within weeks, the navy had purchased or chartered several merchant vessels, armed them, and sent them to guard the Southern coasts. By the year's end, there were more than 260 warships in active duty, and another 100 under construction.[9]

The government also quickly began constructing a riverboat flotilla to patrol the Ohio and Mississippi Rivers—thus fulfilling another of Bates's suggestions. Shortly after the fall of Fort Sumter, Bates's friend and fellow St. Louisan James Eads contacted him about constructing a fleet of iron gunboats to clear the Mississippi of Confederate forces. Eads was uniquely suited for this work, having made a fortune constructing vessels used to salvage sunken treasure and free the river of snags. Bates urged Eads to come to Washington and present his plan to the secretaries of war and the navy. Both approved and, after first assigning the job of construction to crews in Cincinnati, eventually awarded Eads the bid to make St. Louis the site of construction. On October 12, 1861, Eads launched the first gunboat, the *Carondelet*. Three more—the *St. Louis*, the *Louisville*, and the *Pittsburg*—were launched within days, and another three—the *Cairo*, the *Mound City*, and the *Cincinnati*—followed from a separate yard near Mound City, Illinois. All the boats joined the naval flotilla amassing near Cairo, Illinois, where Commodore Andrew H. Foote accepted them into service on January 15, 1862.[10]

Although Lincoln's cabinet secretaries worked swiftly to implement these naval plans, they presented yet another legal problem. Lincoln's April 19 proclamation referred to the naval action as a blockade "in pursuance of the laws of the United States, and of the law of Nations." However, blockades, strictly speaking, were international matters governed by the laws of nations. The general understanding among experts was that a nation could not legally blockade itself. Doing so would be tantamount to recognizing the belligerency of the Confederacy and might invite intervention by foreign powers. Lincoln, however, argued from the start that secession was illegal and that the Southern states had never truly left the Union. If he hoped to maintain that interpretation, then it was essential that he classify the naval action not as a blockade but as the closing of ports—a legally sanctioned action belonging to any sovereign government.[11]

Bates supported the closing of ports, having used that language in his April 15 memorandum. "If their ports be closed," he wrote, "they *must* send their products northward, to the ports of the States yet faithful. . . . At all events, it is the most feasible project for the accomplishment of our main end, that has occurred to my mind." To classify the action as a blockade, however, caused him some trepidation. "There can be no such thing as a lawful blockade of a *friendly* port," he later wrote. "A nation cannot lawfully blockade its own port in its own possession." Welles said much the same thing: "If we blockade those ports, do we not, by that act, admit the nationality of the Confederate States, and a division of the Union? But if we close the ports and guard them, do we not by those acts assert our own nationality and maintain the integrity of the country?" In the end, though, the argument over how to classify the naval action amounted to little more than an exercise in semantics. Lincoln had already called it a blockade. Once the deed was done, there was no way to undo it.[12]

Another, more controversial, legal hurdle that spring involved the president's war powers. The special session of Congress was not scheduled to begin until July 4. In the meantime, Lincoln was free to act on his own initiative. He thus assumed powers generally considered as belonging to the legislative branch to manage a crisis brewing in Maryland. A slave state bordering Washington, D.C., on three sides, Maryland was troublesome for Lincoln from the start. In the days leading up to the inauguration, to avoid an assassination attempt, he was compelled to travel through the city stowed away in the sleeping car of a passenger train. Heavily ridiculed in the national press for sneaking into the capital in disguise, Lincoln swore from then on that he would confront threats head-on and with resolve. That decision heavily influenced his actions a few weeks later in response to a second threat from Baltimore.[13]

With Virginia on the verge of secession, Marylanders were inspired to reconsider their own loyalty to the Union. On April 19, a Baltimore mob assaulted federal soldiers with rocks as they passed through on their way to Washington and burned several railroad bridges leading into the city. Maryland governor Thomas H. Hicks—to the alarm and apprehension of Washington society—then called for a special session of the state assembly to consider the issue of secession. If Maryland went with the South, the capital would be surrounded by enemy forces.[14]

Bates shared his neighbors' concerns. Only a week earlier, in relation to Fort Sumter, he had cautioned Lincoln against excessive military provocation, but now things had changed. The Baltimore mob, he believed, was guilty of "overt acts of treason" and the soldiers had done nothing to provoke such an attack. "We hurt nobody; we frighten nobody; and do our utmost to offend nobody," he wrote. Yet, Marylanders "every day are winding their coils around us, while *we* make no bold effort to cut the cord that is soon to bind us. . . ." Considering the vulnerability of Washington, Bates concluded: "Affirmative & progressive measures are absolutely necessary to our safety."[15]

Lincoln too was exasperated, but he could only arrest the secessionists if they raised arms against the government. "If we arrest them," Lincoln explained to Winfield Scott, "we cannot hold them as prisoners; and when liberated, they will immediately re-assemble, and take their action." If the situation worsened—if there was an organized military resistance on the part of Marylanders, for instance—then Lincoln would be justified in responding proportionately, "even, if necessary," he wrote, "to the bombardment of their cities." Indeed, Lincoln went so far as to surmise that, "in the extremist necessity," the federal government might even be authorized to suspend the writ of habeas corpus.[16]

Matters eventually forced Lincoln's hand. On April 25, Washington breathed a sigh of relief when soldiers redirected around Baltimore finally arrived in the capital. Still, General Scott continued to press Lincoln over what he perceived to be a tangible threat from the Confederates amassing a few miles away in Virginia. What was worse, in four days, the Maryland legislature would convene in Frederick to decide the issue of secession. Frederick was a Unionist stronghold, which boded well for unionists' chances, but because Baltimore remained a hornet's nest of secessionist fever, Lincoln seized the moment and authorized Scott to direct military commanders to suspend the writ of habeas corpus near military lines stretching from Washington to Philadelphia.[17]

This strike against a key component of civilian due process put Lincoln on shaky legal ground. Because he had given the initial order to a military subordinate, the public had no knowledge of it. When news got out, though, it had the potential to spark a firestorm of resistance. Realizing this, two weeks later, Lincoln issued a second, public proclamation suspending the writ of habeas corpus as a wartime necessity. Still, the second announcement limited the suspension to the Florida Keys, where the populace posed a clear and present danger to military personnel. Lincoln had failed to mention his earlier order for Maryland and Pennsylvania. Nonetheless, military personnel interpreted the second order for the Keys as retroactively applying to the states as well.[18]

Bates supported Lincoln's assumption of extralegal war powers, but always with the private acknowledgment that any departure from the regular, peacetime separation of powers be understood as temporary in nature. When the special session of Congress convened—and even more importantly, when the war ended—he expected the separation of powers to be reinstated.

Lincoln's actions regarding habeas corpus were put to the test just four days after he made his second, public proclamation. On May 25, federal officials in Baltimore arrested John Merryman for his involvement in the riotous events of April 19. When Merryman's family appealed to Chief Justice Taney for help in his capacity as federal district judge, Taney issued a writ of habeas corpus to Merryman's captor, General John Cadwalader, commander of Fort McHenry. Cadwalader ignored Taney's writ, citing as justification Lincoln's April 27 military order to Scott, not the more public May 21 proclamation. In response, several days later, Taney issued a scathing in-chambers decision—*Ex Parte Merryman*—that labeled Lincoln's actions an abuse of power and threatened to undermine the administration's efforts to curtail secessionist activity in the North.[19]

In a showdown between the heads of two branches of the federal government, Taney ruled that Section 9 of Article I of the Constitution explicitly stated that "The Privilege of the Writ of Habeas Corpus shall not be suspended, unless when in Cases of Rebellion or Invasion the public Safety may require it." As such, Lincoln had overstepped his constitutional authority by usurping a power explicitly belonging to Congress. The decision presented the cabinet with a further quandary. If as Taney claimed, Lincoln had overreached, then he needed a sound legal argument for doing so; otherwise, the president was in jeopardy of impeachment. To that end, on May 30, Lincoln turned to Bates as the man best situated to provide a formal defense.[20]

Bates's assistant, Titian J. Coffey, anticipated Taney's argument. On April 20, he had preemptively begun a memorandum tracing the history of the constitutional powers of the government in relation to habeas corpus and martial law. Unfortunately for Bates, Coffey's findings ultimately concurred with Taney's. "It would seem, *as the power is given to Congress* to suspend the writ of Habeas Corpus in cases of rebellion or invasion," Coffey concluded, "that the right to judge whether the exigency had arisen, must exclusively belong to that body. . . ."[21]

Written before Taney's own decision, Coffey's memo would clearly cause potential embarrassment if it became public. Bates's own assistant had undermined the president's actions. However, Senator Reverdy Johnson— himself a former U.S. attorney general—had recently published his own opinion defending Lincoln's power to suspend habeas corpus. Lincoln therefore ordered Bates to discard Coffey's report and work with Johnson on an official opinion. Bates thus found himself in a difficult position. As the nation's chief law enforcement officer, he would have the definitive opinion. As a member of the administration, furthermore, Bates had few options but to craft an opinion that upheld his chief's actions—even though they clearly rejected the sound opinion of his own subordinate, whom he very much respected.[22]

The best evidence of Bates's thoughts on habeas corpus prior to his tenure as attorney general came from the pages of his legal journal, which he started keeping in 1847. In the pages of this volume was referenced an obscure 1859 Supreme Court case—*Ableman v. Booth*—which involved a Wisconsin abolitionist who incited a mob to rescue an escaped slave from custody. The abolitionist—Sherman Booth—was arrested by a U.S. marshal and applied for a writ of habeas corpus from a Wisconsin state judge who ordered Booth to be placed under state custody. When the marshal refused to comply, he was fired, and the case wound up before the Wisconsin supreme court, which upheld Booth's release. The marshal then petitioned the U.S. Supreme Court, where Taney ruled that because Booth had violated a federal law, a federal court—not a state court—should have heard the case. The Wisconsin supreme court was in error, then, because a writ of habeas corpus issued by a state authority could not release a prisoner held in federal custody.[23]

Bates's previous notes, then, suggest that he understood habeas corpus as a federal power, but it was an open question as to what branch of the federal government had the right to suspend it. The war, it became clear, was the one variable on which Lincoln's entire case depended. In unchartered legal territory, for the next month, Bates toiled away on his opinion, relying heavily on Johnson's earlier pamphlet for guidance. As Congress assembled for the special session on July 4, it was finally ready, and Lincoln sent the opinion up to the Hill along with his own accounting of his actions.

Taney had argued that Congress's authority to suspend habeas corpus resided in Article I, Section 9, of the Constitution, but Bates found that the language of the article did not explicitly name to whom the powers over habeas corpus belonged. It was not until the Judiciary Act of 1789, he continued, that Congress affirmed its right to that power. If the statute were ever to be repealed, or if the laws were to be suspended, then control over habeas corpus would revert back to the stipulations—or lack thereof—in the Constitution. Put another way, because Congress was unable in recent months to exercise its powers, the president was legally within his right as a separate but equal branch of the government to suspend habeas corpus.[24]

From there, Bates moved to a discussion of the use of martial law as a means of making arrests in the absence civilian authority. The legitimacy for that act, he argued, resided in Lincoln's dual responsibility as both civil magistrate and military chief. Their specific oaths of office separated the executive and legislative branches in ways that Taney must have known.

Legislators swore an oath to support the Constitution while the president swore an oath to preserve, protect, and defend it. The congressional oath was passive, Bates argued, while the presidential one was active. Furthermore, the Insurrection Act of 1807 granted the president the ability to unilaterally suppress insurrections using martial force.

Bates ended with a summation of the case that again affirmed the president's powers granted him by the constitution and, later, by Congress for the express purpose of assertively defending the nation against foreign and domestic enemies. Unlike Taney, Bates's deeper reading of the Constitution and later statutes showed that, in suspending habeas corpus and invoking martial law, Lincoln had acted within the limits of his authority and had upheld his constitutional oath in the process.[25]

The opinion bolstered Lincoln's confidence in his actions, but, for a man of Bates's conservative nature, it had proven difficult to write. Broadly expanding executive power ran counter to Bates's lifelong Whiggishness. He had long championed his old party's safeguard of Congress's role as the dominant power in the national government. Indeed, during the Mexican-American War, both he and Lincoln had been critical of Polk for bypassing Congress in his management of the war. As Bates wrote in 1848:

> Congress is undoubtedly the war power under the constitution, yet the president solely makes the war, and determines for himself, without giving information to or asking the advice of Congress how and where the war is to be conducted, and for what ends and objects it is to be waged. The sovereignty is tersely conceded to the president, and Congress is content to abandon its acknowledged constitutional power over the subject of war, and, like the English House of Commons, vote supplies and men, and money to their sovereign lord, the King, to be dispersed of at his pleasure.[26]

Now, thirteen years later, Bates was compelled in his capacity as the nation's highest legal officer to betray his earlier sentiments. On second glance, though, in his opinion on habeas corpus, Bates was exercising a certain amount of constitutional pragmatism, for the Civil War created constitutional problems unparalleled in the nation's history. Such a drastic state of domestic affairs required that the president's war powers be defined in a way that would guarantee the restoration of peace but that also bent the law a little. Lincoln adapted to this more easily than his conservative colleague, and perhaps put the argument best in his own message to the special session of Congress: "Are all the laws but one to go unexecuted and the government itself go to pieces lest that one be violated?"[27]

Having justified their actions in the first months of the war, Lincoln and Bates now awaited Congress's reply. A few days after the special session convened, Senator Henry Wilson of Massachusetts and Congressman Thaddeus Stevens of Pennsylvania introduced the Indemnity Bill, which retroactively approved the president's suspension of habeas corpus and authorized him to continue to do so in the interests of national security. The bill also shielded military personnel who carried out this policy from legal action by civilians after the return to peacetime. The legislation met some resistance from conservative Republicans like John Sherman and Lyman Trumbull who, despite their overwhelming support for the war, could not in good conscience grant the president powers that they agreed belonged to the legislature. Nonetheless, after several drafts, both chambers finally settled on language and passed the bill as the renamed Habeas Corpus Act in 1863.[28]

The suspension of habeas corpus troubled Bates throughout the remainder of the war. Congress had accepted his argument that in times of war the president enjoyed extralegal war powers. What was more, the new Habeas Corpus Act limited the president to only wielding those powers in places where civilian government was compromised. However, as the conflict intensified, Bates watched radical members of the cabinet and Congress place a greater premium on the use of military tribunals to prosecute rebel sympathizers while Lincoln seemed content to ignore the limitations imposed on him by the Habeas Corpus Act. "There seems to me no excuse for this wanton degradation of the Civil law," he warned Lincoln in June 1863. "I cannot see a motive for these groundless & needless assumptions of arbitrary power, unless indeed the object be to drive the people into despair & anarchy, and thus *make a necessity* for a *Military Dictator!*" In July 1861, though, Bates had no reason to expect that Lincoln would take such a radical turn.[29]

With no significant bloodshed yet to speak of, with Washington firmly in Union control, and with Congress granting the administration authority to hamper secessionist sentiment, Bates had every reason to expect that the limited nature of the war would be enough to bolster Southern loyalists to retake the state governments and deliver the South back to the Union. However, events transpiring near Manassas Junction, Virginia, later that month challenged that hopeful outlook.

9.
Waging War

On August 21, 1861, Julia dashed off a letter to grandson Onward in St. Charles, Missouri, describing life in Washington. She had arrived in the capital in April with daughter Matilda (called Tilly), as well as sons Woodson and Coalter. Shortly afterward, the family moved out of Bates's room at the Willard Hotel and into a Federal-style townhouse. Julia described their new abode as a "retired quiet place" with a magnificent view of the city. There, they entertained members of Congress during the special session that summer, but now "we see few persons . . . tho enough to be pleasant." The house was befitting a person of Bates's stature. From the dormer windows on the fourth floor, one had an excellent panorama of the city and Alexandria in the distance. When the family moved in, the house had an old-fashioned air to it, but Julia had made short work of revitalizing the place. Besides planting a new garden, she also purchased new furniture and redecorated Bates's study—a habit she had first begun at Grape Hill in St. Louis.[1]

While they entertained members of Congress, the family also nervously followed news about the ongoing war in Missouri. With the state convention's adjournment in March, in just a few weeks matters had eroded into outright war. On April 17, Governor Jackson refused to comply with Lincoln's proclamation calling for volunteers. Three days later, secessionists in western Missouri seized the federal arsenal in the town of Liberty. A palpable fear soon spread among St. Louisans that the arsenal in their city was next.[2]

They had good reason to be worried. Since March, Jackson had been undermining unionism in the city. That month, the assembly gave authority over the St. Louis police to a committee chosen directly by the governor. Meanwhile, Jackson secretly reached out to Jefferson Davis for supplies to assist in seizing the arsenal and called a special session of the assembly where he argued that Missourians must prepare to defend themselves against forces that threatened their sovereignty.[3]

A drama also began to unfold surrounding command of the arsenal. Winfield Scott had replaced the previous commander, Major William H. Bell, with Brevet Major Peter V. Hagner, a conservative Unionist. However, Hagner and his direct superior, General William S. Harney, commander of the Department of the West, were reluctant to pursue open conflict with the governor and his acolytes. This reticence drew Hagner into direct conflict with General Nathaniel Lyon, commander of federal troops at the arsenal, who outranked him.[4]

Lyon believed Jackson's machinations were treasonous, and he saw Harney and Hagner's reluctance to strike the enemy as little short of complicity. He thus worked behind the scenes with Frank Blair Jr. to neutralize them both. After the fall of Fort Sumter, and against Hagner's express wishes, Lyon ordered his men to begin fortifying the arsenal grounds while Blair lobbied the Lincoln administration to have Harney removed.[5]

Later that month, after Jackson ordered the militia to muster across the entire state, Brigadier General Daniel M. Frost's secessionist militia descended on St. Louis. Harney, however, ordered Lyon's troops to remain inside the arsenal. His detractors thus had all the proof they needed to remove him, and they were jubilant when Cameron did so. But Harney felt his dismissal unjust and left at once for Washington to clear his name. Meanwhile, Lyon was in command.[6]

On May 10, matters came to a head after Lyon's spies learned that a shipment of arms from the Confederate government had arrived at Frost's headquarters—now christened Camp Jackson. At the same time, Lyon learned that Harney had successfully convinced authorities in Washington to reinstate him. A short window of time existed before he returned to St. Louis and Lyon would have to relinquish command. He thus set in motion a plan to capture Camp Jackson before the commander arrived. The operation, however, did not go smoothly. Frost surrendered without a shot, but as Union soldiers marched their prisoners back to the arsenal, a crowd of civilians swelled around the procession. Shots were fired, and in a matter of minutes, twenty-eight spectators and one soldier lay dead in the street. Over a dozen more were wounded. When Harney arrived the next day, he immediately set about restoring peace while Jackson consolidated his forces throughout Missouri into a single unit and appointed Sterling Price as its commander. Harney counseled St. Louisans to refrain from joining Price's force, and when he and Price met on May 21, the result was a concession from Harney to refrain from outright military provocation.[7]

Bates was kept apprised of these events by informants who regularly wrote him detailed reports of the goings on that he then willingly shared with Simon Cameron. One letter, for instance, described Missourians as under the false impression that Lincoln's government was waging war against them. The news of the Camp Jackson affair did not help matters. The administration needed to work harder to halt the campaign of misinformation. Another letter from Barton described the challenges he and his family endured to defend Bates and the administration. "It is somewhat unpleasant," he wrote, "to have so nearly all of my neighbors differing from me so radically & with such earnestness that they may at any time upon very slight occasion become deadly enemies." Adding to his anguish was the fact that Barton's own brother, Fleming, seemed to be siding with the Confederates. "Though he never says anything to me directly about his own opinions in public matters," Barton wrote of Fleming, "I thought his general talk indicated that he was siding with the foolishness of the Southern treason."[8]

Despite the difficulties, Barton nonetheless continued to ardently defend his father and the administration and was determined to be his father's eyes and ears in the state. During a business trip to St. Louis, Barton called on General Harney—newly returned from Washington—where he gave the timid commander a piece of his mind. "The Harney & Price *truce*," Barton wrote his father, "has thrown us back almost to where we were before the seizure of Camp Jackson; the traitors are running up their flags again & mustering their companies."[9]

Barton was not alone in his anger at Harney's timidness. Lincoln was also discouraged. Following a visit from two delegations of Missouri unionists—one requesting Harney's reinstatement, the other demanding his removal—the president kept the general in command but secretly authorized Frank Blair to relieve him whenever Blair found it expedient. To that end, on May 30, Blair notified Harney of his removal after Blair learned that he had done nothing in response to rumors that Jackson had invited troops from Arkansas to reinforce Price's State Guard. Lyon now formally succeeded him, having been promoted in the meantime by Lincoln to the rank of brigadier general.[10]

It is not clear what, if any, influence Bates had on Lincoln's thinking about the situation in St. Louis. Consumed with writing his opinion on habeas corpus, Bates left only a cursory record of his own thoughts on the matter. A May 20 memorandum in his handwriting suggested five bullet points for securing the state, including retaining Harney, dissolving all paramilitary forces not directly under the command of the president, and sending "large bodies" of soldiers into the state "in order to assure our friends within the state & deter their enemies from further attempts to browbeat & drive them out." When it came to this latter point, Bates was again expressing his conservative temperament. While he condemned Jackson and Price for undermining unionism in the state, he nonetheless sympathized with Harney's attempts to avoid violence. Furthermore, he had a good working relationship with the Blairs, but it is unlikely that Bates condoned Lyon's confrontational style.[11]

That abrasiveness was soon on public display. On June 8, after learning of Lyon's promotion, Jackson and Price reached out to him with overtures of peace. Lyon accepted and offered safe passage to St. Louis for both men and their staffs. Four days later, they sat down with Lyon and Frank Blair in a room at the Planter's House where Jackson offered to disband the State Guard if Lyon would refrain from sending federal soldiers into areas of the state where they were not already stationed. Lyon, however, was in no mood to bargain with traitors. Before storming out of the room, he shouted at the governor, "Rather than concede to the State of Missouri for one single instant the right to dictate to my Government in any matter however important, I would see you . . . and every man, woman, and child in the State, dead and buried."[12]

Events in Missouri now moved rapidly. Jackson and Price departed for Jefferson City while Lyon's forces boarded steamboats and headed up the Missouri River in pursuit. On June 15, they landed at the state capital—now abandoned by Jackson and the secessionists in the legislature for higher ground at Boonville where, two days later, Union forces routed the State Guard and pursued Jackson and his men southwest toward Springfield. Now free of secessionists, the state convention reconvened in Jefferson City, where it pronounced Jackson and his followers as traitors and declared all statewide offices vacant. It then elected Hamilton Gamble as interim governor. With his inauguration a month later, Missouri had fully reversed its earlier course and was now squarely on a Unionist heading.[13]

Bates was pleased at his brother-in-law's appointment as governor. In a letter to Gamble on August 2, he wrote: "I rejoice, my Dear Sir, at the wise course taken by the Missouri Convention—I rejoice for the state at large, because I believe that internal peace & tranquility will soon be restored." That Gamble shared Bates's conservative opinion that state governments, rather than federal forces, should take the lead in putting down the rebellion was not lost on either man. In a letter to Charles Gibson a few days later, Bates surmised that, with Gamble in charge, "there will be no need of Federal troops but to guard against invasion from without & protect some important points within, against any sudden uprising which might be planned." What Bates now envisioned was a partnership between the two governments—a true manifestation of federalism—in which each party bolstered and supported the other. "We must if possible have harmony between the two governments," he continued, "we cannot afford to quarrel." If anyone could forge such a partnership, Bates believed, surely it was he and Gamble.[14]

Julia shared her husband's optimism. "From what we gather by the papers," she wrote Onward later that August, "we have reason to hope your county [St. Charles County] is more settled than has been for several weeks." While the threat to St. Louisans had abated following the exile of Jackson and the inauguration of Gamble, Julia nonetheless spoke for the entire Bates clan in Washington when she wrote that they remained "very uneasy about all of you."[15]

The family in Missouri could have said the same about their relatives in Washington. The Confederate threat to the federal capital had only increased since the special session of Congress earlier in July. In May 1861, the Confederate government moved from Montgomery, Alabama, to Richmond, making northern Virginia the main theater of the war. Meanwhile, forces arriving in Washington quickly transformed the city from a village of muddy avenues leading nowhere into the command center of the Union war effort. "When I came here," Julia wrote, "it was before the Government had any preparations for its own safety & there were no troops except a few companies of District Volunteers. Since then there has been many thousand men—& the wagons necessary for the baggage of camp life." The city had a tangible martial atmosphere. As one newspaper correspondent described it: "Long lines of army wagons and artillery were continually rumbling through the streets; at all hours of the day and night the air was troubled by the clatter of galloping squads of cavalry; and the clank of sabers, and the measured beat of marching infantry, were ever present to the ear."[16]

By June, some thirty-five thousand Union soldiers under the command of General Irvin McDowell were encamped across the Potomac, ready to attack P. G. T. Beauregard's twenty-thousand Confederate soldiers near Manassas Junction. Despite McDowell's superior numbers, when Lincoln ordered him into action, the results were disastrous. On July 16, the Union army began a fifteen-mile march to Manassas that was stalled by felled trees and rumors of snipers, giving the Confederates time to bring up reinforcements. On July 21, both sides clashed on the fields around Bull Run Creek. By 4 P.M., a Confederate assault turned the battle, and the Union forces retreated from the field. The casualties on both sides were staggering. McDowell suffered 481 killed, 1,011 wounded, and 1,216 missing while Beauregard lost 387 killed, 1,582 wounded, and 13 missing. It was the biggest battle, up to that time, ever fought on North American soil.[17]

Bates learned of the disaster while returning from a carriage ride with Julia and the Lincolns. As Julia later recalled the episode in her diary: "After supper we felt so anxious having heard reports that at four o'clock there had been a change in the field and that our men were returning beaten." As they arrived home, former attorney general Edwin Stanton appeared at their door with confirmation of the Union defeat. Promising Stanton that he would pay him a visit later, Bates and Julia then rushed to the White House. Julia joined Mary Lincoln in one of the sitting rooms while Bates went up to the president's office. "All the time I was there," Julia continued, "the door keeper every little while came to announce the death or wounding of some officer or friend."[18]

At 10 P.M., Lincoln adjourned the meeting of his advisors and departed for General Scott's office. Julia and Bates stayed at the White House for a further period, in case Lincoln returned. When he did not, they went home, stopping on the way at Stanton's house. Among Stanton's anxious guests was Louisa Rodgers Meigs, wife of Quartermaster General Montgomery

Meigs, who had departed Washington for Manassas earlier that day. Now, Louisa Meigs pumped Bates for information on the fate of her husband as well as her son, who was an aide to one of the Union generals. Bates knew nothing of either man's fate and, after consoling Louisa Meigs and the couple's friends, went home. As it turned out, both men were safe, but Louisa Meigs's worry nonetheless touched upon a fear Bates and Julia also felt. Earlier that month, their son, John Coalter, had joined the army as a first lieutenant in the Eleventh Regiment of Infantry. Meanwhile, Fleming was flirting with joining the enemy. Indeed, the Bateses were confronted with the same horrors facing thousands of families across the country.[19]

The Battle of Bull Run convinced many Northerners that the war would be long and difficult. On July 22, Lincoln took steps to rebuild the army, ordering General George B. McClellan to come to Washington and take command of McDowell's beleaguered troops. The next evening, he jotted down a nine-point memorandum calling for volunteers for a three-year duration and pushing forward the blockade of the Atlantic states "with all possible dispatch." The president also authorized General John C. Frémont—who recently replaced Harney as commander of the Department of the West—to organize his forces and mount operations "as rapidly as possible, with special attention to Missouri."[20]

The reorganization of the Department of the West, it turns out, was already well underway. When Frémont arrived in St. Louis on July 23, Nathaniel Lyon was busy chasing the remnants of the State Guard to the outskirts of Springfield in southwest Missouri. There, on August 10, along the banks of Wilson's Creek, Lyon ordered an early-morning attack. After seven hours of combat, the Union suffered its second major defeat in a matter of weeks. Over thirteen hundred of Lyon's men were killed, wounded, or missing. Price's losses were nearly equal, but the percentage of casualties was higher for the Union (24.5 percent to 12 percent for the State Guard). Worse, Lyon was killed in the thick of the fight, creating a vacuum in Union command that helped turn the battle. With the Union army suddenly on the retreat in southwest Missouri, Price took the opportunity to bolster his ranks and began menacing the Missouri River Valley. Meanwhile, Confederates from Kentucky threatened southeast Missouri. Lincoln's strategy to vigorously execute the war in the West had suffered a tremendous setback.[21]

Bates, who had been so cautious earlier in the summer, now conceded the need for greater action. "I care not how cautious our commanders may be in securing certain important points (such as this city)," he wrote in September: "But gallant enterprizes are necessary to establish the prestige of the army and thus increase its positive strength. And I have no doubt that a few such enterprizes—even at the hazard of some Regiments—some Brigades—would contribute largely to the general result, and accelerate our final success." Success, however, remained elusive. Since Bull Run, the Union army in the east had lingered along the banks of the Potomac in utter despondency. The public mood reflected the state of the army. As Bates wrote in late September, "We absolutely need some dashing expeditions—some victories, great or small, to stimulate the zeal of the Country, and, as I think, to keep up the credit of the Government."[22]

The hoped-for victories were not forthcoming, however, and in the meantime, emboldened Confederates were running amok. A force of them even patrolled the Potomac just fifty-five miles below Washington. Then there was General Charles Stone's embarrassing defeat in October at Ball's Bluff, where in the dark of night his men mistook a cluster of trees for a Confederate encampment and were ambushed by a Mississippi infantry regiment. Lincoln's good friend Senator Edward Baker was killed in the skirmish, and hundreds of soldiers surrendered when they were forced over the bluffs and into the Potomac River. Bates described the affair as "most unsatisfactory."[23]

The administration itself seemed to have lost direction. "The Administration has no system—no unity—no accountability—no subordination," Bates wrote in his diary after one cabinet session: "Men are appointed, and not trusted—interfered with by side agencies, and so, relieved from all responsibility. Of course [sic] therefore, things run all wrong. . . ." The trouble to which he was alluding was the conduct of Secretary of War Cameron. The Pennsylvania political boss had never been a good fit. Where the country needed efficiency, he brought corruption and ineptitude. The contractors hired by Cameron's department to supply food and clothing to the soldiers made a fortune selling them subpar merchandise, while railroads overcharged the government to ship the items and men across the country. Then it became evident that the department had awarded an unusually large number of contracts without competitive bidding to Pennsylvania firms. Furthermore, a large amount of government shipping was being done on railroads in which Cameron and his assistant secretary had a direct financial interest. So much effort had gone into lining pockets and so little into communication between armies and theaters of war, in fact, that Adjutant General Lorenzo Thomas lamented: "Generals *do not* make reports of their troops, as they ought."[24]

Indeed, army generals were causing the administration a great deal of trouble. In May, under a flag of truce, a Confederate colonel arrived at the gates of Fort Monroe in Virginia and demanded the return of three escaped enslaved people sheltered there. General Benjamin Butler, commander of the fort, refused. The colonel, Butler argued, had forfeited his property rights under the Constitution and was using his enslaved people to wage war against the Union. Every item of "property" withheld from the Confederate army helped the Union cause. By July, the news of Butler's policy spread to the surrounding plantations, and hundreds of enslaved people flocked to the protection of the Union forces at Fort Monroe.

On July 30, Butler wrote to Cameron requesting instructions on what to do with the enslaved people coming into his lines. He refused to consider them property and believed that they should be withheld from their enslavers on humanitarian grounds. Still, he would defer to official directions from Washington. To that end, days later, Congress passed the First Confiscation Act, which allowed military officials to confiscate Southern property, including enslaved people, used to aid the rebellion. But this did not end the matter: Lincoln was reluctant to sign the act, fearing that it would agitate the loyalists in the border states. Bates, for his part, disliked the bill because it continued to define enslaved people as property. A civilian court would need to intervene to determine their status as freed people. In the meantime, the administration would technically become custodian of these individuals—an embarrassment, to be sure, considering that the cabinet stood on the principle that the Constitution did not recognize slavery. In the end, only after strong lobbying by prominent Northern politicians did Lincoln sign the bill. Even so, Lincoln believed that the Confiscation Act's ambiguous language made it almost impossible to enforce and thus refrained from providing Bates with instructions to pass along to U.S. marshals for its implementation.[25]

Uncertainties about the confiscation program, in turn, compelled another Union commander to take matters into his own hands. John C. Frémont faced a difficult situation in Missouri. After the setback at Wilson's Creek, guerilla warfare began to break out in the rural counties. Meanwhile, the troops that Frémont was able to recruit to rebuild Lyon's force were inadequately provisioned, and Frémont soon began wondering if elites in the government with whom he did not get along might be attempting to sabotage his command. Frémont therefore saw in the Confiscation Act an opportunity to leverage his popularity with radical antislavery Republicans against his enemies. Thus, on August 30, building off Butler's work in Virginia, Frémont issued a proclamation emancipating the enslaved people of any persons using them to assist the rebellion.[26]

Frémont's proclamation troubled Bates, not because he disagreed with the antislavery aspects of it—though he would have preferred something less provocative—but because he believed that authority over slavery in the state lay with Missouri's provisional government. The military, he believed, should focus its energies on protecting, not confiscating, property. Lincoln too opposed Frémont's proclamation, but on the grounds that—as commander in chief—only the president had the power to order the military to emancipate enslaved people. Lincoln was not ready to take that step, and he therefore requested that Frémont rescind the offending portion of his proclamation. When Frémont refused, Lincoln personally countermanded it.[27]

Problems with Frémont did not end there. By October, government officials in St. Louis began complaining that the general was insulating himself from all but his close advisors. Led by the Blairs, who had initially championed his selection to head the Department of the West, Frémont's critics now began pressuring Lincoln to remove him. Continuing to serve as his father's eyes and ears on the ground, Barton concurred with Frémont's critics on October 10: "[Frémont] allows Sterling Price (and drink) to out-general him. . . . I hope that he will be recalled & (as Frank Blair phrases it) an *able* man put in his place."[28]

Sterling Price's victory against the Union forces at Lexington, Missouri, in late September exacerbated the suspicions that Frémont's heart was not in this fight. When Frank Blair began criticizing Frémont's inability to secure the state, Frémont briefly had him arrested, prompting Montgomery Blair and Montgomery Meigs to travel to St. Louis at the behest of Lincoln to further investigate matters. Secretary of War Cameron, who had himself begun courting radical Republicans allied with Frémont in the hopes of saving his own job, also traveled to St. Louis later that fall. Like his fellow cabinet ministers, though, Cameron was disheartened by the situation at military headquarters.[29]

In a letter to Gamble on October 3, Bates sympathetically described Lincoln as "an intelligent & virtuous man" but complained that he had "no *will*, no power to command—He makes nobody afraid of him. And

hence, discipline is relaxed, & stupid inanity takes the place of action."
In truth, though, Lincoln was even then reaching the end of his patience.
On October 22, following Blair and Cameron's return from St. Louis, the
president convened an emergency cabinet meeting to discuss the matter.
Secretary of State Seward urged caution; so did Cameron. Chase, too,
was reticent, fearing that removing Frémont would anger the soldiers in
the department who were loyal to the commander. Bates, on the other
hand, emphatically argued that Frémont must go. "None actively support
him, but his own pet officers and contractors," he wrote in his diary. "Yet
strange! both Cameron and Chase gave in and timidly yielded to delay;
and the President still hangs in painful and mortifying doubt." As he had
confided to Gamble, Bates believed that to leave the general in command
would invite criticism that the administration was afraid of its own commanders. "For me," he continued, "I think too well of the soldiers and the
people, to be afraid of any Major General in the Army."[30]

Two days after the cabinet meeting, Lincoln dismissed Frémont from
command in Missouri. The indignation from radical Republicans was expected. Congressman Thaddeus Stevens denounced Lincoln as the puppet
of conservatives, and some radical well-wishers thronged to the general
when he arrived in New York City, leading to speculation that he might
challenge Lincoln for the Republican nomination in 1864. This speculation may have contributed to Lincoln's decision to promote Frémont to
command of the Mountain Department in the Spring of 1862. Still, for
the time being, the insubordinate general was silenced.[31]

Lincoln realized that changes in leadership were needed in more places
than just the Department of the West. Given the rumors of corruption in
the War Department, Cameron seemed a likely candidate for dismissal,
but instead it was Winfield Scott's turn to go. Back in mid-August 1861,
Congress passed a law allowing any officer of the military who had served
forty consecutive years to apply for full retirement. Shortly afterward,
Scott informed Lincoln that he felt his time had come. Lincoln initially
rejected Scott's resignation, but by October 18, he was reconsidering it.
After discussing the matter in cabinet council on November 1, Lincoln and
his ministers visited Scott at the War Department to formally accept his
retirement. According to Bates, all present conducted themselves "chastely
and in excellent taste." Bates himself whispered to the retiring general that
the people across the North were praying for him—a sentiment to which
Scott responded with great emotion.[32]

That same day, Lincoln promoted George B. McClellan to command of all Union armies. A greater contrast with Scott would have been hard to find. An energetic man of thirty-five, McClellan was sometimes known as the Young Napoleon and did everything he could to look the part. More than just aesthetically pleasing, McClellan's record promised a possible turnaround in military fortunes. A graduate of West Point, he had served with great distinction in the Mexican-American War before embarking on a successful private career with the Baltimore and Ohio Railroad. When the Civil War broke out, he rejoined the army and helped secure Northwest Virginia for the Union. After the debacle at Bull Run, Lincoln brought him to Washington to replace Irvin McDowell. In late August, when several military units under his command were combined into the Army of the Potomac, he became second only to Scott in the echelons of the U.S. armed forces. Given his resume, there was simply no better choice to succeed the old man.[33]

Before McClellan could ascend to his new role, however, a small, but significant point needed to be ironed out. It was not clear whether the title commander in chief should apply to the general of the army or to the president. At the start of the war, Scott was referred to both as "general-in-chief" and "commander-in-chief of the army." However, the Constitution gave the latter title to the president when the army, navy, and militias were "called into the actual service of the United States." Lincoln believed that the Civil War now made him both chief magistrate *and* commander in chief, so where did that leave McClellan? Ultimately, the cabinet settled on bestowing on McClellan the specified title of *general in chief.* Lincoln was concerned, however, that Congress had not actually created such an office. In the end, Bates opined that Lincoln had the power to create the office with or without congressional approval. "You are constitutional 'Commander in chief," he counseled the president, "and may make any general you please, your second, or lieutenant, to command under you."[34]

McClellan had a hard time giving up the far grander title of commander in chief. Earlier that summer, as his star began to rise, he wrote to his wife: "I find myself in a new and strange position here—[President], Cabinet, Genl Scott & all deferring to me—by some strange operation of magic I seem to have become *the* power of the land. . . . I almost think that were I to win some small success now I could become Dictator or anything else that might please me." This simpler title of general in chief, however, implied that the president and the secretary of war could countermand any military orders he chose to make. A dictator he was most decidedly not.[35]

If not omnipotent, McClellan was nonetheless resourceful. In a short time, he made Washington almost impregnable, ringing the city with 48 forts equipped with 480 guns, and manned by 7,200 artillerists. He tripled the size of the Army of the Potomac and made frequent visits to the camps, which boosted morale. But when it came to strategy, he often differed with his superiors. Rather than slowly squeeze the South into surrender, as Scott and Bates had suggested, McClellan wanted to instead throw his bloated army at the enemy in an all-out assault.[36]

Bates had his doubts about whether McClellan would succeed at this. On November 19, he dined with Colonel James Henry Van Alen of the Third New York Cavalry and talked of military matters. Rather than expend his resources in a grand battle, Van Alen believed that McClellan would wait until the Confederates' enlistments ran out at the end of the year. A third of their force would disperse at that time, and the other two-thirds would lose the stomach to keep fighting. Afterward, McClellan could undeservedly bask in the glories of a false victory. "This does but confirm my old opinion," Bates wrote in his diary, "that there could be no general battle between the two grand armies."[37]

All was quiet on the Potomac, but military affairs elsewhere gave credence to Bates's concern that McClellan's star might indeed be hitched to the successes of others. On November 7 came news that the army and navy had successfully landed troops at Port Royal Sound, South Carolina. "The victory," Bates wrote, "if properly followed up, and especially, if repeated at other points, will send a chill to the heart of all the southern coast. The spirit of the north, beginning to flag, for lack of some success, will be re-animated. . . ." Then there were leadership changes happening in the west, where, in the aftermath of Frémont's dismissal in Missouri, Lincoln settled on General Henry W. Halleck as the new commander.[38]

If McClellan looked the part of a supreme commander, Halleck looked to be more comfortable in the front of a classroom. Known as "Old Brains," his career had largely been academic. In 1846, he wrote a textbook that highly influenced battlefield tactics early in the Civil War. He was balding, paunchy, and had large, watery eyes that gave way to rumors that he was an opium addict. Bates did not believe the rumors, however, and was relieved to have such a capable man in control of affairs in his home state.

"He is imputed to have high military ability," Bates wrote. "I found him a frank straightforward man." Before leaving for the West, Halleck visited Bates and promised to act in cooperation with Governor Gamble and the Republican state government. He also requested Bates provide him with the names of St. Louisans on whom he could rely as confidants. To that end, Bates wrote to Barton, as well as conservative St. Louis lawyers James O. Broadhead and Samuel T. Glover, suggesting that they call on Halleck when he arrived.[39]

Although the military situation seemed better managed, international affairs now demanded more of the administration's attention. The Union blockade had strained the relationship between the United States and France and Great Britain. Sensing an opportunity, the Confederate government sent a delegation to Europe with instructions to work toward England and France's recognition of the Confederacy. Parliament flirted with the idea, but U.S. minister Charles Francis Adams convinced the English that recognition would put the United States and Great Britain on an unfriendly footing. Meanwhile, in France, U.S. minister William Dayton similarly convinced Emperor Napoleon III to ditch his own plan to recognize the Confederacy. The Union defeat at Bull Run, however, muddled these efforts. Suddenly, public opinion in England swung in favor of recognition of an independent South. Still, when the Confederate delegation pushed for a change in England's policy, Prime Minister Lord Palmerston refused unless the Confederacy won a second, more decisive victory and forced a settlement with the Union. When the North continued to suffer military setbacks that autumn, Jefferson Davis tried again for recognition by sending James Mason of Virginia and John Slidell of Louisiana as new emissaries to England and France, respectively. By October 12, they were on their way.[40]

Union spies had already informed the administration about the new Confederate emissaries. In reaction, Welles dispatched ships into the Atlantic with orders to find and arrest them. On November 7, Captain Charles Wilkes of the USS San Jacinto, stationed in the Caribbean, learned that Mason and Slidell were in the region waiting to board the RMS Trent, a British mail packet intending to run the Union blockade. The next day, near the island of Cuba, the San Jacinto stopped the Trent in international waters, took Mason and Slidell into custody, and delivered them a week later to a prison cell at Fort Warren in Boston Harbor.[41]

Charles Francis Adams later wrote of Northern reaction to the *Trent* Affair: "I do not remember in the whole course of the half-century's retrospect . . . any occurrence in which the American people were so completely swept off their feet." Indeed, when the House of Representatives assembled the next month, their first act was to congratulate Captain Wilkes "for his brave, adroit, and patriotic conduct in the arrest and detention of the traitors, James M. Mason and John Slidell."[42]

On the surface, Lincoln, too, was pleased, but underneath, tensions boiled. At first, the president was concerned about the treatment of the prisoners. As Welles later recalled, Lincoln saw Mason and Slidell as "elephants on our hands, that we could not easily dispose of." The public opinion was so overwhelmingly negative toward them that he feared "it would be difficult to prevent severe and exemplary punishment." For the time being, that was as far as Lincoln went in considering any global ramifications. In the ensuing weeks, however, as the British government began railing over a violation of its maritime rights and demanded a formal apology, the cabinet was forced to revisit the issue.[43]

On Christmas Day, Lincoln called a special session of the cabinet to discuss the *Trent* Affair. He began by reading a letter from Lord Richard Lyons, the British minister to the United States, protesting the arrests on the grounds that Captain Wilkes had decided Mason and Slidell's fate on the quarterdeck of the *San Jacinto* instead of properly taking the matter before a prize court—that is, a court with jurisdiction over captures at sea. Around the table, each cabinet minister then weighed in with their thoughts.

Seward, ever the diplomat, believed that even if Wilkes had erred in not bringing the matter before a prize court, England should not press its luck. There was plenty of precedent in the annals of naval history to support Wilkes's actions, including England's own behavior in the leadup to the War of 1812. Still, England was not the only concern. France too was up in arms. And given the current state of military affairs at home, Seward saw no recourse but to appease the Europeans by releasing the prisoners.[44]

Chase agreed. Great Britain, he felt, had every right to request an apology, and the administration was obligated to comply. "It is gall and wormwood to me," Chase confessed: "Rather than consent to the liberation of these men, I would sacrifice everything I possess." Still, he argued, in its relations with other Atlantic powers, America must act in good faith.

After all, this country would expect no less from Great Britain if the roles were reversed.[45]

Welles, in contrast, believed that by not taking the *Trent* as a prize, Wilkes might be guilty of a breach of protocol, but America owed nothing to Great Britain. Furthermore, he reminded Lincoln that Wilkes was even then being hailed by Northerners as a hero. It would be disastrous for the administration to publicly rebuke Wilkes's actions, and it might discourage other sailors from likewise doing their duty.[46]

Bates weighed in next. After poring over old cases involving America's maritime rights, he concurred with Welles that, because Wilkes had allowed the *Trent* to continue on her way, he was innocent of an offense against the British flag. The bigger concern for Bates was that the European powers might use the affair to intervene in the blockade. "If England can pick a quarrel with us, on the pretense of this seizure," Bates predicted, "France will join with England in forcibly opening the blockade and consequently acknowledging the Confederate States of America and that is war, and we cannot afford such a war." What was worse, he continued, the case might also come before the Supreme Court, which would certainly use the occasion to raise questions over the legitimacy of the Confederacy. As Bates had previously warned Lincoln, a nation could not technically blockade itself, and the administration needed to tread carefully by defining the naval action merely as "the closing of ports." If the case came before the Taney Court, it might judge that the closing of American ports was indeed a blockade, which would then serve as another way for the Confederacy to gain recognition as an independent country.[47]

At the end of four hours, the exhausted men adjourned until the next day. In the meantime, Lincoln weighed his options. The suggestions to release Mason and Slidell were much on his mind; so was the popular support in the North for continuing their incarceration. He even went so far as to draft his own counterargument in support of keeping the prisoners in custody. When the cabinet reconvened, however, Lincoln presented no such argument and instead simply agreed to let the men go.[48]

Except for the protests of a few prominent persons, including Wilkes himself, the response to Mason and Slidell's release was mostly positive. The English, for one, accepted the news as a diplomatic victory and raised no further objections. France, too, put up no further argument. And although Mason and Slidell arrived in their respective missions a few weeks later, both nations kept them at arm's length. Thanks in large part to Seward's

adept understanding of international politics, as well as a cautious interpretation of the facts by Bates and his colleagues—not to mention the
swallowing of their pride—the *Trent* Affair, the most serious threat to
the Union effort in the Civil War, ended in peace rather than world war.[49]

The peaceful conclusion of the *Trent* Affair did not stop Congress from
criticizing the war effort. When the House met on December 2, it unan-
imously congratulated Wilkes for his handling of the affair, but then de-
volved into sniping over the lack of movement on other fronts. Radical
Republicans focused their attention on McClellan and the army's continued idleness. The criticism of the general in chief came down mainly
along party lines, with Democrats defending him against what they took
to be an abolitionist plot to sully his reputation. On December 10, as a
means of getting at the truth, Congress formed the Joint Committee on
the Conduct of the War. Its first act was to invite McClellan to testify a
few days before Christmas. When the time came, however, McClellan
failed to show—he had come down with typhoid fever.[50]

On December 31, the cabinet met again; this time, to discuss the seriousness of McClellan's illness. One proposed solution was to convene a
council of major generals to ensure that someone other than McClellan
understood Union strategy and had a plan of action if he died. This was
absurd, Bates thought. McClellan's illness was problematic, but mainly
because the general in chief had played his cards too close to his chest.
"The strange and dangerous fact exists," he wrote, "that the Sec of War
and the Prest. are ignorant of the condition of the army and its intended
operations!" Had McClellan been more forthcoming with information,
perhaps his presence at these councils would not be so crucial.[51]

In fact, Bates used this opportunity to question the need for a general
in chief at all. Before the war, when America had a single army, Scott had
managed just fine. Now that the Union force was broken into smaller
armies stationed across the continent, as well as a naval flotilla on the Atlantic and Gulf coasts, Bates thought one commander counterproductive.
Instead, he proposed that Lincoln become both commander in chief *and*
general in chief, relying on the secretaries of the army and the navy to
convey his orders to the commanders in the field. Lastly, he urged Lincoln
to assign military men to serve as his secretaries, delivering his orders,
collecting information, and maintaining records. "If I were President," he
told Lincoln, "I *would* command *in chief*—not *in detail*, certainly—and I
would know what army I had, and what the high generals (my Lieutenants)

were doing with that army." For the time being, Lincoln did not take Bates's advice. McClellan remained in command, if in absentia.[52]

The year 1861 had been an incredible one. In just twelve months, the United States found itself in the greatest crisis it had ever faced. Eleven slave states had left the Union, and the four border states teetered on the brink. Washington, D.C., was threatened by its proximity to Richmond, but the army had so far managed to stave off any attempt to separate it from the North. In this unprecedented situation, Bates had legitimized the president's assumption of extralegal powers that, in peacetime, would have been unimagined. International powers had threatened war, but the administration had, at least for the time being, managed to diffuse the tensions. No one could know what the New Year would hold, but all knew that the war would undoubtedly continue. Meanwhile, Bates shared the anxieties of thirty million of his fellow Americans. Several of his sons had, by now, volunteered for service with the Union army, and one had joined Sterling Price's State Guard. As Americans continued to slaughter each other, many began to wonder if reunification was worth the price.

10.
Best and Worst of Times

January 1, 1862, dawned bright and warm in Washington. At eleven, Bates and his children Nancy, Matilda, and Richard made the short trek over to the White House reception. In attendance was the foreign diplomatic corps, in full regalia—"a gawdy show," as Bates later described them. The justices of the Supreme Court were also there, making for an awkward interaction, given Taney's adversarial stance on Lincoln's actions regarding civil liberties. Bates stayed until shortly before noon when the officers of the army and navy arrived—"another gawdy show," he remembered, "worth seeing *for once*."[1]

As they left, the Bates entourage observed a large crowd gathering at the White House gates for admission to the public reception. "I hear that when the gates were opened there was a rush of many thousands, overwhelming the poor fatigued President," Bates later wrote. In contrast, the attorney general enjoyed a quiet afternoon, accepting visits from a few Supreme Court justices, senators, and congressmen. Given the celebratory mood, one almost needed to be reminded that there was a war on.[2]

In the first weeks of the New Year, Bates was consumed by matters devoid of military concerns. He met with several office seekers, including one particularly disagreeable man who criticized Lincoln as an imbecile and asserted that all his political appointments were wrong. Another believed that the president should create an additional assistant secretary of war and that he was just the man for the job. When Bates retorted that he thought Lincoln had too many assistants as is—that what he really needed was a chief of staff—the man "bit at the bait 'as fierce as a rock fish,' not doubting that he is the fittest man in America, to be *chief of the President's staff*."[3]

At this time, Bates also began working on a case scheduled to go before the Supreme Court involving a dispute over land in Missouri. One of the attorney general's chief responsibilities in the mid-nineteenth century was to defend the federal government—or assign lawyers to the job—in all cases brought before the court. This case, *Glasgow et al. vs. Hortiz et al.* had come up from the Missouri Supreme Court and questioned whether a federal land grant of ten acres to William Milburn, William Glasgow Jr., and William C. Taylor, made in the 1850s for the purposes of building a school, superseded an earlier 1812 grant of the same land to Jean Baptiste Hortiz. Because he had been the judge who awarded the grant to Milburn, Glasgow, and Taylor, Bates had a personal connection to the case and thus chose to personally defend them before the court in what he called "the School cases," but he ultimately lost.[4]

It was not until January 10 that Bates had time to attend a cabinet meeting on military affairs. McClellan was still recovering from typhoid fever, and few men outside his inner circle knew anything of the preparations for his grand push against the Confederates. Things fared little better in the West. Of particular concern to Bates was the lack of information regarding Eads's river flotilla being assembled at Cairo, Illinois. The cabinet was unable to discern whether supplies had reached the boats, and Bates raised concern over management of the fleet. "Strange enough," he wrote, "the boats are under the *War* Dept., and yet are commanded by *naval* officers. Of course, they are neglected—no one knows anything about them." As a solution, Bates proposed placing the flotilla entirely under the command of the navy with orders that it cooperate with the army—as was the case with the blockade on the seacoast. But more than that, he once again stressed that Lincoln should assume full control over his armies and reorganize the chain of command, and he now proposed that the cabinet take a formal vote on the measure.[5]

The motion failed on the votes of Cameron and Lincoln, both of whom worried that the creation of a general staff would hurt the pride of the commanding generals. Of course it would hurt their pride, responded Bates. "They wish to give but not receive orders." If the generals openly questioned the orders of the commander in chief, he argued, then they should be dismissed and replaced with more compliant men.[6]

Bates was becoming increasingly troubled by Lincoln's timidity. It was the president's duty to command his officers. "He has no more right to refuse to exercise his constitutional powers," Bates wrote, "than he has to assume powers not granted." Posterity, he wrote, would be the judge of Lincoln's management of this crisis: "If he will only trust his own good judgement more, and defer less, to the opinions of his subordinates, I have no doubt that the affairs of the war and the aspect of the whole country, will be quickly and greatly changed for the better."[7]

What Bates did not know was how much Lincoln was consumed with these concerns. Later that same day, the president privately told Montgomery Meigs, "General, what shall I do? The people are impatient; Chase has no money and he tells me he can raise no more; the General of the Army has typhoid fever. The bottom is out of the tub. What shall I do?" Like Bates, Meigs counseled Lincoln to bring in subcommanders to bypass McClellan. To that end, on January 12, Lincoln summoned Generals Irvin McDowell and William B. Franklin to a cabinet meeting. McClellan, however, learned of the gathering and insisted that he had recovered enough to attend. Lincoln therefore postponed the meeting until the next day, but the general in chief's contributions proved to be a further disappointment. After some pressure from Meigs, McClellan agreed to have Don Carlos Buell move against Confederates in Kentucky—an action that Lincoln endorsed—but still stubbornly refused to divulge his own plans for the Army of the Potomac.[8]

McClellan's intransigence inspired Lincoln to finally take matters into his own hands. First, he replaced Simon Cameron with former attorney general Edwin Stanton. Then, two weeks later, Lincoln issued General War Order Number One calling for an advance of all Union forces against the enemy on February 22. In case there was any doubt to whom Lincoln's ire was directed, the order specifically called out McClellan: "The General in Chief, with all other commanders and subordinates, of Land and Naval forces, will severally be held to their strict and full responsibilities, for the prompt execution of this order."[9]

Bates applauded the president's newfound boldness. In Stanton, Bates believed he had found a kindred spirit. The two had first met on March 6,

1861—the day Bates took the oath of office as attorney general—when Stanton graciously took time to show him around the office and introduced him to members of the Supreme Court. Later that summer, during the Battle of Bull Run, Bates and Julia spent part of the evening at Stanton's home commiserating with friends. "[He] is a man of mind and action," Bates wrote of Stanton a few weeks after his nomination. "He is well [received] by all, except that some of the army officers think that he is too peremptory—He'll cure them of that pretty soon—for he will assuredly, speak to them *in orders*."[10]

Bates was similarly optimistic about Lincoln's orders to the military. They would, he hoped, cure the idleness of Washington society, which had turned to gossip while Congress searched for ways to force more personnel changes in the administration. Specifically, attention turned to Seward and Welles, the latter of whom Bates described in his diary as "not strong or quick, but . . . an honest and faithful man." Bates felt similarly about Interior Secretary Caleb Smith, whom he learned from a member of Congress was about to be indicted for taking bribes in return for patronage positions. "If there be any truth in the story," he wrote, "I incline to think that it must be the work of some vile understrapper of an *office broker*, who screws money out of the needy applicant, under the pretense that he uses it to bribe the Secretary."[11]

Actions of other cabinet members were more troubling. Montgomery Blair, for instance, had recently taken to contradicting Bates at every turn during cabinet meetings. And as for Seward, Bates would not publicly lend his voice to those both inside and outside of the administration lobbying Lincoln to replace him, but, privately, he had plenty of misgivings. In September 1861, for instance, Seward took over management of civilian arrests under the suspension of habeas corpus, but his department made few actual arrests, spending much of the time instead sorting out arrests already made by others. In Bates's mind, while Seward talked tough—going so far as to tell Lord Lyons, the minister from Great Britain, that he had more power to arrest seditionists than Queen Victoria—rarely did he seem to deliver on his threats.[12]

Bates was frustrated over what he saw as Seward's meddling in his own business. He was taken aback, for instance, by a letter he received on February 5, 1862, from the assistant district attorney at Philadelphia. The US marshal there had received orders from Seward transferring all prisoners accused of piracy to Fort Lafayette. By statute, however, the marshal and the district attorney answered to the attorney general, not the secretary of state. Not only did Bates feel that Seward was overstepping his authority, but he also had not bothered to consider the legal ramifications of his orders. Moving prisoners, under normal circumstances, required a writ of habeas corpus, but because that right was suspended, the U.S, marshal in Philadelphia was uncertain how to proceed. Had the order gone through Bates's own office, Seward's ineptitude might have been avoided and the administration saved from undue embarrassment.[13]

Bates raised the matter with Lincoln, who promised to speak to Seward. In the following weeks, however, nothing changed. Instead, Seward began exhibiting a personal resentment toward Bates. "Mr. Seward's deportment has been reserved and suspicious towards me," he wrote in his diary on February 25. Suspecting that Seward's pettiness stemmed from the Philadelphia matter, Bates resurrected it with Lincoln. Seward, Lincoln said, had been directed to sort things out with Bates, directly. "He has never at any time, spoken to me on the subject," Bates responded. Seward's flippancy "surprised and mortified" Lincoln, according to Bates, and he shortly afterward transferred management of civilian arrests to the War Department—presumably because military officers would be making the arrests but also, perhaps, because of the State Department's inability to properly manage the program.[14]

Animosity in the cabinet showed no sign of abating, but one reprieve from the pressures of work was Barton's visit to Washington on January 24. Bates was immensely pleased to have his oldest son staying with him, for it brought joy into the house. There was reason, too, for celebrating: a few weeks earlier, Gamble had named him to the Missouri Supreme Court. Likewise, Bates soon learned, Lincoln had appointed his youngest son, Woodson, as a cadet at West Point. Another reprieve was the long-awaited movement of the Union armies later that month. Lincoln's war order had finally forced McClellan's hand. The general now vowed to march the army against the Confederates in front of Richmond. When combined with simultaneous movements out west, Bates hoped: "It is impossible that we should *fail* every where; and if we succeed in half the instances, the rebellion will be effectually crippled."[15]

The change in fortunes started in the West rather than the East. In Tennessee, on February 5, Brigadier General Ulysses S. Grant and Flag Officer Andrew Foote forced the surrender of Fort Henry on the Tennessee River. A week later, they took neighboring Fort Donelson on the Cumberland. In a matter of days, the Union had taken a third of Albert Sidney Johnston's Confederate army prisoners and divided the other two-thirds. Meanwhile, the Union Army of the Ohio threatened Nashville, which surrendered on February 23, making it the first Confederate state capital to fall into Union hands. Then, a few days after that, Columbus, Kentucky, surrendered to the Union Army of the Mississippi. In a matter of a month, the stars and stripes flew once more over most of Kentucky and Tennessee.[16]

In the coming weeks, the Confederacy's fortunes continued to decline. In late February, Union forces in Missouri, now under the command of General Samuel R. Curtis, drove Sterling Price's State Guard into Arkansas. There, on March 8, in a reversal of the army's fortunes at Wilson's Creek, Curtis won a resounding victory at Pea Ridge. A month later, on April 6, Albert Sidney Johnston struck at Grant's forces near Corinth, Tennessee, at a little crossroads with a log church called Shiloh. In one of the biggest battles of the war, Johnston was killed and the Confederates driven from the state. The next day, forces under the command of John C. Pope overtook the Confederates on Mississippi Island Number 10— securing a long-standing impediment to Union efforts to hold the river.[17]

News of these victories set off a wave of celebration in the North, with Bates joining in the jubilation. "This great victory," Bates wrote of Shiloh, "with all its armaments and munitions, must break the heart of the rebellion. And, followed up, with speed and energy, as doubtless it will be, will I hope, speedily lead to a general submission of the people in the revolted states." New Orleans, he now hoped, could be taken "without a useless waste of blood." His words proved prophetic. On April 29, after the Union navy overran Confederate batteries at the mouth of the Mississippi River, the Crescent City fell into Union hands without a fight. Only the citadel of Vicksburg now stood in the way of full control of the river.[18]

While things were looking up in the West, Union efforts in the East had stalled. To the consternation of many, McClellan moved slowly against the Confederates in Virginia, giving Joseph E. Johnston's forces time to position themselves between the Union army and Richmond. The news of McClellan's bungle was too much for Bates. In his diary, he mocked the general's folly: "Upon the whole it seems as if our genl. went with his finger in his mouth, on a fool's errand, and that he has won a fool's reward." Lincoln was also losing patience. Perhaps the general's workload was too great for him. To that end, on March 11, the president relieved him of the position of general in chief but left him in charge of the Army of the

Potomac. In the meantime, Lincoln and Stanton finally took charge of the military situation—just as Bates had wanted all along.[19]

As Lincoln tried to infuse life into the Army in the East, Congress was busy redefining the meaning of the war. The second session of the Thirty-Seventh Congress was preoccupied with linking slavery to the rebellion. Not everyone, however, supported this effort. Democrats were appalled by the drift away from preserving the Union, while talk of abolition threatened to split the Republican Party between its conservative and radical factions. Border statesmen were particularly concerned. Lincoln, meanwhile, kept his cards close to his chest. He remained aloof when visitors to the White House implored him to support the antislavery efforts in Congress. In February, however, he refused to grant clemency to convicted slave trader Captain Nathaniel Gordon—whose ship, along with its cargo of nine hundred enslaved people, had been apprehended by the navy off the coast of Africa in 1860, and who was facing a sentence of death. Many in the North saw Lincoln's refusal to interfere in Gordon's execution as his first real strike against slavery. Bates himself advised against interfering in the case, but not out of any move to put the administration on a firm antislavery footing. "The President," he wrote, "has no right to stop the course of law, except on grounds of excuse or mitigation found in the case itself—and not to arrest the execution of the statute merely because he thinks the law wrong or too severe." Nonetheless, events in the following months only reinforced the perception that Lincoln's public stance on slavery was changing.[20]

Following the string of Union victories in the West, on March 6, Lincoln proposed to Congress that the federal government assist loyal slave states in adopting gradual programs of emancipation. Doing so, Lincoln reasoned, "substantially ends the rebellion." Democrats condemned the proposal while Republicans applauded it, if not all for the same reasons. Conservatives liked the gradual nature of Lincoln's plan, but radicals believed it would eventually morph into full abolition. And when Lincoln's proposal came up for a vote, every Republican except Thaddeus Stevens—who thought the plan too timid—voted for it.[21]

Outside of Congress, Lincoln's proposal was met with mixed reaction. Abolitionists were skeptical. William Lloyd Garrison believed that gradual emancipation would stonewall more immediate schemes, while Lincoln spent an arduous hour convincing Wendell Phillips that the policy would bring about the death of slavery. Border statesmen, on the other hand, told the president that their states would never go along with the plan unless it was accompanied by mandatory colonization. Bates sympathized with his fellow border statesmen but feared that their outright rejection of Lincoln's plan might push him to embrace the abolitionists. To that end, on March 15, he implored Lincoln to stand firm against the pressures from both factions. "You have taken your positions cautiously," Bates urged, "now maintain them bravely, and I will sink or swim with you."[22]

Lincoln, at first, heeded Bates's advice. When, in early April, Congress passed a bill for compensated emancipation in the District of Columbia, he signed it only after trying unsuccessfully to make the process more gradual and endorsing a push by conservatives to include a plan for voluntary colonization. Then, in May, after General David Hunter, commanding Union forces occupying the sea islands off South Carolina, further stirred the hornets' nest by issuing an edict immediately freeing those enslaved people coming into his lines, Lincoln revoked it and rebuked Hunter for not conferring with him first. Despite these efforts, however, something in Lincoln was indeed beginning to change. In his rebuke of Hunter, for instance, the president left open the possibility of issuing a similar order in the future. When the time came, though, Lincoln stressed that he, not a subordinate, would do it.[23]

The situation in Virginia made it increasingly likely that Lincoln would have to issue such an order. After letting Johnston slip through his fingers at Manassas, McClellan shipped the army south to Fortress Monroe. From there, it prepared to march up the peninsula toward Richmond. By the first week of April, Union forces were set to crush the Confederates facing them at Yorktown. For some reason, however, McClellan laid siege to the town rather than fight directly. Lincoln opposed the idea, believing that it would only exacerbate the criticism in Washington that McClellan had no stomach for a fight. In the end, however, the general's plan won out.[24]

Bates feared from the start that the Peninsula Campaign would fail. He thought the choice to keep the army between the York and the James Rivers was folly. Instead, he felt the army should split in two, with one section remaining on the peninsula and the other crossing south of the James, taking Norfolk, and marching on Petersburg. But alas, McClellan "has such a morbid ambition of originality that he will adopt no plan of action suggested by another—He must himself invent as well as execute every scheme of operations."[25]

Bates's opinion of McClellan only worsened with time. In late April, he attended a party at Senator Benjamin Wade's home where John A. Gurley, a Universalist minister, denounced McClellan's hesitancy and questioned his loyalty. Bates did not share that suspicion—"With more charity," he wrote in his diary, "I conclude that he is only a foolish egot." Nonetheless, he sympathized with the angst at McClellan's sluggishness. Events in early May reinforced those feelings. When Johnston pulled his men back from Yorktown to Richmond, McClellan pursued, but the advance was bogged down by rains that turned the roads into a sea of mud. It was not until May 20 that the army got within miles of Richmond, and yet McClellan would not attack out of fear that he was outnumbered by the enemy two to one.[26]

Bates seethed at the army's glacial pace, but at least one good thing had come of the campaign: Confederates had abandoned Norfolk, and the navy yard was once more in Union hands. Hoping to see the destruction up close, Bates accepted Secretary Welles's invitation to accompany him on an inspection in mid-May. The navy yard was in ashes, but so too was the dreaded ironclad *Virginia* (formerly the *Merrimack*). Of greater interest to Bates, though, was the party's decision to visit McClellan's headquarters, where he had an opportunity to confer with the general one-on-one. The decline in Confederate fortunes in the West, Bates proposed, might induce Johnston and his army to reinforce their compatriots there rather than put up a fight in front of Richmond. McClellan disagreed, however, and the conversation ended without the general giving the attorney general's suggestions much weight. After all, Beauregard's evacuation of Corinth a few days later made the whole conversation moot. Instead, on May 31, the stalemate in the East finally broke when Union and Confederate soldiers clashed at Seven Pines. Unnerved by the sight of mangled corpses on the battlefield, McClellan once more determined to lay siege to the city. Meanwhile, on the Confederate side, Johnston was seriously wounded, and Jefferson Davis soon replaced him with Robert E. Lee, who, unlike his predecessor, resolved no longer to flee from the Union siege guns.[27]

Events now moved at a precipitous rate. Starting on June 26, Lee attacked McClellan in what became known as the Battle of the Seven Days. Each time, the Army of the Potomac successfully repulsed Lee, but in every instance, McClellan picked up and retreated until, on July 1, after the

Battle of Malvern Hill, the army entrenched at Harrison's Landing on the James River, where it stayed until it could be ferried back to Washington. In a matter of weeks, the Peninsula Campaign had completely failed.[28]

Lincoln spent much of the month emboldening McClellan by assuring him that he in fact outnumbered the Confederates. When, however, McClellan—nursing his wounds at Harrison's Landing—sent a message to Stanton laying the blame for his misfortunes on the administration, Lincoln decided to personally intervene. Traveling to Virginia, Lincoln was treated to a grand review of the army before meeting with McClellan to discuss the recent setbacks. Surprisingly, McClellan used the opportunity to present Lincoln with another letter—this one detailing his personal views on the state of the war. Recently, Congress had decided to pass a second Confiscation Act that, unlike the first, freed all enslaved people upon their seizure by the Union army and allowed them to join the military as hired workers. In McClellan's eyes, this was a point of no return, and he warned Lincoln that under no circumstances could the soldiers enforce such a law. If property must be taken, it must be paid for, since any other course of action would appear as piracy in the eyes of an already agitated Southern populous.[29]

Even now, Bates and Lincoln retained a degree of uncertainty as to the legality of the confiscation acts. To better comprehend the situation, they lobbied Francis Lieber, professor of history and political science at Columbia University, and an expert on the laws of war, for his opinion. The distinguished professor responded in the New York and Chicago papers, arguing that because war was a conflict between men, it naturally stripped away their legal status, putting them on an equal footing. Therefore, when a fugitive from slavery came within Union lines claiming to have escaped the enemy and requesting asylum, their enslaved status fell away "like scales."[30]

Lieber's opinion alleviated the president's concerns. After requesting Congress clarify that the confiscation laws would only apply to current rebels and not their descendants, Lincoln signed the Second Confiscation Act along with the Militia Act, which allowed him to call up three hundred thousand nine-month militiamen from the states, including Black soldiers when white men could not be found. Both laws were tremendous steps in the ongoing fight over slavery and aligned well with Lieber's opinion on the use of enslaved people in time of war.[31]

As for McClellan, Lincoln waited a few days after receiving his Hampton Roads letter before naming Henry Halleck as the new general in chief and formally closing the door on McClellan's return to his former position. Although the president exhibited some of the same concerns over the confiscation acts, by no means would he be dictated to by a subordinate—even one as popular with the soldiers as McClellan.[32]

Bates held McClellan in no great esteem, but he sympathized with the general's concerns over the recent turn of events. The confiscation acts were dangerous, he felt, in that, like Lincoln's actions regarding habeas corpus, military commanders might manipulate them to encroach upon individual liberty. Grudgingly accepting Lieber's opinion that confiscation was legal during war, Bates nonetheless argued both in an 1861 letter to Seward following passage of the first confiscation act and in a later opinion to Cameron that, to avoid abuses to civilian rights, it was essential that a civilian court adjudicate whether confiscated property belonged to loyal or disloyal persons. If the former, then compensation was in order.[33]

By summer 1862, Bates was growing increasingly concerned that his conservative views were falling on deaf ears. He was alarmed at Republicans like Thaddeus Stevens who argued that because the Southern states had seceded, they had forfeited their constitutional right to protection of property. Then, on July 22, as the cabinet discussed continued support for gradual, compensated emancipation and colonization, Lincoln outdid Stevens. A week earlier, he had divulged to Seward and Welles that he was considering issuing an executive order emancipating all Southern enslaved people that came into Union lines. He now read to the assembled ministers the first draft of his proposed order, which cited almost word-for-word the main points of the Second Confiscation Act and stated that those enslaved people who fell under its provisions would "thenceforward, and forever, be free."[34]

The one consolation for Bates was that, in its first draft, the Emancipation Proclamation did not negate existing efforts at gradual emancipation. Indeed, one day before he first raised the idea to Seward and Welles, Lincoln tried again to get border statesmen to accept a gradual compensation plan, but he was no more successful the second time than the first. Nonetheless, when Lincoln introduced the Emancipation Proclamation, he told the cabinet that he intended to move ahead with submitting a compensation plan to Congress when it reconvened in December. If they still refused, the Emancipation Proclamation would serve as insurance in Lincoln's strike against slavery.[35]

Reaction to emancipation was as mixed in the cabinet as it was in Congress. Chase approved it but believed the president should have simply allowed his military commanders to spearhead the effort in their respective departments. Blair, on the other hand, was appalled, believing that the proclamation would sink the Republican Party in the upcoming midterm elections. It was left to Seward to propose a compromise. While he supported the proclamation, Seward agreed that now was not the time to issue it. McClellan's setbacks in Virginia would make the proclamation appear like a desperate act. Better to wait for a decisive victory. And so, as Lincoln later explained to artist Francis Bicknell Carpenter, "I put the draft of the proclamation aside . . . waiting for a victory."[36]

Bates kept his thoughts on the proclamation to himself, failing even to record the event in his diary. Perhaps he did so because there was no reason to expound on a policy that—for now, at least—was merely hypothetical. He was also preoccupied with other projects. One of those was the extension of the Missouri Pacific Railroad into southwest Missouri. The road stretched from St. Louis to Rolla, but the construction company tasked with its extension to Springfield had defaulted on payment of interest on its bonds. By law, the state of Missouri seized control, but if 125 miles of track was not laid by June 1863, the federal government would take ownership. Gamble wanted to keep the railroad in state hands and, in April, dispatched Bates's old friend, Charles Gibson, to convince the attorney general to lobby Lincoln to have the federal government complete the project as a military necessity before turning it over to the state.[37]

Bates was easily swayed—his deference for his brother-in-law played a large part in winning him over. Ever a Whig, Bates also understood the importance of railroads to economic progress and Union victory. By May, he was lobbying for affidavits from military personnel favorable to the project. William T. Sherman, for one, extolled on the railroad's importance to keeping Missouri and the American West in Union hands. Other generals wrote much the same. In late June, Bates forwarded these letters to Stanton with the admonishment that "your consent alone is necessary to the accomplishment of a work of immense value to the nation." The business, he explained, would be crucial in ending the rebellion in Missouri: "I beg you, my Dear Sir, decide the matter at once—for or against. If *for*, the people of the South West may hope for repose and the resumption of their ordinary labors; if against, they will dread the repetition of the scenes of last year."[38]

Stanton's reply had the bluntness of a man busy with more pressing concerns. "If this work depends, as you state, upon my consent," he scribbled, "it shall not fail of accomplishment. I will execute with alacrity any order the President may be pleased to sign, and am not aware of any occasion for delay after he shall make the order." Nonetheless, Bates's lobbying paid off. On July 11, Lincoln issued an order extending the rail line to Lebanon, Missouri. Stanton was then given command over the project and took possession of the company.[39]

Another preoccupation for Bates that summer was the continuing decline in Union fortunes in the East. In late August, John C. Pope's Army of Virginia clashed with Lee on the old battlefield of Manassas. Lee outmaneuvered him and forced the army to withdraw to Washington. Particularly galling were the actions of McClellan who, although ordered by Halleck to rush to Pope's defense, instead kept the Army of the Potomac at Alexandria. The cabinet was in an uproar. Stanton said McClellan should be court-martialed; Chase thought McClellan should be shot. On August 30, both men visited Bates at his home to get his endorsement on a memorandum requesting that Lincoln remove McClellan immediately. Bates agreed, but only if he was allowed to draft a more deferential version. Eventually signed by Chase, Stanton, Interior Secretary Caleb Smith, and Bates, the memorandum stated that it was no longer safe for McClellan to command any army of the United States.[40]

As acts of the cabinet went, this letter was on par in its presumptiveness with that of Seward's attempt to govern the administration from the spring of 1861. When presented with the opportunity to sign it, Welles refused, and was shocked that Bates had lent his hand to it, fearing that Stanton and Chase, whom Welles saw as radicals, had gotten to him. In truth, Bates was not influenced by radical pressure so much as by recent news from Gamble of a Confederate invasion of Missouri for which Bates needed the help of the other cabinet members. Nevertheless, the attempt to overthrow McClellan failed. Instead of removing him, Lincoln instead directed McClellan to shield Washington from the danger posed by Lee, who in early September led his army into Maryland. On September 17, the bloodiest single day of fighting in U.S. military history, both armies engaged in near point-blank combat on the banks of the Antietam Creek near Sharpsburg. Although the battle is often seen as a draw, by nightfall on September 18, Lee's army limped back into Virginia, leaving McClellan in command of the field.[41]

It was not the victory that anyone hoped for, but as Bates wrote to Gamble on September 21, "I am thankful for even small favors!" The best news to come out of it, Bates thought, was that Coalter, who had been in the thick of the fighting, came through unscathed: "It looks as if he were protected by a guardian providence." Meanwhile, Lincoln was determined to make more of the battle than simply the repulsion of a Confederate invasion. The next day, he called a special cabinet meeting to discuss the fallout from Antietam, and again brought up his proposed emancipation proclamation. Over the previous months, he had tried to persuade the border states to accept gradual emancipation. Their rejection of that plan, however, convinced him that he would have to act without them. Taking his draft proclamation from its place in his desk drawer, Lincoln explained that, as the armies converged on Sharpsburg, he made a promise to God that, if the battle went in the Union's favor, he would use the occasion to strike at slavery. He then read his now-revised proclamation. In the two months since he had first proposed it, Lincoln had added lengthy snippets from the Second Confiscation Act and the Militia Act banning military officers from returning fugitives from slavery to their enslavers. He also stipulated that any slave state that put down its arms and returned its representatives to Congress before January 1, 1863, would be exempted from the policy. Furthermore, Lincoln added clear language supporting gradual, compensated emancipation in the border states and expressed his intent to pursue agreements with foreign countries to create colonies where the newly freed people would be exported.[42]

Lincoln had made his decision, but he still wanted the opinions of his cabinet. Seward and Chase recommended inserting language giving the proclamation an indefinite lifespan; Blair supported the spirit of measure but still questioned its expediency; and Welles could think of no argument against it other than to doubt whether it would effectively shorten the war. When it was his turn, Bates insisted that emancipation be attached to a firm policy of colonization. It was right, Bates thought, to pursue treaties with Central American countries, and the administration should highlight to these countries the benefits of receiving the former enslaved people— many of whom were "well advanced in arts and knowledge, and a few, who are educated and able men." In working out an agreement, however, he stressed the necessity of classifying freed Black people as emigrants, not colonists. The former term implied an irrevocable split with their country of origin while the latter suggested an obligation by the United States to see to their welfare. Likewise, any formal treaty should glean from the foreign country a promise to treat these emigrants humanely, "guaranteeing to them 'their liberty, property and the religion which they profess.'"[43]

Bates wanted the impossible. The government simply could not unload the newly freed Black people on another country and still demand their humane treatment. It is possible that, knowing this, Bates was fishing for a solution that would isolate radicals and make emancipation palatable to a sizable population of moderates and conservatives. It is also notable that Bates lacked the political savvy to realize that political support for such a scheme was rapidly declining outside of the border states. In the following days, it also became clear that no one in the cabinet, aside from Blair, shared Bates's hopes for a compulsory plan. Lincoln, for instance, insisted that Black deportation be voluntary and without expense to the former slave, but he shared with Bates the hope that agreements—preferably in the form of treaties—could be procured from foreign countries protecting their inalienable rights. Welles and Seward agreed with Lincoln in sentiment but questioned whether a treaty was necessary.[44]

In his views on colonization, Bates might have hoped—unlike Welles—that emancipation could be made palatable enough to hasten the end of the war. Indeed, his comments about colonization were an expression of Northern conservative antislavery principles that accepted emancipation as now a military necessity but rejected any notion of racial equality. That point of view was on full display among Bates's neighbors back home in Missouri. Gamble had, so far, kept them loyal, but his hold was tenuous. As war gripped the southern and western counties, emancipation and the prospect of Black and white people comingling risked pushing Missouri into the arms of the Confederacy.[45]

Regardless of his motives, one thing is clear: Bates believed that Black and white people could not cohabitate peacefully. As he had when freeing his own enslaved people a decade earlier, he saw colonization here as a humane measure meant to give Black Americans the greatest chance at escaping the prejudices that gripped both North and South. For the time being, Lincoln agreed. In August, he stated as much in remarks to a deputation of freed Black people at the White House. Addressing the question of why they should voluntarily leave the country, Lincoln reasoned, "You and we are different races. We have between us a broader difference than exists between almost any other two races. Whether it is right or wrong I need not discuss, but this physical difference is a great disadvantage to us both, as I think your race suffers very greatly, many of them by living among us, while ours suffer from your presence. In a word we suffer on each side."[46]

One hundred days separated Lincoln's issuing the preliminary Emancipation Proclamation and his signing the official version on January 1, 1863. In that time, the president experienced pressures on all sides lobbying him to do everything from rescinding the proclamation to expanding it. Bates, meanwhile, began to accept the inevitable and used this time to press Lincoln to have civilian courts oversee the confiscation of enslaved people. Still spoiling over the fact that the previous spring Lincoln had transferred civilian arrests from the State Department to the War Department, Bates wrote directly to Lincoln in November insisting that his office be authorized to instruct and direct attorneys and marshals on the matter of property seizures. The president seemed receptive. Later that day, he issued an executive order authorizing military personnel to defer to civilian officers in these matters. In the coming weeks, however, Bates did not exercise much control over the policy. Military commanders continued to manage the policy on the ground while Stanton—to Bates's consternation—refused to relinquish control, and Lincoln made no attempt to force him.[47]

By now, jealousies among the cabinet members had become evident to anyone who cared to notice. Bates often suspected Chase, Seward, and Stanton of undermining his authority on legal matters while Chase suspected Seward of supplanting his authority on financial concerns. Welles saw corruption in Chase's handling of fiscal matters, and Blair disliked anyone who challenged his or his family's hold over Republican politics. These internal divisions, for the most part, were neutralized by Lincoln, who remained above the fray, but as time went by, Seward again found himself the primary target of forces in Washington seeking to shake up the administration.

The impetus for this new opposition to Seward lay with the continued military setbacks late that year. After McClellan failed to crush Lee's army following the battle of Antietam, in November Lincoln replaced him with Ambrose Burnside, who, for three days in mid-December, ordered a disastrous assault on Lee's army, which had dug into the hills above the town of Fredericksburg along the Rappahannock River. The loss at Fredericksburg set off a wave of discontent in Washington that eventually settled on the secretary of state. To improve Union fortunes, many persons reasoned, more shakeup was needed at the highest levels of government. Radical Republicans, fed by inside news from Chase about Seward's closeness to Lincoln, once more pressured the president to dismiss him. Doing so, they felt, would bring into alignment those factions of the party that, while distrusting each other, distrusted Seward more.[48]

Seward offered Lincoln his resignation on December 16, but Lincoln did not immediately accept it. Instead, three days later, with Seward absent, he confronted both his cabinet and the secretary's congressional critics. In these deliberations, Bates defended Seward, although not from any personal loyalty. Rather, he believed that, except for the congressional power of advice and consent, Lincoln had no obligation to heed the demands of Congress regarding the hiring or firing of advisors. Blair and Welles agreed. Lincoln then concurred, giving deference to the sacred principle of separation of powers. The cabinet crisis, as it came to be known, ended the next day when Chase—clearly the ringleader of the anti-Seward forces—offered his own resignation. The rest of the cabinet had already conceded that their personal feelings toward Seward were not worth disrupting the balance in the cabinet. Now, Lincoln noted, Seward and Chase's resignations canceled each other out. The public dispute was unfortunate, coming as it did only days after a terrible loss for the military and a little over a week before the Emancipation Proclamation went into effect. Nonetheless, if there was a silver lining, it was that, from then on, Lincoln worked harder—albeit not always successfully—to better accommodate the ideas of his cabinet ministers.[49]

Bates treated these internal squabbles as a distraction from the greater issue of the rollout of the Emancipation Proclamation, several matters of which still concerned him. First was the fact that the proclamation was a war measure. If peace came before the South was completely occupied, slavery would likely survive. Then there was the matter of compensation and colonization. Only Haiti and Liberia had agreed to take Black immigrants, but most of them were not interested in relocating there. Finally, Lincoln had, until then, been supportive of compensation, but in his annual address to Congress, he threw doubt on the idea by acknowledging the astronomical price tag that accompanied it. Pressing ahead, despite these unresolved matters, was especially alarming to Bates when considered alongside the clauses of the proclamation arming Black soldiers. He had long harbored fears that the war would devolve into a servile insurrection. Firmly believing in the superiority of the white over the Black race, he now expressed to Lincoln his belief that, if armed and sent into battle, the sacrifice of Black soldiers to the cause of the Union would obligate the government to reward them with full citizenship. Colonization and compensation had to be resolved before then, for it would be incredibly difficult to implement them afterward.

In raising this concern, Bates was harkening to an opinion he had written for Chase the previous month on American citizenship. In August 1862, the revenue service steamer *Tiger* detained the schooner *Elizabeth & Margaret* because its captain, David Selsey, was a Black man. A 1793 law required vessels doing coastal trade be licensed to U.S. citizens, and the Dred Scott decision said that Black men could not be citizens. The collector of customs referred the matter to Chase, who in turn asked Bates for an opinion on Selsey's citizenship. Bates spent two months poring over legal tracts on the subject and concluded that, while American lawyers had previously based citizenship on political participation, such a definition excluded a large swath of the population. White women and children, for instance, were traditionally considered citizens. If that were so, then Black people born with free status in the United States must be considered likewise. Although Bates stressed that this opinion applied only to the case of Selsey—meaning it should not be construed as applying to recently emancipated enslaved people—his closing line stated that "the free man of color . . . if born in the United States, is a citizen of the United States."[50]

Bates's opinion was received enthusiastically by antislavery advocates. The *New York Times* believed that it nullified the Dred Scott decision. Its popularity among abolitionists, though, worried Bates, for it threatened his pet project of colonization. Hence his efforts, in late December, to get Lincoln to find a solution to colonization and compensation or drop the clause of the proclamation enrolling Black men into the military. Lincoln carefully considered Bates's suggestions and, over the next few days, vacillated over whether to drop the offending passage. At one point, he even scribbled the word "out" in the margins next to it. In the end, however, when Lincoln sent the final draft to the printer, he left the passage in. Meanwhile, as a solution to the temporary nature of the Emancipation Proclamation, Lincoln proposed to Congress a thirteenth amendment permanently outlawing slavery. He offered no such solutions to the other issues. Bates, for his part, supported an amendment, but he simply could not accept Lincoln's insistence that, even with compensation and colonization unresolved, emancipation was still going forward.[51]

New Year's Day festivities commenced at the White House at 11 A.M. Much like the previous year, the cabinet assembled early and mingled with military officers, foreign diplomats, and members of Congress before the public arrived. For three hours, Lincoln shook hands in a receiving line. Then in the afternoon he went to his office to sign the official Emancipation Proclamation. Among the witnesses to this watershed event were Seward and his son, Frederick, Senator Charles Sumner, and Lincoln's secretaries, Hay and Nicolay. The president's hand, swollen from pressing flesh all morning, shook as he prepared to affix his signature. Perhaps he also felt the weight of history. But steadying himself, Lincoln turned to Seward and said, "If my name ever goes into history it will be for this act, and my whole soul is in it." He then dipped his pen in an inkwell and slowly and steadily signed his name.[52]

The gravity of the event was clear to several members of the administration. In his diary, Gideon Welles wrote, "This is a broad-step, and will be a land-mark in history." Nicolay, too, jotted down his impressions: "Slavery caused the war: it is with the sword of his war power under the Constitution that President Lincoln now destroys the right arm of the rebellion." For Nicolay, though, of greater concern was what came next. "This day is also the initial point of the separation of the black from the white race," he surmised: "The two races cannot live together under the contingencies of future growth and expansion." Lawmakers, he concluded, should now set themselves to solving "the problem of an eventual exodus from the United States, and a successful and prosperous colonization within the tropics of this continent of the black nation today liberated by the president's wise and just decree."[53]

Bates concurred. Back in 1859, in a letter to Missouri Republicans recalling his long-time membership in the Colonization Society, he wrote that he considered colonization to be "both humane and wise." This same belief underlay his approval in September 1862 of Lincoln's efforts to treat with foreign governments for the creation of "safe and convenient places of refuge for the free colored population of this country." America's free Black expatriates, Bates thought, would provide foreign governments with an influx of free labor that, possessing skills learned in the United States' rapidly industrializing economy, would modernize their preindustrial economies. Colonization would also provide a solution to the problem of freeing an entire race of beings who nonetheless were viewed as inferiors by most of their white neighbors. In the months since the preliminary Emancipation Proclamation, however, nothing substantive had come of Lincoln's efforts with foreign nations, and although he had gone so far as to endorse a contract to use federal funds to export five thousand Black men and women to Haiti as late as December 31, his abandonment of colonization from the official Emancipation Proclamation led Bates to conclude that prospects for colonization were now dead.[54]

Bates was present at the White House celebrations on New Year's Day, but it is unclear whether he stayed to watch Lincoln sign the proclamation. Other persons in the room left written records, but in his diary, Bates was uncharacteristically silent. This omission might be attributed to his busy social calendar, or it may have been a telltale sign of his disappointment with the course of the war. Emancipation, in whatever form it took, would change everything. But the reality that the official version of the proclamation allowed former enslaved people to join the armed services boded ill for Bates's hope for a prudent, conservative management of the war. Perhaps, then, Bates realized on that January day that the Emancipation Proclamation marked the first major ideological separation between himself and Lincoln.

11.

Radicalism Ascendent

On February 21, 1863, Bates, fatigued from the responsibilities of public office, composed a short letter to his granddaughter in Missouri. "I have been at very hard work," he wrote, "[and] have so many things to think of that I sometimes forget, for a while, even those I love best." Bates was indeed overworked. During January, he and Julia attended only a single social gathering at the White House, at which the guest of honor was vaudeville sensation Tom Thumb. Otherwise, the attorney general was so overworked that he often lost track of time, compelling his daughter, Tilly, to come daily to retrieve him from the office.[1]

His time was consumed mainly by the *Prize Cases*, a matter before the Supreme Court regarding the Union blockade. The plaintiffs argued that Lincoln had no power to enact a blockade because Congress had not formally declared war. Richard Henry Dana Jr., who led the administration's defense, rebutted that war existed whether Congress declared it or not. Bates was apprehensive about the outcome, at one point acquiescing to the advice of defense attorney William Evarts to stall the case as long as possible in the lower courts to buy time for Lincoln to appoint his own justices to the Supreme Court. Now, with the court on the verge of a decision, Bates was also troubled by the conduct of Dana and Evarts's co–defense attorney, Charles Eames, whose opening remarks were too theatrical for the court's austere tastes. Justice Noah Haynes Swayne, for one, warned Bates that several justices questioned whether Eames had ever before argued a case, while Taney brought up Eames's failure to acquit General Fitz John Porter in a court-martial the previous year, suggesting that if Porter had chosen Eames as his counsel, Porter deserved his fate.[2]

The court ultimately upheld Lincoln's war powers, but it was a troubling victory for Bates. It verified his earlier opinion on habeas corpus, but it also gave the president a blank check to employ the military against rebellious individuals in the future. Bates wanted the Union preserved, but not at the sake of permanently altering the law. The decision also sent an important message. Two years into the war, with three Lincoln appointees on the bench, the court was finally shedding its earlier conservatism and was beginning to interpret the laws to meet the immediacy of the moment.[3]

Given the gradual shift in politics toward radicalism, Bates saw his position as a conservative advisor to the president as more important than ever. To that end, Lincoln's order in November to military commanders deferring to civilian courts in confiscation cases gave Bates some hope that he would soon take command of the policy. In January, he therefore drafted instructions ordering U.S. marshals to make the seizures, taking special care that probable cause existed before the confiscation took place. Bates then ordered the marshals to maintain records of all property seized and immediately inform the local district attorney, who would defend the marshal in court. If the court found the marshal in error, the property would be returned to the owner. If implemented as Bates had dictated, the plan would have effectively inserted the civilian courts into the war effort. However, the War Department had no intention of relinquishing its control over the policy, and Lincoln made no attempt to intervene on Bates's behalf. While he did not doubt his personal friendship with the president, Bates began to wonder if Lincoln was "under constant pressure of extreme factions and of bold and importunate men."[4]

These "bold and importunate men"—the radical Republicans—although not always united on all political matters, were nonetheless, by 1863, endeavoring to use immediate emancipation and arbitrary arrests to expand the power of the federal government. The goal, conservatives theorized, was to argue that the slave states had committed suicide by seceding from the Union. They could then be reorganized as federal territories, allowing radicals to confiscate property and disenfranchise those who aided and abetted the rebellion. The theory seemed outlandish, but the Supreme Court's ruling in the *Prize Cases*, as well as the War Department's intrusions in matters belonging to civilian courts, made Bates a believer.[5]

Radical influence was on full display in Missouri. Following its victory at Pea Ridge, Curtis's army descended on the town of Helena, Arkansas, where its cache of cotton was a potential windfall for Northern traders. During the summer and fall of 1862, businessmen arrived with bribes for the soldiers to turn over the lucrative commodity. Curtis worked hard to maintain order and was rewarded by Lincoln with promotion to replace Halleck as commander of the Department of the Missouri, but his successor at Helena reversed much of his earlier progress.[6]

In his new position, Curtis—himself a radical Republican—butted heads with the conservative governor Gamble. Even though Curtis was no longer in command at Helena, Gamble's men used the continued corruption there to discredit him. On February 5, Colonel Thomas Ewing—a Gamble ally—arrived in Washington to implicate Curtis in the cotton fiasco, accusing the general of allegedly depositing $100,000 from cotton sales in a private bank account in Chicago. Then on February 24 came Missouri senator John B. Henderson and Missouri congressman John S. Phelps, both lobbying for Curtis's removal. Beyond the military necessity, Henderson believed that getting rid of the general would quash the radicals in the state and assure his own reelection. For his part, Bates agreed.[7]

Curtis's loyalists did not simply let the conservatives have their way; they also arrived in Washington to lobby Lincoln in his defense. On February 12, Charles D. Drake called on Bates. Self-righteous and opportunistic, Drake had been pro-slavery during the first year of the war, but when the political winds shifted, he defected to the Republicans and was now in the early stages of organizing a radical faction in Missouri. Bates did not record their conversation, but the obstacles that Drake and his radical allies in Missouri had created for Gamble gave him some misgivings about the political situation at home.[8]

Lincoln ultimately sided with the conservatives, removing Curtis and replacing him with Edwin V. Sumner, a conservative division commander in the Army of the Potomac. Although Bates had always seen his role as advisory in nature, in a rare moment of boldness, he decided that, if Stanton held no qualms about going over his head to influence Lincoln on legal matters, then Bates could involve himself in military affairs in his home state. Thus, on March 7, he began a short correspondence with Sumner advising the commander on political matters in the state. Honor and glory, Bates wrote, awaited the man who brought order to the chaos in Missouri: "That glory is now within your reach, & to be attained, not so much by those high fighting qualities . . . as by the less conspicuous labors of the wise statesman—prudence, moderation, firmness, conciliation." Sumner, for his part, welcomed Bates's advice and invited him to write again. To that end, a week later, Bates counseled the general to undermine the radicals by allying with Gamble: "If you & he cordially cooperate & mutually sustain each other, there can be no opposition, there or here, strong enough to give either of you an hour's uneasiness."[9]

Bates hoped that Sumner's appointment would be a turning point in Missouri's political affairs. It was not to be, however. On March 21, Sumner died suddenly while on his way to St. Louis, and Curtis stayed on until a replacement was found. On April 23, Bates again wrote Gamble, reassuring him: "I have not despaired. I still hope & believe, that there will soon be a change for the better, in Mo, as elsewhere." In May, after more prodding by prominent conservatives, Lincoln replaced Curtis with another conservative, John Schofield. By then, however, the radicals had become a force to reckon with for the foreseeable future.[10]

Outside of Missouri, the military situation in the East only dampened Bates's mood. Back in January, he and Julia welcomed a visit from their son, Coalter, then serving in the Army of the Potomac. He stayed a month, and when he left on February 19 for Fredericksburg, Bates ruminated on the conditions to which his son was returning. "Seldom has an army so brave, so strong, and so well appointed, had so hard a fate," he wrote: "it has been forced, by the stupid slowness and persistent blunders of its commanders, always to 'fight backwards' and at disadvantage." To address those blundering commanders, Lincoln, in late January, replaced Ambrose Burnside with Joseph Hooker, whose bravado, Bates hoped, would bring about decisive victory. Indeed, he even lobbied to have Coalter join Hooker's staff so that the young man could witness the longed-for victories. However, when in April Hooker tried to entice Lee into a battle, Lee attacked him near a mansion known as Chancellorsville in the northern Virginia wilderness and, after two days' hard fighting, forced Hooker to retreat. Within a week, the Union army was out of Virginia, and morale in the North again plummeted. Coalter arrived at headquarters just in time to be present at Chancellorsville, but while Bates was not worried about his son's well-being, he noted instead that, although his son owed Hooker for his promotion, it looked like Hooker himself would last no longer than his predecessors.[11]

The one consolation was the progress out west. On April 20, news arrived that the Union riverboat flotilla had successfully run the guns at Vicksburg and was now south of the city. "As soon as we are masters of the River," Bates wrote, "the tide of the war must turn." His mood lightened further a month later when Grant took Jackson, Mississippi. It was now only a matter of time, Bates expected, before Vicksburg fell. When it did, it would "break the heart of the rebellion." The thought presented a moment for reflection. From the beginning, Bates argued that control of the Mississippi would decide the fate of the rebellion. He was pleased to see his theory realized. His only regret was that victory had not come sooner, to avoid "rivers of blood, and great heaps of ashes."[12]

Bates's poor health and his confinement to home for a matter of weeks dampened some of his contentment. Overwork was partially to blame, but so too was Bates's concern for his son, Richard—called Dick—who had recently been made deputy solicitor of the Court of Claims. Dick was prone to low self-esteem, and Bates hoped his new position would improve his son's mental status. When it did not, J. D. McPherson, the assistant solicitor of the court, suggested that Bates and Julia take him on a sojourn to St. Louis. Bates followed McPherson's advice, and a few weeks later happily recorded in his diary that both father and son were improving nicely, thanks in no small part to the family's decision to avoid news of the war as much as possible. He could not, however, avoid hearing on July 6 of the victory three days earlier at Gettysburg, Pennsylvania, where General George Meade, who recently replaced Hooker, repulsed Lee's second invasion of the North in the biggest battle of the war. A day later, Vicksburg surrendered to Grant, cutting the Confederacy in two. The war, it seemed, was turning.[13]

On July 23, Bates and Dick felt well enough to return to Washington. With Julia, Tilly, Sarah, Julian, and Onward, they boarded a train to Chicago and then took a steamboat across the Great Lakes. While in Chicago, Bates learned of the state of national politics during his absence. Orville Hickman Browning—whom Governor Richard Yates of Illinois had appointed to the Senate to finish out the term of the late Stephen A. Douglas (who died in 1861)—warned Bates that radical Republicans were scheming to reconstruct the Union by returning the seceded states to territorial status. Bates hoped Browning's fears were exaggerated. The leaders of the Republican Party were enlightened men, he thought, who "will not fail to see, in such a course, their own defeat and downfall." Back in the office on August 1, however, Bates found that Browning's fears were not at all farfetched.[14]

The radical shift in Republican politics was most notable in the divisions within the cabinet. Back in May, Bates's friend Isaac Newton warned him that the Blairs were orchestrating to replace all members of the cabinet except Welles. Bates advised Newton to ignore these intrigues, but privately acknowledged that the Blairs hated Seward and Stanton, were jealous of Chase, and were dissatisfied with himself because he refused to be their puppet. True, Bates sympathized with Blair regarding Seward, Stanton, and Chase, believing that—however much the three men disagreed on other issues—they were thoroughly radicalized on the administration's emancipation policy. Allowed by Lincoln to bypass the conservative members of the cabinet, they now took their business directly to the president, only in retrospect seeking consensus from the rest of the cabinet. But Bates was no man's puppet. He had his qualms with the radicals in the cabinet but would not intrigue to have them removed.[15]

Bates would not work toward their removal, but he nonetheless worried that Seward and Chase's influence would undermine his own position as a conservative advisor to Lincoln. At first, he hoped that victories in the West would alleviate some of the radical pressures on the president. Missouri could serve as a test case. There, General Schofield endorsed Gamble's gradual emancipation plan and allowed the state militia to manage internal affairs. He also ordered the military to refrain from interfering with the return of fugitives from slavery. All of this paid handsomely. As James Rollins reported to Bates that fall, excepting a few guerilla units in the West, "there is not a regularly authorized or organized band of Confederate soldiers in the state; there never will be again!" The rising threat now, he warned, was the radicals in the assembly, who were discontented with Gamble's conservative policies.[16]

In late September, Lincoln gave the conservatives in Missouri an important boost when he rejected the demand from a delegation of Missourians led by Charles Drake to remove both Schofield and Gamble from power. Almost gleefully, Bates wrote of Drake and his followers, "From all I can hear, I think they are conscious of defeat and degradation." However, far from ending their intrigues, Bates believed that Lincoln's actions would embolden the radicals to try harder to obstruct the governor's policies. Still, he reassured his brother-in-law, "My policy with them is a war policy. I refuse flatly to hold social, friendly intercourse with men, who daily denounce me and all my friends, as traitors, allies of the public enemy."[17]

It was about this time that Bates and other conservatives began disdainfully referring to the radicals as "Jacobins," after the ruling party in the French Revolution who used demagoguery, intimidation, and divisiveness to erode the ideals of freedom and equality. Unlike their earlier French counterparts, however, the radical Republicans, Bates observed, "for the most part, [are] mere ignoramuses, destitute alike, of sincerity, zeal, courage and knowledge." Drake, he believed, was a perfect choice to lead them, for he was completely devoid of principle and acted only according to political expediency.[18]

Despite rejecting the demands of the Missouri radicals, Lincoln appeared to embrace their ideals in other ways. "Sometimes [Lincoln] almost yields to my remonstrances," Bates wrote Gamble back in April, "and then, seem to get the better of him the influence of extreme politicians." Gamble was freer with his opinion. While meeting with Lincoln in August, he felt rebuffed by the president, who catered instead to several radicals who called in the middle of their conference. While returning to St. Louis, Gamble wrote Bates: "I have hitherto thought [Lincoln] to be an honest man. I retract the opinion." The president, he now felt, was "a mere intriguing, pettifogging, piddling politician."[19]

Whether Lincoln was actively courting them, it was clear to Bates that, in Washington at least, the radicals had friends in high places. He had little doubt as to who was fueling their intrigues. After the meeting with Lincoln in September, Drake had retired to the home of Chase, who invited Bates to dine that evening. He declined, though, knowing full well that his conservative ideas were not in vogue at Chase's table. Gamble too believed Chase the fountainhead of conservative woes. When Drake first went to Washington earlier that year, Gamble observed, it had been at Chase's invitation. "All the revolutionary papers in the state would support Mr. Chase for the Presidency against Mr. Lincoln or anybody else," Gamble warned, "and they are all of one mind in seeking the over throw of the state government."[20]

Standing up to the radicals, though, was a political risk for Lincoln. In late October, he told Bates that he feared he no longer had any friends in Missouri—a sentiment that Bates vehemently denied. Conservatives had the upper hand, Bates explained, thanks to Lincoln's refusal to unseat Schofield. If Lincoln continued to give his unequivocal support to Missouri's provisional government, then he would easily carry the state in 1864. Gamble, however, was less certain that the radicals were beaten. He was also losing faith in Schofield, who was backtracking on compensated emancipation. "My spirit chafes within me," Gamble wrote, "when I think of the Government of the State assailed by daring and unscrupulous revolutionists and supported only by a hesitating, halting General who is afraid to do his duty."[21]

Clearly, Gamble was sinking under the pressures of office, but Bates continued to send words of encouragement. The upcoming judicial elections—scheduled for early November, and in which Barton was a candidate—would, Bates believed, relieve Gamble's anxieties. "Already we have extinguished the enemy's lightning," Bates wrote, "and if we carry the election week after next, we will silence his thunder." He continued to believe that Lincoln's earlier rebuff of the radicals strengthened the conservatives' position. "Discard all Jacobins over whom your authority extends, & defy them boldly," Bates counseled: "Fear nothing here, for the extremists in the East, will soon be taught by their fears, to denounce their brethren in Mo."[22]

The election took weeks to determine, but in the end the conservative judicial candidates won 43,180 to 40,744. The victory was bittersweet, however. Conservatives controlled the judiciary, and their candidate, John B. Henderson, was elected to a full term in the U.S. Senate. However, radical Benjamin Gratz Brown also won election to the Senate, and Drake's compatriots won several state offices.[23]

In late November, while Lincoln and most of the cabinet ventured to Gettysburg for the dedication of a new military cemetery, Bates stayed in Washington to handle a delicate family matter. Their sojourn to St. Louis earlier that summer had done Dick well, but his demons returned with the onset of autumn. On November 12, he left Bates's house for his office and stumbled home drunk around 3 A.M. After breakfast the next morning, Dick went out again, this time not returning home for over a week. "The terrible conviction is forced upon us," Bates wrote, "that he has abandoned himself to shame and ruin, and is no longer worthy to be a husband or a son."[24]

Bates believed in second chances. Even now, he would not abandon his son. With his father's blessing, Dick resigned his position in the Court of Claims and, after Secretary Welles awarded him a commission as an acting ensign, left for the North Atlantic Fleet in late December on what Bates described as "a new experiment for his reformation and redemption." Meanwhile, his wife stayed behind with Bates and Julia, who promised to look after her as if she were their own child.[25]

Dick's departure happened during a flurry of activity at the Bates home. Eads and his wife stayed with them while Eads consulted with the Navy Department on plans for more iron boats. Then came Bates's sister, Sarah, for a visit. George Smizer, a family friend, brought them news of Fleming—still serving in Sterling Price's Confederate army—whom Smizer had sighted in Mobile. Lastly, in late December came Coalter, who had remained on General Meade's staff following Hooker's departure and who witnessed firsthand the Battle of Gettysburg earlier that summer.[26]

The presence of family and friends brightened Bates and Julia's spirits, but while they played host in Washington, back in Missouri another family tragedy was unfolding. On December 16, Gamble fell on the icy steps of the governor's mansion and broke his right arm, which he had injured the previous summer. Taking to his bed, he soon developed pneumonia and died on Sunday, January 31, 1864. To the end, he promised to continue fighting against the radicals who had hounded him throughout his tenure.[27]

As he had forty years earlier with the loss of his brother Frederick, Bates took Gamble's passing hard. "He stood, like a lighthouse on a rock in the edge of a stormy sea," Bates wrote, "not only to give warning of the danger, but to resist its violence." By the word "danger," he was again alluding to the radicals and their leader, Drake, who, Bates noted, did not attend the funeral services for Gamble. But whether Drake's absence was another manifestation of the schism between conservatives and radicals, Bates could not say. Still, he was inspired by the eulogies offered for his late friend. Believing that Gamble's high character in the face of adversity had undermined the radicals, Bates now took upon himself his brother-in-law's mantle as conservative standard-bearer.[28]

Gamble's death removed one of the few remaining impediments to radical ascendancy in Missouri. A few weeks later, Lincoln removed the other. Since the previous fall, Schofield had slowed down recruitment of Black soldiers and had placed the policy in the hands of provost marshals, many of whom were themselves slave owners. Lincoln warned him to tread a moderate ground, but when Schofield did not alter his policy, the president—who needed radical support in the coming election—removed

Schofield and replaced him with William Rosecrans. Within months, Black recruitment was up in the state, owing to federal protection of Black families against reprisals from angry slave owners, sounding the death knell for slavery in Missouri.[29]

Bates long feared that the recruitment of Black troops would create a potent voting bloc for radicals and burgeon the power of the federal government. The radicals would then use that power to pursue equal rights for formerly enslaved people. By February 1864, as Congress began debating proposals to repeal the fugitive slave law and pass constitutional amendments guaranteeing all persons born in the United States equality before the law, his fear was becoming a reality. "Surely Cicero was right," Bates wrote, "when he said that 'in every Civil war, success is dangerous, because it is sure to beget arrogance and a disregard of the laws of the government." The radicals, he continued, "have opened up to themselves a boundless source of power. When the constitution fails them, they have only to say 'this is a time of war—and war gives all needed powers!'"[30]

Despite Bates's criticisms, if Lincoln hoped to be renominated by the Republicans, he had to give some credence to radicals' rising influence. At first, many of them turned to Chase, who actively courted them and whom conservatives despised. Lincoln, in private, called their scheme "fiendish," to which Bates—seeing himself as the most influential conservative in the cabinet—offered some advice. If Lincoln continued to obstruct radicals' whims, Bates believed, he would win the support of the same conservative and moderate coalition that put him in office four years earlier. That done, the radicals would "find that they dare not openly oppose him," and "their effort will then be to commit him to as many as possible, of their extreme measures, so as to drive off his other friends, until he is weakened down to their level."[31]

On February 15, Senator Lyman Trumbull, although by no means a radical himself, proposed one of those "extreme measures" when he introduced a thirteenth amendment to the Constitution declaring that neither slavery nor involuntary servitude shall exist within the United States or its territories and giving Congress the power to enforce the amendment through appropriate legislation. While he supported the language ending slavery, Bates had some reservations about this proposal. First, Congress had already passed a thirteenth amendment during the secession crisis, which forbade the federal government from interfering with slavery in the states. That amendment was technically "still open to acceptance by the States." Then there was the passage in the new amendment regarding admitting slavery as a punishment for crimes wherein the "offender shall have been duly convicted." Bates was concerned that the language ignored the principle of sui generis, which barred the transfer of legal status beyond one generation, and could possibly condemn generations to convict slavery. This later criticism amounted to splitting hairs, but at its heart, it was another example of Bates's attempt to slow the hasty and unthinking actions of the radicals.[32]

As winter turned to spring, that intrigue continued to threaten the Republican presidential nomination. In late February, Bates learned from his pardon clerk, Edmund C. Stedman, that Chase men in New York were organizing radical clubs throughout the North, but as yet, those groups were only united in their opposition to Lincoln; they had yet to commit to an alternative candidate. "Then, so far," Bates reasoned, "it is only an effort to unite all the outs against the ins." A few days later came rumors that Secretary of the Interior John P. Usher—who replaced Caleb Smith in early 1863, and who was politically aligned with Chase—and Senator Samuel Pomeroy of Kansas were working to embarrass Lincoln by publishing a pamphlet declaring the president unfit to be the nominee. The circular went out at the same time as the Maryland Republicans held their state convention, condemning the conservatism of the administration, which Bates thought amounted to little more than "intermeddling impudence" but nonetheless provided clear evidence of another border state giving in to radical impulses.[33]

Ultimately, Chase's men failed to unite the radicals, and they underestimated Lincoln's popularity with the Northern public. Meanwhile, Chase was personally damaged by a resolution introduced in the House by Frank Blair Jr. calling for an investigation of his department's mishandling of contraband cotton. Chase again offered Lincoln his resignation, which the president again rejected, but on March 5, Lincoln secured a greater prize when Chase withdrew his name as a candidate for president. Far from celebratory at Chase's implosion, though, Bates rightly guessed that the radicals would simply look elsewhere for a candidate. Some flocked to Ulysses S. Grant, but he quashed their hopes when he refused to stand for office if Lincoln intended to run. They next turned to John C. Frémont, but although he was well-liked in the North, they soon realized that he too could not compete with Lincoln's popularity. As summer grew near, it was clear that—as Bates had predicted—Lincoln had adroitly managed all factions of his party into supporting him for another four years.[34]

Between conflicts with the radicals, Bates was also embroiled in a torturous legal dispute before the Supreme Court involving the question of the federal government's power of imminent domain. The matter involved a silver mine near San Jose, California, the ownership of which was disputed by two companies—the New Almaden Company and the Quicksilver Mining Company. In 1863, the court threw out the New Almaden claim, prompting Bates to recommend that Lincoln seize the mine. Both companies protested, however, and the president backtracked. A new decision was needed, and in 1864, the three aggrieved parties brought their arguments back to the court.[35]

For the first time since taking office, Bates chose to personally appear on behalf of the administration. He made several prolonged speeches back-to-back over a two-day period, which were, as he later wrote, some of the most important of his tenure as attorney general—mainly because, until then, the members of the court had assumed him "unable or afraid to encounter the leading members of the bar." His opponents were impressed. Former attorney general Jeremiah Black, for one, was taken aback at the effectiveness of Bates's argument. In the end, however, the corruptive influence of Bates's opponents—several of whom were stakeholders in the New Almaden company—overwhelmed his argument, and the court ultimately ruled in their favor.[36]

Bates was disappointed at the ruling, mainly because he believed the justices stood to profit from siding with a private corporation. He had little time, however, to reflect on it, for he was already preoccupied with another political scandal in his hometown. This time, it involved his friend, Presbyterian minister Samuel McPheeters, who had suffered heavily for maintaining his neutrality in the war. The fact that McPheeters's older brother, William, was a member of Sterling Price's army, along with his own refusal to take sides, led many of his congregants to doubt his true allegiances, and in December 1862, they convinced Curtis to banish him from Missouri. McPheeters protested to Lincoln. With Bates's help, he managed to convince the president to rescind the order. Lincoln, too, doubted McPheeters's loyalty, even after Bates vouched for him, but would not go so far as to allow the military to involve itself in church affairs.

Nonetheless, to appease the radicals in Missouri, Lincoln also allowed Curtis to remove the preacher if he truly felt the Union cause was threatened. In April 1863, when McPheeters refused to take a loyalty oath, Curtis denied the preacher's reinstatement. There matters rested until McPheeters and his friends again petitioned Lincoln for his reinstatement. Irritated that the matter had gone on this long, and that both sides somehow believed the president of the United States could determine who could preach in a St. Louis pulpit, Lincoln reinstated McPheeters on December 31, 1863. Bates felt vindicated, believing that he played no small part in convincing Lincoln to overrule his military commander. Still, it was fast becoming clear that the radicals were creating new political battlegrounds upon which to throttle their enemies.[37]

Personal matters also plagued Bates. Dick was showing improvement in his new position. So much so that in March, Rear Admiral Samuel Lee expressed his intention to make him judge advocate of the squadron. But now, changes "in the conduct and personnel" of Bates's own office began to trouble him. On April 28, his longtime assistant, Titian J. Coffey, resigned his position. The loss of a favorite staffer at such a crucial moment in his public life took a physical toll on the seventy-year-old attorney general, and a few days later he suffered a minor stroke that caused temporary paralysis and impaired his speech for three days. Although Bates personally made little of the episode, his family was alarmed. Barton and Julian, worried that their father's fate might resemble that of their late uncle Gamble, urged Bates to resign at once and come home. "You are not required to sacrifice your health and comfort for any good which you may possibly do in your present position," Barton implored. There were younger men capable of doing the job, and besides, he continued, referencing the radicals, "Mr. Lincoln does not need you as an adviser (for if the public understanding be correct, he 'puts his foot down' [& into it] not only without the concurrence but also without consultation with the cabinet)."[38]

Bates took his son's entreaties to heart, but in the end, he chose to stay until Lincoln's election was assured. As summer progressed, that eventuality became increasingly more likely. Stationed with the Army of the Potomac, Grant was harassing Lee in the northern Virginia wilderness, shedding thousands of lives at an alarming rate, but Lee refused to retreat. By late summer, Lee's forces entrenched just outside of Richmond at Petersburg, where both sides prepared for a siege. Meanwhile, Sherman's

Army of the Tennessee was advancing daily toward Atlanta. Within a matter of months, it seemed, Confederate forces in Georgia and Virginia would be on the verge of annihilation.[39]

Despite the mounting casualties—over eighteen thousand in the Wilderness campaign alone—which caused some Northerners to criticize Grant as a butcher, as well as the apoplexy of Washington society when, in mid-July, Jubal Early's small Confederate army nearly breached the city's defenses, Bates was pleased at the military victories. He was likewise relieved to find that his son, Coalter, "is still without a wound, in all this carnage." More good news came in September when Atlanta surrendered, and Phil Sheridan decimated Early's army in the Shenandoah Valley. For extra measure, in late October, Union forces in Missouri fended off a final raid by Price's army. The Army of the Potomac was stuck in front of Petersburg, but elsewhere Confederates were melting away, giving a weary North reason to believe that, if it stayed with Lincoln, victory was assured.[40]

By then, the radicals had grudgingly given their support to Lincoln. Back in May, searching for an alternative candidate, some in Cleveland had nominated Frémont. In a public address afterward, however, they offered to support Lincoln if the administration would, in turn, promise to give more effort to enforcing equal rights in the South. Meanwhile, a month later, Lincoln sailed to renomination at the National Union Party convention in Baltimore. No longer plagued by a possible intraparty challenger, the president began cleaning house. He accepted Chase's resignation later that month. Then, in July, he pocket vetoed the radical Wade-Davis Bill, which would have enacted a Reconstruction plan that denied Southern states sovereignty until they disenfranchised Confederate soldiers and sympathizers and 50 percent of the populous complied with a loyalty oath that swore they had never taken up arms against the Union.[41]

Although angry at these moves, radicals were left with little choice but to vote for Lincoln in November. The Democrats had nominated George McClellan as their candidate and called for immediate cessation of the war and a negotiated peace, both of which were nonstarters for radicals. Then in September, with the Union military victories in Georgia and Lincoln's acceptance of Montgomery Blair's resignation, the matter was settled for many holdouts. Yet despite radicals' cold embrace of Lincoln, and the president's veto of the reconstruction bill, Bates nonetheless chose to see Lincoln's dismissal of Blair as little more than a sacrifice for political gain. In truth, Blair had known for some time that he was a political liability and gave Lincoln an undated letter of resignation back in July to be used when Lincoln deemed it necessary. While Bates had never entirely been on Blair's side—given their past disagreements—he nonetheless wrote, "I think Mr. Lincoln could have been elected . . . in spite of [the radicals]. In that event, the Country might have been governed, free from their malign influences."[42]

As election day approached, some radicals joined conservative Republicans in stumping for Lincoln. Meanwhile, McClellan failed to shake his party's call for an immediate negotiated peace. "I am convinced that the *man* cannot support the party," Bates wrote of McClellan, "nor the *party* the man." Lincoln agreed, stating back in late August that the Democrats would either nominate a war candidate on a peace platform or a peace candidate on a war platform. Either way would be problematic for them. With McClellan hopelessly at odds with his own party, on November 8, voters gave Lincoln a second term in a landslide: 212 electoral votes to 21.[43]

Under the surface, Republicans were fractured, but in their overwhelming victory in 1864, they at least gave the appearance of being unstoppable. Bates personally felt heavily bruised by the late campaign. Lincoln's concessions to radicals on military matters in Missouri, as well as the dismissal of Blair, had only been the start. His policies on race were the greatest point of contention for the attorney general. Back in May, after Confederates massacred surrendering Black soldiers at Fort Pillow, Tennessee, Bates openly chastised the president for arming them in the first place. "I knew something of the cherished passions and the educated prejudices of the Southern people," Bates wrote, "and I could not but fear that our employment of negro troops would add fuel to a flame already fiercely burning." Then, in August, Lincoln ignored Bates's entreaties to reprimand General Butler for not returning confiscated property to loyal Virginians, angering Bates to the point that he wrote in his diary his fears that Black people would undoubtedly use their newfound rights to subjugate whites civilly, socially, and politically: "I do not believe that the negroes desire that the Whites shall be reduced to slavery; but if, by the destructive processes of the war, their own personal freedom can be accomplished, we cannot expect them to reject that consummation."[44]

Bates's discontent did not end with the issue of race, however. Later that fall, he sparred with Stanton over civil rights and the new treasury secretary, William Pitt Fessenden, over continuing Chase's policies on confiscated cotton. His continued estrangement from Seward, with whom he had previously enjoyed a cordial relationship, was also disconcerting. Then in late November—a month after Chief Justice Taney died following a long illness—Lincoln recommended Chase as his replacement. In years past, Bates had been highly critical of Taney. Now, however, he eulogized the late chief justice as "a man of great and varied talents, a model of a presiding officer; and the last specimen within my knowledge, of a graceful and polished old fashioned gentleman." He could not so easily say the same for Taney's successor.[45]

Having for so long held the Supreme Court in high regard and given his previous record as a land judge, the architect of the Missouri judicial branch, and the nation's chief legal officer for the past three years, Bates hoped that he might be named chief justice. Lincoln, however, went with Chase in order to appease radicals whom he needed to pass his legislative agenda in the second term. He may also have been motivated by the age gap between the fifty-six-year-old Chase and the seventy-one-year-old Bates. Furthermore, while Bates and Lincoln largely agreed on matters of Reconstruction, Lincoln possessed a remarkable ability to change his mind according to the situation at hand, whereas Bates had failed to demonstrate the same capability.[46]

The shock of being passed over for chief justice had a similar sting to losing the Republican presidential nomination four years earlier. If nothing else, it reinforced the entreaties of Bates's family that he was no longer needed in the administration. He had resolved to remain until Lincoln's reelection. That was now accomplished. With the radicals now ascendent in the cabinet, Bates could no longer provide Lincoln meaningful counsel. Having come to these conclusions, on November 22, Bates made the decision to leave office. Three days later, in the presence of the cabinet, he formally submitted to Lincoln his letter of resignation. The last three years had been the most arduous of Bates's entire life. With the Union on cusp of victory and Lincoln reelected, but with the radicals now in full command and the republic on the verge of tremendous social change, Bates was going home.[47]

12.
Final Battles

On December 1, 1864, Bates prepared to leave Washington for the last time. Julia and Tilly had gone to West Point to visit Woodson while Nancy remained with her father to supervise the packing and transportation. That night, father and daughter moved to a room at the Metropolitan Hotel, where Bates entertained friends and colleagues. The next day, Bates made last calls on several members of the government, including the new postmaster general, William Dennison, and Edwin Stanton, who now dropped all pretense of adversity and adopted an air "especially civil." Stanton promised to do all in his power for Bates's sons still on active duty. At the White House, Bates took his leave of Seward, Welles, and Usher. Lincoln escorted him from the office with a manner "affable and kind" and promised to write. That night, more friends called at the hotel to say their goodbyes, and in the morning, Bates and Nancy boarded a train for St. Louis, by way of Philadelphia, where they picked up Julia and Tilly. Home, and retirement, beckoned.

The weather remained decent throughout the four-day trip, but as the train drew close to Missouri, it suddenly grew colder. Within days, the winter snows began. It might have been a portent of things to come, for although Bates thought he was returning to the tranquil Elysium of political retirement, one more battle lay ahead.[1]

Bates found his home state much changed. Union military officers were in charge and were quickly reshaping civilian life. In the western part of the state, a chaotic situation existed where neighbors took sides and lives were upended by, first, armies marching against one another and, later, by violent vigilante groups. In St. Louis, two converted prisons bulged with men arrested by federal forces for allegedly assisting the rebellion. Others found themselves disenfranchised for refusing to take an oath of loyalty to the Union. As a result, in the election of 1864, over fifty thousand fewer Missourians cast a ballot than in 1860. Whereas in that earlier contest the state went for Douglas for president and Jackson for governor, four years later, Lincoln and Thomas Fletcher, the radical Republican gubernatorial candidate, carried the state by nearly forty thousand votes.[2]

German Americans, who had been marginalized in St. Louis before the war, now held important bureaucratic posts in the new state government with the duty of promoting Missouri as a veritable utopia for farmers, capitalists, and free laborers. The latter group was of particular importance in the postwar economy and, as such, influenced the successful passage in the late election of a referendum calling for a new state constitutional convention with the express purpose of outlawing enslaved labor in the state. The convention was also tasked with a less-celebrated mandate— permanently disenfranchising and punishing persons guilty of treason. Over the ensuing months, instead of amending the current state constitution, the radicals wrote a new one, alarming conservatives who railed against the illegality of the convention. In time, this growing chasm between people who had once joined hands in defense of the Union would cause a political realignment in the state that put people like Bates in league with the very partisans they had opposed before the war.[3]

Bates intended at first to watch the proceedings of the state convention from the sidelines. He had long realized that his philosophy of government was out of style, writing to the Western Sanitary Commission Fair in 1864 that he had begun to "suspect myself to be little or nothing better than an *old fogy*." Moreover, his family demanded much of his attention. As he had feared, his salary as attorney general had barely provided for their needs, and his miniscule savings made returning to Grape Hill unfeasible. In February 1865, Bates borrowed $18,000 from Barton to purchase a new house, which offered many of the same amenities as his previous one, including space for a garden and a library, where he could spend time in quiet contemplation and, perhaps, write his memoir.[4]

Privately, though, he could not avoid political matters. He expressed to his friends and family his fears at the radical takeover of the state government—a government he had personally helped to frame in 1820. In 1863, he had underestimated the resiliency of the radicals as a faction; in 1864, he watched as they co-opted the highest levels of government; now, they were on the cusp of reshaping society; someone had to stand up to them. After a short time, he decided to publicly lead the conservative effort against the Missouri radicals. It would be a harder political battle than any he had fought as attorney general.[5]

On December 20, Bates ruminated in his diary on terms such as *radical* and *loyalty*. "Radical," he concluded, now meant "adhesion to my clique," and a "radical politician" believed "the good of the people is the Supreme Law, and he is the only judge of what is good for the People!" Like the secessionists of 1860, Bates saw the radicals as a small band of fanatics who had managed to assume control of the government by professing their love of personal liberty while suppressing dissent. As for the imminent state convention, Bates believed it to be "a gathering of Demagogues, designed to throw society into anarchy, and then to gamble for a better system." Power not freedom, he claimed, was their ultimate prize, and the convention was a convenient means of achieving it.[6]

For the time being, this was Bates's only mention of the radicals and the upcoming convention. Rather than speak out publicly, he silently waited to see whether his suspicions about their motives would prove true. The answer came a few weeks later when the convention got to work. On January 11, 1865, it accomplished its primary mission, passing an ordinance abolishing slavery three weeks ahead of Congress's passage of the Thirteenth Amendment. Of sixty-six delegates, only four voted against it. The next day, Governor Fletcher endorsed the ordinance, declaring it to be the law of the land.[7]

Bates supported emancipation but found the ordinance wholly unnecessary. The convention Gamble called in the spring of 1863, he believed, had adopted a sufficient plan for gradual emancipation that would eradicate slavery in seven years. Only wait another five, and slavery would be no more. Given this fact, Bates surmised that the true reason for the ordinance was for launching the radicals' true course to secure "the ascendancy and permanency" of their faction. Indeed, when the convention remained seated after its stated aim was accomplished, rumors began circulating that the radicals would next announce the nullification of the old constitution and the creation of a new one along with another ordinance vacating all state offices not currently held by radicals. Having been called, therefore, "ostensibly to enfranchise the enslaved people and punish rebels," Bates lamented in his diary, the radicals now "assume to remodel the State and dispose of all its interests."[8]

Bates was deeply rankled by the fact that radicals sought to discard the constitution that Bates had personally helped to draft forty-five years earlier. Still, he did not publicly make his criticisms known. Instead, that same month, several of Bates's friends, acknowledging his recent status as the country's chief legal officer and his high regard in St. Louis society, began lobbying him to write a memoir of his experiences over the last seventy years. For some time, he admitted, he had considered such a project, but in the end had rejected it. He distrusted his ability to recount the past objectively and saw himself as far more suited "to state a principle, in accurate terms, and maintain it by logical argument, and to pass judgment upon a man or measure, and support it with such power as the facts of the case and the principles involved in it, may warrant." Ever an attorney, he would remain one, prosecuting what he believed to be gross violations of his fellow Missourians' civil liberties.[9]

Having thus made the decision to raise his voice in opposition to the radical threat, he then made the new constitution his primary target. The question remained; what newspaper should provide the vehicle of that prosecution? Only a paper bold enough to oppose the convention's extralegal measures without fear of reprisal would suffice. Bold criticism from the press, however, was severely lacking these days. Still, Bates surmised, editors would only hold out for so long before they spoke up to these wrongdoings. Until then, Bates would have to be patient. A few weeks later, though, a series of exchanges in the local papers between Governor Fletcher and Major General John C. Pope, the new commander of Union forces in St. Louis, over whether to continue martial law in the state, forced Bates's hand.[10]

On February 20, Lincoln wrote to Fletcher with suggestions for hastening an end to hostilities in Missouri. Despite a few cases of bushwhacking on the western frontier, intelligence suggested that there no longer remained a viable threat to Union forces in the state. As for those unfortunate cases in the west, Lincoln suggested, the people themselves could likely handle them. Time had come, Lincoln told Fletcher, to hand management of military affairs over to the state militia.[11]

Fletcher disagreed. Responding to Lincoln on February 27, he suggested that, of all theaters of war, the situation in Missouri was the worst. To prove his point, he used the example of a village in western Missouri recently wracked by inhumane acts of butchery. Forty or fifty men—Fletcher identified them as farmers—were murdered as they worked in their fields by marauders who made no distinction between old and young, fit or infirm. For this unfortunate community, he wrote, the war in Missouri was truly a war of neighbor against neighbor. The survivors would most certainly reject the idea that they make "a covenant with the accessories of the slayers of their kindred." Furthermore, the governor argued, promises of peace were easily broken. Only months earlier, rebel prisoners had violated their paroles and had joined Price's raid in the southwest. Others had fled to the woods "to become banditti." What would stop these men from again taking up arms when they learned that the convention in St. Louis sought to disfranchise them? No, Fletcher told Lincoln, "We want no peace with rebels but the peace which comes of unconditional submission to the authority of the law." That justice was only achievable so long as the military tribunals continued.[12]

Although Fletcher personally disagreed with Lincoln, he nonetheless recognized the gravity of a personal request from the president of the United States. He therefore presented Lincoln's proposals to Pope to obtain his opinion. Pope sided with Lincoln, citing the recent elections in 1864 as sufficient proof that the people of Missouri were "prepared to meet and settle any questions affecting the welfare and prosperity of the State." The citizenry, Pope concluded, were ready to take command of their own fate.[13]

In a stunning reversal, Fletcher now issued a proclamation stating that "there no longer exists within the state of Missouri, any organized force of the enemies of the Government of the United States." Acting upon Lincoln's suggestion, he invited all loyal citizens of the state to unite behind the civilian government and "make common cause against whomever shall persist in making, aiding, or encouraging any description of lawlessness." Finally, Fletcher added, military tribunals would no longer prosecute accused traitors. Judges and justices of the peace would now exercise that authority.[14]

Bates applauded Fletcher's decision to reestablish civilian law, but his elation quickly vanished after radicals in the convention, learning of the governor's proclamation, responded with a scorching condemnation. Speaking for many radicals, the editor of the *Missouri Democrat* argued that martial law was "still in force and will remain in force as long as there exists the least necessity for its exercise." A week later, he warned his readers to avoid interpreting Pope's response to Fletcher as encouraging immediate withdrawal of federal troops. Instead, the editor claimed that Pope had told him personally that he intended only "to transform the military into a police force." Civil courts might try criminals, Pope clarified, but if convicted, the military would carry out sentencing. Then on March 20, as if to confirm the *Democrat*'s claims, Pope issued Special Orders No. 15, declaring that the military would continue to both apprehend and prosecute criminals. Far from reestablishing the sovereignty of the people, Pope had legitimized the supremacy of the military over civilian law. It was a wholly absurd order, Bates judged, clearly the work of a timid general overpowered by "the truculence of the Convention!"[15]

Bates had now privately begun outlining a potential rebuttal to Pope's general order. Clearly, the influence of the radicals was too much for the general. They had infiltrated the highest levels of the military, and only Fletcher's half-hearted resistance kept them from overtaking all levels of the state government. Given the seriousness of the situation, Bates felt that the time had come to intervene.[16]

On April 6, a letter addressed by Bates to the people of Missouri appeared in the pages of the *Missouri Democrat*. Purposefully choosing the same newspaper that only weeks earlier had argued for continuing martial law, Bates wrote that, although it seemed more and more likely that the Union would be preserved, Missourians' civil liberties, at the hands of the radical Republicans, were in jeopardy. Contrary to the opinion of the *Democrat*'s editor, Pope's letter and Fletcher's proclamation immediately suspending martial law had been the proper course of action, and Pope's about-face occurred because of pressure from radical factions. The argument now coming from Pope and the radicals, that martial law was the only means of suppressing violence by bushwhackers, was, Bates argued, little more than a ploy to mislead the public through fear and intimidation and allow the radical clique to consolidate its power over the state.[17]

Giving credence to Bates's assertion that a state of war no longer existed, three days later, on April 9, Lee surrendered the Army of Northern Virginia to Grant at Appomattox Court House. With Richmond in ashes and only a few scattered Confederate forces still active, the American people could finally look to Reconstruction. Before Bates could use the occasion to reinforce his theory that the Missouri radicals were unnecessarily continuing martial law to consolidate power, however, news arrived in St. Louis of the death of Abraham Lincoln in Washington at the hands of an assassin—thus undermining any argument he might make that the United States was once again at peace.

The shock of Lincoln's death reverberated throughout the country. For Bates, the loss was personal. "Besides the deep sense of the calamity which the nation has sustained," he wrote in his diary, "my private feelings are deeply moved by the sudden murder of my chief, with and under whom I have served the country, through many difficult and trying scenes, and always with mutual sentiments of respect and friendship. . . . I mourn his fall, both for the country and for myself."[18]

On April 19, Bates attended a packed memorial service for Lincoln at the Second Presbyterian Church. Despite the collective outpouring of grief, he could not help fearing that the radicals would certainly "make party capital out of [Lincoln's] flagitious murder." A month later, the military trial of the assassins became a test case for their continued suppression of civilian law. On May 25, Bates wrote in his diary, "Such a trial is not only unlawful, but it is a gross blunder in policy: It denies the great, fundamental principle, that ours is a government of *Law*, and that the law is strong enough, to rule the people wisely and well." If the radicals could submit Lincoln's assassins to an impartial tribunal, what would stop them from submitting rebel sympathizers in Missouri to the same fate?[19]

Bates's next public letter, published the same day as the memorial service, expanded on these thoughts. In the early days of the war, Bates had helped Lincoln assume powers previously belonging to Congress, but legitimizing the president's suspension of habeas corpus and invoking martial law had never sat well with Bates. Now, four years later, he was more willing to express his personal feelings, especially when he saw the radicals using martial law as a means of consolidating power. "There are some members of [the convention]," he asserted, "who ought to know and do know that martial law is simply no law at all." The term, he concluded, was merely "a nickname for arbitrary power, assumed against law."[20]

The danger in this policy, Bates argued, lay in the opportunity it provided for a military commander to assert his authority over the people. To prevent that calamity, it was crucial the people understand that "the military is subordinate to the civil power and can act only as the minister and servant of the law." The Missouri state convention already wielded significant influence over civilian and military authorities; it was likely that, were it to continue in peacetime to enforce martial law, it would operate "without any fear of punishment [from a higher authority] for [its] misdeeds."[21]

In between Appomattox and the publication of Bates's second letter, the convention passed a new state constitution that confirmed Bates's greatest fears. Aside from the role martial law played in the constitution's conception, conservatives had several concerns. Article II, Section 3 denied any person the right to vote who had participated in or aided the rebellion against the United States. Examples of disloyalty were numerous and included sheltering or sympathizing with rebel troops, holding office in the Confederate government, and taking up arms against the state, which many persons loyal to the Union had done when they opposed Clayborne Fox Jackson's administration in 1861. Any person who performed one of these acts was disenfranchised, barred from serving in public office or holding a position as a trustee, director, or manager of any corporation, or from serving in positions such as educators, lawyers, members of school boards, and even clergymen. Sections 4 and 5 authorized the legislature to generate lists of qualified and unqualified voters. Civil rights would be returned, however, to anyone who took a new "iron clad" oath—so called because it was nearly impossible for those who had abetted the late rebellion to take it. Simultaneous with the introduction of the new constitution was another ordinance ousting all judges, court clerks, circuit attorneys, sheriffs, and county recorders from their offices by May 1. The governor would then appoint seat holders who had taken the loyalty oath. New officers could be elected to full terms starting in 1866.[22]

The constitution would be put to a referendum on June 6. In the meantime, conservatives and radicals began debating its merits in the news columns. "Let it have a free and fair discussion before the people," exclaimed the *Missouri Democrat*, "and this so far as in us lies it shall have—and there is no doubt about its triumphant adoption." Drake did not share the *Democrat*'s optimism. He was nervous that conservative condemnations might be enough to sink its passage and warned his cohorts to prepare a vigorous defense. "Disloyalty in Missouri is in the last ditch," Drake wrote, "and will die hard" if ratification was successful: "Look forward, then, in the next fifty nine days, to the severest struggle we have yet had to make."[23]

Drake intended to use the next few months to make sense for average Missourians the constitution's most controversial sections. In so doing, he became the leading voice among the constitution's supporters, just as Bates's first two letters made him the natural leader of the opposition. Drake's first letter and the subsequent publication of Bates's third essay, then, served as the first shots in Bates's final political battle.[24]

Bates's third public letter touched upon the disfranchisement clause of the constitution, which conservatives argued was not so much extralegal—the convention was, after all, called for the express purpose both of eradicating slavery and securing franchise rights for loyal citizens—as it was poorly written. In its present wording, it was almost impossible to differentiate a loyal person from a disloyal one. This, Bates surmised, was by design. The radicals sought to enact their own standard of loyalty. Put another way, "no man can be loyal who is not a Radical." True loyalty, however, could only be defined as allegiance to the rule of law, "not a blind devotion to a clique or faction."[25]

Turning next to the ousting ordinance, Bates sought to paint the convention as a revolutionary assembly. In his fourth letter, he reminded his readers that the original 1864 referendum that brought the convention into being was a call for the constitution's amendment, not its overthrow. Since both emancipation and disfranchisement were accomplished through ordinances, not amendments, in Bates's mind, the convention was guilty of attempting a coup. The radicals, he argued, were employing "a new and extraordinary power, not belonging to any department of the state government nor to all of them combined." The "radical revolution," then, began with the discarding of the original constitution, and was accomplished by the forced removal of any opponent of the radicals elected under the old constitution.[26]

Drake did not sit idly by while Bates sullied the reputation of the convention. He directly responded to these accusations with all the cunning of an experienced lawyer and politician. In response to Bates's assertion that the convention was attempting a coup, Drake conceded that the convention had acted wrongly when it accomplished emancipation and disfranchisement through ordinance rather than amendment. However, he absolved himself of any personal wrongdoing, explaining that the convention passed these measures while he was absent from the proceedings. The damage done, however, and the ordinances now the law of the land, the only way to correct the error was to nullify the current constitution altogether and replace it. The 1865 constitution, Drake asserted, was created through legal means and with the best of intentions, and it deserved to be ratified.[27]

Despite Drake's best efforts, Bates's criticisms had an effect. Several prominent radicals who had earlier supported the convention came out against it. Fletcher, for one, worried that some of the constitution's provisions were so ironclad that future generations would have trouble amending it. In a letter to the *Missouri Democrat*, he wrote that he had therefore chosen to vote against it. After reading this announcement, Bates gleefully observed, "'The rats are running from the burning house.' Governor Fletcher [has] waked up, from the drunken dream of radicalism, just in time to smell the smoke of the kindling fires, and save [himself], by timely flight, from the coming conflagration."[28]

As the election drew near, the constitution's fate was still uncertain. To bolster his previous arguments, Bates published two more essays—now choosing as his vehicle the more conservative *Missouri Republican*. He recapped his earlier argument against martial law and continued to press upon the convention's revolutionary nature before asking the people to choose wisely in the coming vote. The constitution, he avowed, was not the property of any one clique or faction. It belonged to the people and must serve all the people equally. Having begun his crusade to champion civilian rule, he concluded by promising, "I will continue to make the best defense I can of the only valuable inheritance left to us by our fathers— liberty according to law."[29]

If Drake's essays failed to gain traction, Bates's also had mixed results. One writer to the *Missouri Democrat* called him a feeble old man—his apparent ravings against the radicals being attributed to "the influence and promptings of accumulating years which strengthen prejudices as they weaken the reason." Another called him a traitor, declaring him the leader of the enemies of the truly loyal people. Yet another defended Bates, describing him as "as honorable and pure a man and patriot as lives in Missouri" and urging readers to "swear and vote . . . though it is evident [the reader] would do wisely to vote no."[30]

Most Missourians appeared sympathetic to Bates's cause, and this fact was not lost on the radicals, who were doing everything possible to halt the conservative momentum. One St. Louis citizen noted in his diary rumors that in some regions of the state, conservatives were being disenfranchised regardless of whether they had taken the loyalty oath. Radicals were also clearly pressuring Fletcher, who now reversed his criticisms of the constitution and embraced the ousting ordinance, which allowed him to remove conservative election judges and replaced them with radicals.[31]

Despite these last-ditch efforts, early indications were that the conservatives would carry the day. Bates noted in his diary that the vote in St. Louis County was overwhelmingly against the constitution. Drake, he wrote, "is plucked bare, and cast down upon his own dunghill," and "all the prominent members of the Convention are sunk into contempt and the whole party in this state, I think has received its death blow." Yet in a stunning reversal of fortune, after weeks of ballot counting, on July 1, Missouri secretary of state Francis Rodman certified the results as 43,670 votes in favor, 41,808 against. By a slim margin of 51 percent, the new constitution became the law of the land on July 4.[32]

For Bates, the ratification of the new constitution was bittersweet. On the one hand, his cause was lost. On the other, conservatives had carried his hometown of St. Louis and had come within striking distance of defeating the constitution altogether. The radicals had won by allowing soldiers to cast absentee ballots and empowering partisan poll judges to reject suspect votes. Nonetheless, the ratification of the constitution, along with the radicals' hold over the state legislature, served to further remind Bates that he no longer possessed the prowess he once had as a political leader. He took some solace when, later that summer, a small group of conservatives carried on his cause—St. Louis archbishop Peter R. Kenrick, for instance, ordered his priests to refuse to take the loyalty oath—but his own fighting spirit and his health was, for the second time in a year, severely taxed by his battle with the radicals.[33]

As summer turned to fall, Bates's poor health sapped him of much of his strength. As he noted in his diary, his breathing had become increasingly labored and the pain in his chest was almost unbearable, prompting the family to send for a doctor. Although he was confined to bed for days, by slow degrees, he eventually rallied and, on September 4, celebrated his seventy-second birthday. On this occasion, he reflected, "there remain now, of the 12 children brought up by my parents, only two of us—my sister Margaret M. Wharton . . . now 80 years, and myself." If his recent political defeat had not done so already, his age and health were constant reminders that he was a member of a generation rapidly disappearing from the earth. In that vein, his daughter, Nancy, noted during his last illness that he found peace with God and was prepared to leave the world in the hands of a younger generation. The death of his sister on December 11, coinciding with a relapse of his breathing malady, reinforced his thoughts on his own mortality.[34]

Bates's frailty, however, did not stop him from lending moral support to persons carrying on the banner of conservatism. Starting in October 1865 and extending into the New Year, he began corresponding with Republican senator James R. Doolittle of Wisconsin, then positioning himself as a moderate in the congressional debates over Reconstruction. Then in February 1866, he wrote to President Andrew Johnson, pledging support for him in his fight against the radicals and urging him to resist their efforts to reduce the Southern states to territories and put them under military rule. Speaking for all conservatives, Bates wrote, "We believe that you are a patriot—an earnest, sincere brave man—determined to fulfill all the legal duties of your station 'as you understand them.'" To that end, he counseled Johnson to reject the renewal of the Freedman's Bureau Bill—even though that agency had very little authority in Missouri—and be vigilant, lest the radicals "degrade you, if they can, by forcing you to recant & falsify the wisest & best measures which you have devised, for the good of your country & your own historic fame." For his support, Johnson made it a priority to call on the aging former attorney general when he came to St. Louis in September 1866. Along with the president were Secretaries Seward and Welles, both of whom Bates embraced with great emotion.[35]

As Reconstruction progressed, new life was breathed into the conservative cause. In Missouri, the process began as early as 1865 with the unexpected pairing of conservatives and disenfranchised rebel sympathizers, then in 1867 it blossomed into a political movement when Senator Benjamin Gratz Brown—himself turning away from radicalism—called for a new policy of universal amnesty. Bates could not personally engage in this fight, but a few months earlier, he did write a public article in support of Brown's position. Still, for a time, it was an uphill climb for conservatives as Drake, incensed by Brown's betrayal, challenged and ultimately defeated him for reelection.[36]

Despite Drake's victory, the radical phalanx was weakened by this infighting, and his popularity lasted only a short while longer. Although equality had never really been embraced by radicals in Missouri, at the national level, it had become their signature policy. As time progressed, however, white Americans tired of the long battle for equality began to quash Black Americans' attempts to build upon the gains made in the 1866 Civil Rights Act and the Fourteenth and Fifteenth Amendments. Railroads then replaced the freed man as the pet project of Republican state governments. In Missouri, Drake's influence was dealt a particularly heavy blow in March 1869 when moderate Carl Schurz challenged radical Benjamin F. Loan for the Republican nomination to the U.S. Senate. Rightly seeing Schurz's campaign as dividing the party, Drake traveled to Jefferson City to confront him. Schurz, however, masterfully handled the radical senator, forcing him to publicly lose his temper and launch into an ethnic tirade against Germans—a consistently loyal Republican voting bloc. Embarrassed, Drake left the state capital to avoid witnessing Schurz's inevitable victory. Consequently, in November, the radicals in Missouri suffered heavily at the polls. And although Ulysses S. Grant won the presidency and subsequently nominated Drake as chief justice of the Court of Claims, the radical leader's plummet from grace was nothing short of meteoric.[37]

The new conservative movement—now being styled the Liberal Republican movement—was fully realized in 1871 when Missouri became the springboard for launching a national effort to take back the Republican Party. In the previous year conservatives officially broke from the state party and submitted their own ticket in the elections; the result was the successful elevation of Gratz Brown to the governorship. By 1872, a national movement was underway in both North and South that ultimately nominated Brown as vice president on a Liberal Republican ticket challenging Grant for a second term.[38]

The Liberal Republicans failed to unseat Grant, but they were successful at rolling back radical Reconstruction. In 1875, in Missouri, they overhauled the 1865 state constitution, finally eliminating from that document the draconian clauses for which Bates had fought so vociferously. Now, the charter defended civil liberties for all citizens and called for free and fair elections. Most notably, the 1875 constitution lifted the requirement of a test oath for public and private offices.[39]

Bates did not live to see the overhaul of the state constitution. He was likely discouraged by Drake's rise to the Senate, and although he had been pleased with Grant's conduct in the last days of the war, Bates's sentiments are unknown regarding the general's rise to the presidency. After all, in the battles between Congress and the president over Reconstruction, Bates had sided with Andrew Johnson. Furthermore, like many of his fellow conservatives, Bates's white supremacist belief that the Black and white races could never coexist amicably was closely aligned with that of his friend Frank Blair Jr., who ran against Grant in 1868 for vice president on the Democratic ticket.[40]

Following that presidential contest, in December 1868, Bates was once again wracked by bronchitis. Although he had rallied in the past, this time his health steadily worsened. "My father still lingers," Barton wrote to James Eads on December 23, "taking no pleasure in life—only enduring it." Julia was likewise unwell, Barton noted, "but she is patient and cheerful, always doing something for others' comfort or happiness." Meanwhile, Nancy had taken over management of the home. By March 1869, Bates's prognosis was grim. Julian, who served as attending physician, informed the family that this would likely be Bates's final illness. On March 25, 1869, the children assembled at the home on Morgan Street, and later that day, surrounded by friends and family—including Fleming, with whom he had reconciled after the war—Edward Bates died at the age of seventy-six. The loss was hardest on Julia and Nancy, who helped nurse Bates through his final illness. Soon after he breathed his last, Nancy was reported to have said to her mother, "His troubles are over, but ours have fairly begun." On March 27, Bates's remains were interred in a receiving vault at Bellefontaine Cemetery. A month later, he was removed to a private burial plot near Julian's home in Florissant. The previous July, Bates had drawn up his last will and testament. To Julia, he left most of his estate except for one-third of his lands in Carondelet, which he gave to Barton. He also forgave his children any debts they might owe him.[41]

In the days following his death, individuals that had previously been estranged from Bates by his comments against the radicals openly mourned his loss. "Such men as Edward Bates have seldom lived," eulogized his friend, James O. Broadhead, at a meeting of the St. Louis Bar Association. Throughout Bates's long life, Broadhead noted, the late statesman had always been a true, upright, charitable, and kindhearted man. "He had a wonderful equipoise of character, not so much the result of education as of native instinct." While Bates was not above personal difficulties and controversies, Broadhead noted, he was separated from lesser men by his ability to meet adversity without compromising his own integrity. "With all his gentle nature," Broadhead concluded, "he was without exception, the bravest man I ever knew."[42]

Samuel T. Glover also gave a public eulogy recalling Bates as a man of integrity. "Few men," he wrote, "have passed through the turmoil of active public and private life for fifty years and left a name that may so well defy even the tongues of malice." Though agreeing with Broadhead that Bates's moral character would be long remembered in the hearts of his contemporaries, Glover believed it was Bates's strong defense of the U.S. Constitution that would be of lasting significance. "Would to God," Glover prayed, "that among our leading and most influential citizens that have taken 'oaths' to support the Constitution there were found a greater number who employed the care that he did to comprehend its meaning."[43]

Bates represented a moral fiber and character, Glover argued, that would be forever lacking in subsequent generations. Indeed, he recalled the words of a friend who walked with him in the procession that accompanied Bates's coffin to Bellefontaine Cemetery. "Mr. Bates," Glover observed, "belonged to a generation that had passed away." It should be the business of all good citizens, Glover therefore pressed, to venerate Bates's name and merits for all time.

Glover's proposal was soon realized. In 1876, his friends immortalized Bates in a twenty-two-foot-tall statue unveiled at the opening of Forest Park. Bates's likeness stood atop a red granite pedestal displaying medallions depicting James Eads, Hamilton Gamble, Charles Gibson, and Henry Geyer, all of whom had been prominent characters in the preservation of the Union. The statue stood on the highest knoll in the southeast corner of the park but was relocated to the western entrance in the mid-1930s, where it remains to this day. In its current setting, Bates faces east as if to portray him as a favorite son of the West who never forgot his Virginia roots. Such could also be said of his political philosophy. He never forsook those Jeffersonian principles that were engrained in him from his youth. When the opportunity came for him to exert his influence on government—first as leader of the Missouri Whig Party and later as attorney general in the Lincoln administration—radical pressures only strengthened his ideals. And when he returned to St. Louis in 1864, much the same man who had left four years earlier, he fought vehemently to make those principles relevant once more. He did not live to see the resurgence of his conservatism, but the statue in Forest Park is nonetheless a lasting tribute to his importance as a founding father of Missouri.[44]

Julia survived Edward by eleven years. On October 16, 1880, she passed away, like her husband before her, in the company of her children and grandchildren. A week later, she was laid to rest in the Coalter family plot in Bellefontaine Cemetery. Wrote the *New York Times* in memorial: "She was a woman of rare virtues and accomplishments, and possessed all the gentle graces of a model American matron." On May 14, 1906, Bates's remains were relocated once more to Bellefontaine where, today, he rests alongside Julia in the company of several of their children, including Nancy, Julian, Charles, and Fleming. In the center of the plot are Julia's brother, John David Coalter, and sister-in-law, Mary A. Means, and not far away in another plot lay Julia's sister, Caroline, and her brother-in-law—and Bates's dear friend—Hamilton Gamble.[45]

The Coalter family plot at Bellefontaine is a quiet place near a bluff overlooking the muddy Mississippi River. Edward Bates's entire adult life was, in some way or another, connected with the waterway. As a young man, he had lost his friend and law partner in a duel on a sandbar in the middle of the river. As a state representative and Whig Party leader, he had seen the Mississippi as the lifeforce of his hometown and had advocated for public funds to maintain and promote its vibrant riverboat commerce. As attorney general, he fought to keep it out of rebel hands and utilize its central geographic location to divide and conquer the Confederacy. As his life had begun along the banks of one river—the James in Virginia—so it ended along a second. It was fitting, given all of this, that he should forever watch over the great artery of the nation he helped to preserve.

Conclusion

In 1862, radical Republican congressman Owen Lovejoy spoke at New York's Cooper Union on the causes of the Civil War. He was frustrated at Abraham Lincoln's unwillingness to link the downfall of slavery with the preservation of the Union. He then used the analogy of two horses pulling a buggy to describe the radical and conservative factions vying for the president's attention. "The [radical horse]," he observed, "in the shafts is a most superb animal . . . [he] can clear ditch and hedge, high spirited and fast. . . . The [conservative] creature behind is a very different kind of animal: he can do nothing but hold back . . ."[1]

By the second year of the war, Lincoln—perhaps surprising Lovejoy—agreed. A few months after the congressman's speech, in his annual address to Congress, the president expounded upon the root difference between the factions of his party. Having just laid out his plan for gradual, compensated emancipation, he now singled out conservatives directly when he said, "The dogmas of the quiet past, are inadequate to the stormy present." Those who clung to old modes of thought ignored the extraordinary times the Civil War had wrought. "We must rise with the occasion," he urged: "As our case is new, so we must think anew, and act anew. We must disenthrall our selves, and then we shall save our country."[2]

As Adam I. P. Smith observed, a "sentimental attachment to an idealized past" was a particular quality of mid-nineteenth-century conservatism. These conservatives venerated their own revolutionary past while reacting negatively to "revolutionary changes" in the present. Put another way, the radicals of the past had lived long enough to become opponents of change.[3]

If, indeed, conservative unionists were identified by their attempt to hold back the tide of change, then Edward Bates accurately fits the description. Everything he did in politics was compelled by an awareness of his sacred duty to defend and preserve the principles of the Revolutionary generation—the generation of his father, Thomas, who had sacrificed so much to create the nation Bates and his siblings inherited. It was even more important to preserve it considering that, before long, Bates's generation would pass it on to their children and grandchildren. It was this sentiment that Lincoln proposed in 1861 when he asked his Southern brethren to harken to "the mystic chords of memory, stretching from every battle-field, and patriot grave, to every living heart and hearthstone." Bates and his fellow conservative unionists took Lincoln's words to heart and stood opposed to attempts to use the extraordinary situation presented by the Civil War to fundamentally alter the way Americans viewed not only their country but their system of government as well.[4]

The Civil War was not the only instance that showcased Bates's conservatism. His steadfast belief that his ideals were right, if not always popular, guided him throughout his public life. It prompted him to oppose the populist instincts of the Jacksonians in the 1830s. It also explained why he remained with the Whig Party in the mid-1850s, long after it ceased to be a contender in national politics. It led him to oppose abolitionists in the antebellum years and radical Republicans during the Civil War, and it explained why he personally took on the radicals in his home state during the early days of Reconstruction. As the *Bangor (Maine) Daily Whig and Courier* put it in August 1865, Bates "was conservative when conservatism meant '*not* to agitate' the question of free soil in national territories,—when it meant *not* to interfere with the extension of slavery over the whole broad Union. He was conservative when conservatism meant *not* to oppose new Missouri compromise lines and the extension of slavery to the Pacific. He was conservative when, after the war commenced, conservatism meant *not* to protect and employ escaped slaves, *not* put arms into the hands of loyal black men, and *not* to proclaim emancipation to the millions of slaves belonging to the rebels. And he is conservative now when conservatism means *not* to give the freedmen the full rights of men, but to stop half way in our professed desire to vindicate the principles of the Declaration of Independence . . ."[5]

As the later part of the above quote implies, Bates's conservatism is also complicated. This is particularly the case on the issue of race. Born to a family of enslavers in Virginia, and enslaving Black people himself during the antebellum years, he nonetheless assisted Lincoln in his efforts to end slavery nationwide. In the years before the war, he voluntarily emancipated his enslaved servants and fought in court to free others, and as attorney general, he paved the way for equal rights through his opinions on citizenship. Yet, while his public actions helped shape a new world for Black men and women—while he helped to build a new nation where the Declaration of Independence's famous lines on equality applied universally to all Americans—Bates was too rooted in the past to see Black Americans as his equal or to understand the full potential of the movement he helped to shape.

Bates's conservatism is no less complicated when examining other aspects of his political career. He opposed Polk's overreach during the Mexican-American War but legitimized Abraham Lincoln's curtailment of civil liberties during the Civil War. He also opposed secession but cautioned against using excessive military force to suppress the rebellion. He claimed to be above politics but assisted Gamble, as well as others in Missouri, in undermining Gamble's political opponents in the state. He claimed to have a good working relationship with his fellow cabinet members but privately resented Seward, Chase, and Stanton for their closeness with Lincoln and for meddling in the affairs of Bates's office. Indeed, it could be argued that because Lincoln gave many of his responsibilities to other cabinet ministers, Bates was—by and large—ineffective as attorney general.

The criticism that Bates and his fellow conservatives were wrong on matters of race is fair. Less so is the claim that he was an inadequate member of the Lincoln administration. The age of the active attorney general at the head of the Justice Department was still over a decade away. Bates, like his predecessors, saw his role as advisory in nature. Furthermore, as an advisor to the president, Bates was effective at the start of the war, when his ideas about a Southern counterinsurgency were more mainstream and when persons such as Seward and Stanton had yet to carry influence with Lincoln. He was also ahead of others—including Winfield Scott, who usually gets credit for the Anaconda Plan—in proposing that the Union effectively isolate the Confederacy by taking command of western rivers and blockading southern ports.

Bates was most effective at safeguarding the right of due process. As mentioned elsewhere, the Civil War tested the Constitution as never before. That it did not break under the pressure is thanks, in no small part, to people like Lincoln and Bates. Bates knew from history how easily such wars could end in tyranny. But unlike Northern copperheads and Southern Confederates, Bates did not believe that Lincoln was such a dictator. He did, however, think that the president was being manipulated by men who sought those powers for themselves. The unprecedented military buildup was an enticing tool in their hands, and this was particularly galling given the fact that Bates's opinion on habeas corpus was responsible for legitimizing the use of martial law in the first place. Reinstating civilian courts in areas no longer in rebellion was therefore the best means of thwarting radical intentions. One speculates on how Bates might have reacted to efforts by the government to neutralize domestic threats in the twentieth and twenty-first centuries.

Bates figures prominently in very few modern cultural depictions of the Lincoln administration. Doris Kearns Goodwin's *Team of Rivals* gives him, perhaps, the greatest attention, but the 2012 motion picture *Lincoln*, based on Goodwin's book, mentions Bates only once, and then merely as an obstacle to universal emancipation—the central issue of the film. To be fair, the setting of the film is the winter and spring of 1865, a time when Bates was already out of the cabinet. Furthermore, the film is correct to imply that Bates and his fellow conservatives questioned the legality of Lincoln's emancipation policies in peacetime. Still, in the end, Bates was important, in that he was an exemplar of the ideals and policy positions of thousands of Northern conservatives. And while their radical counterparts have been previously examined in scholarly articles and books alike, conservatives were not, until very recently, given the same consideration. As more studies come about, we are beginning to see just how truly fascinating, and multifaceted, were Edward Bates's life and times.

NOTES

BIBLIOGRAPHY

INDEX

NOTES

Introduction

1. Hofstadter, *American Political Tradition*; Williams, *Lincoln and the Radicals*; and Benson, *Concept of Jacksonian Democracy*.
2. Bailyn, *Ideological Origins of the American Revolution*; Banning, *Jeffersonian Persuasion*; Silbey, *Respectable Minority*; Baker, *Affairs of Party*; Foner, *Free Soil, Free Labor, Free Men*; Holt, *Political Crisis of the 1850s*; and Howe, *Political Culture of the American Whigs*.
3. Gienapp, *Origins of the Republican Party*; Kohl, *Politics of Individualism*; Smith, *Stormy Present*; and Astor, *Rebels on the Border*; Lynn, *Preserving the White Man's Republic*.
4. Appleby, *Inheriting the Revolution*, 3–6.
5. Randall, "Is the Lincoln Myth Exhausted?"; Goodwin, *Team of Rivals*; Hendrick, *Lincoln's War Cabinet*; Donald, *Lincoln's Herndon*; Pratt, *Stanton*; Thomas and Hyman, *Stanton*; Van Deusen, *William Henry Seward*; Cain, *Lincoln's Attorney General*; Niven, *Gideon Welles*; Niven, *Salmon P. Chase*; Blue, *Salmon P. Chase*.
6. Clinton, *Mrs. Lincoln*; Emerson, *Giant in the Shadows*; Mason, *Apostle of Union*; Parrish, *Frank Blair*; Cook, *Civil War Senator*; Stahr, *William Seward*; Stahr, *Stanton*; Stahr, *Salmon P. Chase*; Kahan, *Amiable*

Scoundrel; Marvel, *Lincoln's Autocrat*; Epstein, *Lincoln's Men*; Zeits, *Lincoln's Boys*.

1. Son of Virginia, Father of Missouri

1. Huton, *Seventeenth Century Colonial Ancestors of members of the National Society Colonial Dames, XVII Century*, 18; Bates, *Bates et al.*, 66, 72, 103; Davis, *Tidewater Virginia Families*, 425–26.
2. Bates, *Bates et al.*, 73–74.
3. *Heads of Families at the First Census of the United States Taken in the Year 1790*, 9.
4. Bates, *Bates et al.*, 66; FB to CWB, July 19, 1812, in Marshall, *Life and Papers of Frederick Bates*, vol. 2, 228.
5. Bates, *Bates et al.*, 22–28, 37, 40–65.
6. Middlekauff, *Glorious Cause*, 542; TFB to FB, October 31, 1801, in Marshall, *Life and Papers of Frederick Bates*, vol. 1, 3–5.
7. Appleby, *Inheriting the Revolution*, 56–89; Bates, *Bates et al.*, 59; EB, "To the People of Missouri," *Missouri Intelligencer*, June 29, 1826; TFB to FB, November 30, 1800; FB to TB, January 14, 1802; Thomas Jefferson to FB, February 4, 1807; Albert Gallatin to FB, October 13, 1804; Albert Gallatin to FB, December 28, 1804; FB, Oath of Office as Land Commissioner, December 3, 1804; Albert Gallatin to FB, July 6, 1805; Marshall, *Life and Papers of Frederick Bates*, vol. 1, 9, 54, 91; TB to Thomas Jefferson, March 6, 1801, Thomas Jefferson Papers, Library of Congress, Washington, DC; Bates, *Bates et al.*, 12–13, 59.
8. *American Almanac and Repository of Useful Knowledge for the Year 1844*, 242.
9. Cain, *Lincoln's Attorney General*, 1.
10. Primm, *Lion of the Valley*, 9–11; Johnson, *Broken Heart of America*, 26–30; Irving, *Astoria*, vol. 1, 142–43.
11. Primm, *Lion of the Valley*, 118–19, 136,
12. Wade, *Slavery in the Cities*, 64–65, 101–2, 193, 208, 224.
13. Astor, *Rebels on the Border*, 17; Bates, *Bates et al.*, 26; Marshall, *Life and Papers of Frederick Bates*, vol. 1, 26–28; FB to RB, March 24, 1808; FB to Meriwether Lewis, April 5, 1807, Marshall, *Life and Papers of Frederick Bates*, vol. 1, 26–27, 99, 315; Carter, *Territorial Papers of the United States*, vol. 14, 115–321; Holmberg and Buckley, *By His Own Hand*.
14. Marshall, *Life and Papers of Frederick Bates*, vol. 1, 31.
15. William E. Foley, "Charles Gratiot," in Christensen et al., *Dictionary of Missouri Biography*, 347–48; Foley, "Edward Hempstead," in Christensen et al., *Dictionary of Missouri Biography*, 391–92; FB to Edward Hempstead,

January 22, 1810, Marshall, *Life and Papers of Frederick Bates*, vol. 2, 124–25, 260; William Clark v. Jeremiah Connor, Circuit Court Records, WASHU; Perry McCandless, "Thomas Hart Benton," in Christensen et al., *Dictionary of Missouri Biography*, 59.

16. Perry McCandless, "David Barton," in Christensen et al., *Dictionary of Missouri Biography*, 32

17. Jo Tice Bloom, "Rufus Easton," in ibid., 271–72.

18. Gaines, "'True Lawyer' in America," 133–34; Scott, *Address Delivered to the Law Academy of Philadelphia*, 4.

19. Darby, *Personal Recollections*, 400–401; "Joshua Barton & Edward Bates," *Missouri Gazette and Public Advertiser*, March 22, 1820; Marshall, *Life and Papers of Frederick Bates*, vol. 1, 24–25; Cain, *Lincoln's Attorney General*, 8.

20. Horder, "Duel and the English Law of Homicide," 419.

21. Appleby, *Inheriting the Revolution*, 40–45; Statement of Facts by Thomas Hart Benton and Edward Bates, Duel between Joshua Barton & Thomas Hempstead, August 11, 1816, Benton Papers, MOHIST.

22. Dearinger, "Violence, Masculinity, Image"; Brown, *Southern Honor*, 353; Statement of Facts by Thomas Hart Benton and Edward Bates, Duel between Joshua Barton & Thomas Hempstead.

23. Primm, *Lion of the Valley*, 116–17; Charles Lucas to THB, August 11, 1817, Benton Papers, MOHIST; Charles Lucas to THB, September 20, 1817, Benton Papers, MOHIST; Primm, *Lion of the Valley*, 117.

24. L. E. Lawless to EB, August 18, 1820; EB to L. E. Lawless, August 18, 1820, Bates Family Papers, MOHIST.

25. March, *History of Missouri*, 381–82, 388–90; Shoemaker, *Missouri's Struggle for Statehood*, 31–41, 55–57; Nagel, *Missouri*, 42–43; Van Atta, *Wolf by the Ears*.

26. Culmer, *New History of Missouri*, 136–37.

27. March, *History of Missouri*, 391–95; Shoemaker, *Missouri's Struggle for Statehood*, 62–65.

28. March, *History of Missouri*, 398–400.

29. *St. Louis Enquirer*, April 15, 1820; "To the People of Missouri," *St. Louis Enquirer*, May 10, 1820; March, *History of Missouri*, 400.

30. *St. Louis Enquirer*, April 29, 1820; *Journal of the Missouri State Convention* (1820), 3–4; Billon, *Annals of St. Louis*, 397–98.

31. Shoemaker, "David Barton," 528, 539; *Journal of the Missouri State Convention* (1820), 28–33.

32. *Journal of the Missouri State Convention* (1820), 48.

33. Shoemaker, "First Constitution of Missouri," 134–41.

34. Ibid., 18–19, 34, 36; Nagel, *Missouri*, 46–47; Wiecek, "Missouri Statehood," 124; James Monroe, "Proclamation Admitting Missouri to the Union," August 10, 1821, Richardson, *Messages and Papers of the Presidents*, vol. 2, 95–96.

2. *Congressman*

1. Stevens, "Alexander McNair," 10.
2. Keller, "Alexander McNair and John B. C. Lucas," 241–44.
3. Stevens, "Alexander McNair," 13.
4. Ibid., 14; Jones, *William Clark*, 254–55.
5. Nagel, *Missouri*, 104; Stevens, "Alexander McNair," 14; Howe, *What Hath God Wrought*, 142–43; Alexander McNair, Special Session Message, June 4, 1821, Leopard and Shoemaker, *Messages and Proclamations*, vol. 1, 18–19; Nagel, *Missouri*, 105–6; McNair "Message to the Missouri Senate," November 8, 1821 in *Missouri Republican*, January 12, 1826; EB, "Address to the Voters," *Missouri Republican*, June 5, 1822; "List of the Members of the Next Legislature, Chosen at the Late Election," *Missouri Republican*, September 18, 1822; Shoemaker, "David Barton, John Rice Jones and Edward Bates," 527–43.
6. "August Election," *St. Louis Enquirer*, June 17, 1822; "A List of the Members of the Next Legislature, Chosen at the Late Election," *Missouri Republican*, September 18, 1822; Missouri State Constitution (1820), MOARC; Primm, *Lion of the Valley*, 120–21; Erwin, *St. Charles, Missouri*, 78–79; *Journal of the House of Representatives of the Second General Assembly of the State of Missouri* (1823), 63–77, 98; *Journal of the Senate of the Second General Assembly of the State of Missouri* (1823), 31, 119.
7. *Journal of the Senate of the Second General Assembly of the State of Missouri* (1823), 105, 120, 178–79.
8. Ibid., 31–36.
9. Bates, *Bates, et al.*, 31, 76; Portrait of Julia Bates (née Coalter) as a young woman, MOHIST; Lithograph of Edward Bates, ca. 1855, MOHIST.
10. EB to FB, May 15, 1823, Marshall, *Life and Papers of Frederick Bates*, vol. 2, 313; *Marriage Records for St. Charles, 1807–1854*, Missouri Marriage Records, MOARC.
11. Dick Steward, "Joshua Barton" in Christensen et al., *Dictionary of Missouri Biography*, 35.
12. David S. Barton to John Hardeman, December 15, 1823, Switzler Collection, MOHIST; Edward Dobyns to the Editor of the *Cincinnati Commercial*, February 16, 1877, Duels Collection, MOHIST; Darby, *Personal Recollections*, 21.
13. Bates, *Bates, et al.*, 31, 76.

14. EB to FB, June 30, 1824, Marshall, *Life and Papers of Frederick Bates*, vol. 2, 315–16.

15. *Missouri Republican*, August 2, 1824; Marshall, *Life and Papers of Frederick Bates*, vol. 1, 37–38.

16. EB to FB, August 24, 1824, ibid., 318–19 (emphasis in original).

17. "Hamilton Rowan Gamble," Christensen et al., *Dictionary of Missouri Biography*, 329.

18. "Governor Bates's Address," *Missouri Intelligencer*, November 27, 1824.

19. Leopard and Shoemaker, *Messages and Proclamations*, vol. 1, 83; Darby, *Personal Recollections*, 40–42.

20. Rader, *Civil Government*, 209; EB to C. I. Walker, February 10, 1859, *Collections of the Pioneer Society of the State of Michigan*, vol. 8, 565; Bates, *Bates, et al.*, 24; Stevens, *Centennial History of the Missouri*, 477.

21. EB, "To the People of Missouri," *Missouri Republican*, July 8, 1826.

22. Thomas Jefferson, "First Inaugural Address," March 4, 1801, Richardson, *Messages and Papers of the Presidents*, vol. 1, 322; Breen, *Character of the Good Ruler*; Cunningham, *In Pursuit of Reason*, 239–40; Ellis, *American Sphinx*, 202–3.

23. Remini, *John Quincy Adams*, 71; Bates, "To the People of Missouri," *Missouri Republican*, July 8, 1826.

24. Ibid.

25. *Missouri Republican*, August 10, 1826; Holt, *Political Crisis of the 1850s*, 17–22.

26. Map of the City of Washington in the District of Columbia Established as the Permanent Seat of the Government of the United States of America, ca. 1818, LOC; Lewis, *Washington*; John Poppel, Engraver, Chamber of Representatives Washington / C.R., DEL, John Poppel, SC, Washington DC, 1851, photograph.

27. *Journal of the House of Representatives of the United States*, vol. 21.

28. Howe, *What God Hath Wrought*, 261–66; Johnson, *Soul by Soul* and *River of Dark Dreams*.

29. THB to FB, October 31, 1801, Bates Family Papers, MOHIST; "Confirmation of Sale of Enslaved people," Marshall, *Life and Papers of Frederick Bates*, vol. 2, 225; "Confirmation of a Sale of Enslaved people," ibid., 314; "Inventory for Thornhill," *National Register of Historic Places*, 7; EB to FB, September 1, September 29; EB to FB, October 13, 1817; EB to FB, July 19, 1818; EB to FB, August 18, 1818, Bates Family Papers, MOHIST; *U.S. Census*, 1810; *U.S. Census*, 1830; Mutti Burke, *On Slavery's Border*, 17–51, 309; *Missouri Republican*, May 17, 1827.

30. EB to JCB, February 25, 1828, Edward Bates Papers, VHS.

31. Darby, *Personal Recollections*, 119.

3. Party Leader

1. EB to HRG, February 17, 1829, Bates Family Papers, MOHIST.

2. Cain, *Lincoln's Attorney General*, 40–41.

3. Summers and Dallmeyer, *Jefferson City, Missouri*, 43; Violette, *History of Missouri*, 131; "Heritage of Jefferson City," *City of Jefferson, Missouri*, http://www.jeffersoncitymo.gov/live_play/history_heritage/index.php (last accessed July 17, 2019); E. Sachse, Drawing of Jefferson City Missouri, 1844–1850, Marson S. Carson Collection, LOC; Sketch of Jefferson City, 1859, Summers Collection, MOARC; Viles, "Missouri Capitals and Capitols: Second Article," 233–36.

4. *Journal of the Senate of the State of Missouri, Seventh General Assembly* (1831), 41, 51, 54, 56, 83–84, 92, 123, 125; Cain, *Lincoln's Attorney General*, 41–43.

5. *Journal of the House of Representatives of the State of Missouri, Seventh General Assembly* (1833), 55.

6. Chambers, *Old Bullion Benton*, 160–63; Cain, *Lincoln's Attorney General*, 43; Mering, *Whig Party in Missouri*, 52–57.

7. Remini, *Henry Clay*, 225–28; Marshall, "Strange Stillbirth of the Whig Party," 446; Mering, *Whig Party in Missouri*, 52–57.

8. Jefferson, *Notes on the State of Virginia*, 172; EB, "Agriculture in the West," *New York Times*, November 17, 1853; Kohl, *Politics of Individualism*, 26–27.

9. *Missouri Intelligencer*, April 11, 1828; EB, "To the People of Missouri," *Missouri Republican* (St. Louis), June 8, 1826; John Quincy Adams, First Annual Message to Congress, in Richardson, *Messages and Papers of the Presidents*, vol. 2, 316.

10. Ward, *Andrew Jackson*, and Pessen, *Jacksonian America*.

11. EB to Abiel Lenoard, April 4, 1831, Leonard Collection, SHSMO; Mering, *Whig Party in Missouri*, 22.

12. Neels, "Barbarous Custom of Dueling," 21–23.

13. Chambers, *Old Bullion Benton*, 179.

14. *History of St. Charles, Montgomery and Warren Counties*, 193; Cain, *Lincoln's Attorney General*, 50–51; Nagel, *Missouri*, 108–9.

15. Mering, *Missouri Whig Party*, 23; *Boon's Lick Times* (Feyette), May 16, 1840.

16. Mering, *Missouri Whig Party*, 49–51; Dubin, *United States Gubernatorial Elections*, xxxiii; Davis and Durrie, *Illustrated History of Missouri*, 118–19; Holt, *Rise and Fall of the American Whig Party*, 115; Holt, *Political Crisis of the 1850s*, 22–28.

17. J. C. Edwards, "St. Charles County," in Williams, *History of Northeast Missouri*, vol. 1, 573.

18. Johnson, *Broken Heart of America,* 34–35; Primm, *Lion of the Valley,* 138–39.

19. Johnson, *Broken Heart of America,* 35; Booth, "Archeology at the Arch," 25.

20. Booth, "Archeology at the Arch," 25; Primm, *Lion of the Valley,* 134; Johnson, *Broken Heart of America,* 54–55; Johnson, *Shopkeeper's Millennium,* and Howe, *What Hath God Wrought.*

21. J. C. Edwards, "St. Charles County," in Williams, *History of Northeast Missouri,* vol. 1, 573; EB, *Diary: 1846–1852,* June 3, 1846, February 12, 1847, MOHIST; Edward Bates former residence, Photograph by William Swekosky, 1940, Swekosky Notre Dame College Collection, MOHIST.

22. *Journal of the Senate of the State of Missouri, Seventh General Assembly,* 82, 89; *Journal of the House of Representatives of the State of Missouri, Seventh General Assembly,* 116, 140; House Committee on Roads and Canals, *Harbor at St. Louis: To accompany bill, H.R. No. 451,* 23rd Cong., 1st Sess., January 2, 1834; House Committee on Roads and Canals, *Report of Charles Gratiot, Chief Engineer, Army Corps of Engineers attached to House Report No. 425,* 23rd Cong., 1st Sess., April 16, 1834, 4–5; House Committee on Commerce, *Letter from the Secretary of War transmitting the information required by a resolution of the House of Representatives respecting the Harbor of St. Louis,* 2.

23. *Journal of the Senate of the State of Missouri, Seventh General Assembly,* 82, 89; *Journal of the House of Representatives of the State of Missouri, Seventh General Assembly,* 116, 140; House Committee on Roads and Canals, *Harbor at St. Louis: To accompany bill, H.R. No. 451,* 23rd Cong., 1st Sess., January 2, 1834; House Committee on Roads and Canals, *Report of Charles Gratiot, Chief Engineer, Army Corps of Engineers attached to House Report No. 425,* 23rd Cong., 1st Sess., April 16, 1834, 4–5; House Committee on Commerce, *Letter from the Secretary of War transmitting the information required by a resolution of the House of Representatives respecting the Harbor of St. Louis,* 2; Williams, "Chicago River and Harbor Convention, 1847," 608.

24. Williams, "Chicago River and Harbor Convention, 1847," 609; Fergus, *Chicago River and Harbor Convention,* 12; Cronon, *Nature's Metropolis,* 63–64.

25. Fergus, *Chicago River and Harbor Convention,* 52–68.

26. Ibid., 50, 169.

27. Ibid., 69, 140.

28. Ibid., 141.

29. Ibid., 81–84.

30. Ibid., 84.

31. EB, *Diary: 1846–1852*, July 10, 1847.

32. Ibid., November 7, 1847; December 10, 1847; December 20, 1847.

33. Ibid., June 22, 1848.

34. Recollections of Frederick M. Colburne, May 17, 1899, St. Louis Fires Collection, MOHIST; Journal of Sally Smith Flagg, May 18, 1849, Ibid; *Missouri Republican*, May 19, 1849.

35. Recollections of Mrs. J. L. Carner, 1909, St. Louis Fires Collection, MOHIST; *Missouri Republican*, May 22, 1849; Recollections of Frederick M. Colburne, May 17, 1899, St. Louis Fires Collection, MOHIST; Primm, *Lion in the Valley*, 174–75; Moore, "New Perspectives," 47.

36. EB, *Diary: 1846–1852*, May 18, 1849 (capitalization in original); Thomas Easterly, "Ruins of the Great St. Louis Fire, 17–18 May 1849," Daguerreotype, 1849, Easterly Daguerreotype Collection, MOHIST.

37. 1820 Federal Census; 1830 Federal Census; 1840 Federal Census; 1850 Federal Census; Rosenberg, *Cholera Years*, 1–4; Said, *Orientalism*; International Medical Corps, "Basic Facts on Cholera," last modified May 3, 2011, http://www.internationalmedicalcorps.org/Page.aspx?pid=475&gclid =CN-09pPGyqgCFUMUKgodiyRduQ.

38. Charles Peabody, *Travel Diary*, December 28, 1848, MOHIST; Hyde and Howard, *Encyclopedia of the History of St. Louis*, vol. 2, 681.

39. Rosenberg, *Cholera Years*, 104–5; Peabody, *Travel Diary*, February 24, 1849; D. M. Pollock to Brother Peterson, July 6, 1849, Missouri History Papers, MOHIST.

40. Rosenberg, *Cholera Years*, 120; EB, *Diary: 1846–1852*, June 24, 1849.

41. *Missouri Republican*, April 15–May 11, 1849; Proceedings of the Committee of Public Health, June 28–29, 1848, MOHIST.

42. EB, *Diary: 1846–1852*, July 1–11, 1849.

43. Primm, *Lion in the Valley*, 151; Humphreys, *The Cholera*, 12.

44. EB, *Diary: 1846–1852*, June 3, 1846; February 15, 1847.

45. Primm, *Lion of the Valley*, 175; Booth, "Archeology at the Arch," 25, Proceedings of the Committee of Public Health, June 27, 1848; Snow, *On the Mode of Communication*, and Johnson, *Ghost Map*; Primm, *Lion in the Valley*, 163; 1840 Federal Census; 1860 Federal Census.

46. Bates, *Bates et al.*, 76; EB, *Diary: 1846–1852*, June 14, 1849.

47. EB, *Diary: 1846–1852*, July 5, 1845; January 30, 1848; December 5, 1848; December 10, 1848; February 3, 1849.

4. Conservative Reformer

1. John Tyler, Fourth Annual Message to Congress, December 3, 1844, in Richardson, *Messages and Papers of the Presidents*, vol. 4, 345; Clary, *Eagles and Empire*, 57–61; Silbey, *Storm over Texas*, 3–4.

2. James K. Polk, Inaugural Address, March 4, 1845, in Richardson, *Messages and Papers of the Presidents*, vol. 5, 2230; Clary, *Eagles and Empire*, 62–64.

3. Clary, *Eagles and Empire*, 60–61, 94–95; Borneman, *Polk*, 133–49.

4. Nevins, *Polk*, 80–86; Clary, *Eagles and Empire*, 93–95; 100–101.

5. EB, *Diary: 1846–1852*, May 16, 1847.

6. Ibid.

7. Ibid., May 22, 1847; Greenberg, *A Wicked War*, 107; Holt, *Rise and Fall of the American Whig Party*, 248–49.

8. Howe, *What Hath God Wrought*, 806–7.

9. EB, *Diary: 1846–1852*, March 13–14, 1848.

10. Mering, *Whig Party in Missouri*, 57; Nagel, *Missouri*, 125; Mutti Burke, *On Slavery's Border*, 94–95; Tyler, *Freedom's Ferment*, 468–76.

11. Phillips, *Rivers Ran Backward*, 21–48; Earle, *Jacksonian Antislavery*, 4, 6; Mering, *Whig Party in Missouri*, 57; Darby, *Personal Recollections*, 30, 152, 171; Broadhead, "A Few of the Leading People," 289.

12. Johnson, *Broken Heart of America*, 73–74; Primm, *Lion of the Valley*, 175; "Luke Lawless, Charge to the Grand Jury after McIntosh Burning, 1836" in Waldrep, *Lynching in America*, 55–57; *Missouri Republican*, May 25, 1836.

13. Oates, *Fires of Jubilee*.

14. Johnson, *Broken Heart of America*, 76–9; Simon, *Freedom's Champion*.

15. Phillips, *Freedom Speech of Wendell Phillips*, 8; Stone, *Martyr of Freedom*, 4; AL, "Address before the Young Men's Lyceum of Springfield, Illinois," Basler, *Collected Works*, vol. 1, 108–15.

16. Gerteis, *Morality and Utility*.

17. VanderVelde, *Redemption Songs*.

18. Cobb, *An Inquiry into the Law of Negro Slavery*, vol. 1, 217; Stevens, *St. Louis*, 99–100, 370–71; Delaney, *From the Darkness Cometh the Light*.

19. EB, *Diary: 1846–1852*, April 15, 1848.

20. 1840 Federal Census; 1850 Federal Census; 1860 Federal Census; Edward Bates to Frederick Bates, September 29, 1817, Bates Family Papers, MOHIST; Edward Bates, Receipt to J. B. C. Lucas for the hire of Chloe, William H. Semsrott Collection, MOHIST; EB, *Diary: 1846–1852*, April 15, 1848.

21. Phillips, *Rivers Ran Backward*, 64–65, 226–28.

22. Holt, *Political Crisis of the 1850s*, 30–36.

23. EB, *Diary: 1846–1862*, February 8, 1847; February 22, 1848; April 23, 1848.

24. Ibid., April 5, 1848.

25. Howe, *What Hath God Wrought*, 831.

26. EB, *Diary: 1846–1852*, August 5, 1848.

27. Howe, *What Hath God Wrought*, 831–34.

28. EB, *Diary: 1846–1852*, December 31, 1848.
29. Ibid., December 2–4, 1848; December 31, 1848.
30. Ibid., February 3, 1849; February 15, 1849.
31. Ibid., March 3, 1849.

5. Winter of Discontent

1. Ibid., July 3, 1851; Holt, *Political Crisis of the 1850s*, 39–40.
2. Howe, *What Hath God Wrought*, 689–90, 767–68; McPherson, *Ordeal by Fire*, 58–61.
3. Holt, *Political Crisis of the 1850s*.
4. Freeman, *Field of Blood*, 167–69.
5. Remini, *Henry Clay*, 730–62; Daniel Webster, "The Compromises of the Constitution," March 7, 1850, in Tefft, *Speeches of Daniel Webster*, 519–71; Remini, *Daniel Webster*, 694–95.
6. EB, *Diary: 1846–1852*, March 15, 1850; McPherson, *Ordeal by Fire*, 70–75; Hamilton, *Prologue to Conflict*.
7. Phillips, *Missouri's Confederate*, 164–78; Chambers, *Old Bullion Benton*, 341–56.
8. EB, *Diary: 1846–1852*, November 28, 1850 (emphasis in original).
9. Ibid., August 23, 1849.
10. Mering, *Whig Party in Missouri*, 173–6; Holt, *Rise and Fall of the American Whig Party*, 561.
11. EB, *Diary: 1846–1852*, December 22–24, 1850.
12. Henry S. Geyer to J. B. Crockett, January 13, 1851; Henry S. Geyer to J. B. Crockett, January 14, 1851, as quoted in EB, *Diary: 1846–1852*, January 18, 1851; "From Jefferson City," *Palmyra Weekly Whig*, January 30, 1851.
13. Holt, *Rise and Fall of the American Whig Party*, 561; Cain, *Lincoln's Attorney General*, 14, 50; EB, *Diary: 1846–1852*, April 24, 1850; January 11, 1851.
14. EB, *Diary: 1846–1852*, January 18, 1851.
15. Holt, *Rise and Fall of the American Whig Party*, 596.
16. Ibid., 565–66; EB, *Diary: 1846–1852*, Marginal Note, December 22, 1850; Mering, *Whig Party in Missouri*, 177; "Letter from Mr. Geyer," *Palmyra Weekly Whig*, February 27, 1851; EB, *Diary: 1846–1852*, February 20, 1851; February 22, 1851.
17. EB, *Diary: 1846–1852*, April 29, 1851; March 10, 1852; October 30, 1852; November 15, 1851.
18. Ibid., May 29, 1851; July 9, 1851.
19. Ibid., September 28, 1851; November 27, 1851.
20. Ibid., May 15, 1851 (emphasis in original).

21. Ibid., May 31, 1851; "The Largest Slaveholders," *St. Louis Intelligencer,* May 31, 1851.

22. EB, *Diary: 1846–1852,* December 24, 1850.

23. "Letter of the Hon. Edward Bates," *The Republic* (Washington, DC), December 12, 1850.

24. EB, *Diary: 1846–1852,* June 6, 1847; April 29, 1851; *Missouri Republican,* May 14, 1849.

25. "Grand Lodge of Missouri," *Charleston, Missouri Courier,* June 1, 1863; Anbinder, *Nativism and Slavery,* 38; EB, *Diary: 1846–1852,* November 28, 1850; Neels, "We Shall Be Literally Sold to the Dutch," 25.

26. EB, *Diary: 1846–1852,* February 8, 1847; August 28, 1851; January 12, 1852; McPherson, *Battle Cry of Freedom,* 106–8.

27. EB, *Diary: 1846–1852,* January 23, 1852; *Missouri Republican,* March 28, 1852; Boernstein, *Memoirs,* 178; *Missouri Republican,* March 31, 1852; Neels, "We Shall Be Literally Sold to the Dutch," 26.

28. Mering, *Whig Party in Missouri,* 181–87; "Debate in the Whig Convention," *Glasgow Weekly Times,* May 6, 1852.

29. Proceedings of the Whig State Convention," *Glasgow Weekly Times,* April 29, 1852.

30. Chambers, *Old Bullion Benton,* 384–87; EB, *Diary: 1846–1852,* March 31, 1851; Mering, *Whig Party in Missouri,* 181–90; *Hannibal Journal,* November 4, 1852.

31. Gienapp, *Origins of the Republican Party,* 38–39, 70; Holt, *Rise and Fall of the American Whig Party,* 956; *Missouri Glasgow Times,* September 14, 1852; Mering, *Whig Party in Missouri,* 191.

32. EB, *Diary: 1846–1852,* July 4, 1851; *Missouri Glasgow Weekly Times,* May 20, 1852, February 1, 1855.

33. Gienapp, *Origins of the Republican Party,* 172; EB, *Diary: 1846–1852,* March 22, 1855; Mering, *Whig Party in Missouri,* 208–9.

34. Gienapp, *Origins of the Republican Party,* 172–77.

35. Richardson, *To Make Men Free,* 8–13; Mering, *Whig Party in Missouri,* 209–11.

36. Holt, *Rise and Fall of the American Whig Party,* 977–78.

37. "Speech of Edward Bates," *Alexandria Gazette and Virginia Advertiser,* September 17, 1856.

38. Holt, *Rise and Fall of the American Whig Party,* 977.

39. "Speech of Edward Bates," *Alexandria Gazette and Virginia Advertiser,* September 17, 1856.

40. "Coverage of the Whig Convention," *St. Charles Republican Intelligencer,* October 9, 1856; Cain, *Lincoln's Attorney General,* 83–89.

41. Wilentz, *Rise of American Democracy*, 692–706; Foner, *Free Soil, Free Labor, Free Men*; Gienapp, *The Origins of the Republican Party*; and Holt, *The Political Crisis of the 1850s*.

42. "Editor's Correspondence," *Glasgow Weekly Times*, January 22, 1857.

43. EB to Schuyler Colfax, May 31, 1858, Schuyler Colfax Collection, ALPLM.

6. Candidate

1. Harrold, *Border War*, 164–65.

2. Ibid., 166–70; Potter, *Impending Crisis*, 213.

3. James Buchanan, Inaugural Address, March 4, 1857, Richardson, *Messages and Papers of the Presidents*, vol. 5, 432.

4. Johnson, *Broken Heart of America*, 91, 99–105; McPherson, *Battle Cry of Freedom*, 170.

5. McPherson, *Battle Cry of Freedom*, 171; Howard, *Report of the Decision*, 399–454.

6. Beale, *Diary of Edward Bates*, 115; Jones, *Birthright Citizens*.

7. Potter, *Impending Crisis*, 307–17.

8. Ibid., 318–25; Smith, *Presidency of James Buchanan*, 40–46.

9. Holt, *Political Crisis of the 1850s*; Beale, *Diary of Edward Bates*, 1–2.

10. Beale, *Diary of Edward Bates*, 9.

11. Smith, *Stormy Present*; Williams, *Horace Greeley*, 210–11; "Edward Bates," *New York Daily Tribune*, November 14, 1859, 4; Cain, *Lincoln's Attorney General*, 95; *Evansville Daily Journal*, November 12, 1859, 2.

12. Gerteis, *Civil War St. Louis*, 66; Smith, *Francis Preston Blair*, and Parrish, *Frank Blair*.

13. Smith, "Schuyler Colfax," 383–98; Colfax, "Kansas—The Lecompton Constitution."

14. WHS, *Freedom in the New Territories*, March 11, 1850, United States Senate, http://www.senate.gov/artandhistory/history/resources/pdf/Seward NewTerritories.pdf (last accessed July 12, 2012); Seward, "The Irrepressible Conflict," *New York Tribune*, October 25, 1858.

15. Blue, *Free Soilers*, and Niven, *Salmon P. Chase*, 99–128, 140–52.

16. Beale, *Diary of Edward Bates*, 15.

17. Wilentz, *Rise of American Democracy*, 525–29; Beale, *Diary of Edward Bates*, 11.

18. EB to Schuyler Colfax, June 16, 1859, Schuyler Colfax Papers, ALPLM; Beale, *Diary of Edward Bates*, 17, 36.

19. Beale, *Diary of Edward Bates*, 46.

20. Randall, *Diary of Orville Hickman Browning*, vol. 1, 380; Donald, *We Are Lincoln Men*.

21. Beale, *Diary of Edward Bates*, 50–51; 67–68; 71–72.

22. Ibid., 74; EB to Schuyler Colfax, December 13, 1859, Edward Bates Collection, ALPLM.

23. EB to Schuyler Colfax, December 13, 1859, Edward Bates Collection, ALPLM; Cain, *Lincoln's Attorney General*, 102–3; Luthin, *First Lincoln Campaign*, 58–9; Beale, *Diary of Edward Bates*, 77–81.

24. Beale, *Diary of Edward Bates*, 77–81, 83–85; Gordon, *Honorable Edward Bates*; "The Presidency: A Survey of the Field," *New York Daily Tribune*, April 7, 1860.

25. Beale, *Diary of Edward Bates*, 12; "Presidential Candidates: Hon. Edward Bates of Missouri," *New York Times*, February 17, 1860.

26. *Missouri Democrat*, May 4, 1860; Beale, *Diary of Edward Bates*, 125–27.

27. "Immense Gathering of the Republicans," *New York Times*, May 16, 1860; Johannsen, *Stephen A. Douglas*, 749–59.

28. "Immense Gathering of the Republicans," *New York Times*, May 16, 1860; Remini, *The House*, 137–38; Johnson, *Proceedings of the First Three Republican National Conventions*, 86.

29. Johnson, *Proceedings of the First Three Republican National Conventions*, 102–103.

30. Republican Party Platform of 1860, May 17, 1860, Peters and Wooley, *American Presidency Project*.

31. Johnson, *Proceedings of the First Three Republican National Conventions*, 108.

32. Ibid., 111–12.

33. Ibid., 114–15.

34. Ibid., 116.

35. *Missouri Democrat*, May 19, 1860; Beale, *Diary of Edward Bates*, 128; Johnson, *Proceedings of the First Three Republican National Conventions*, 148–53.

36. Thomas, *Abraham Lincoln*, 120; AL, "Printed Resolution and Preamble on Mexican War: Spot Resolutions," December 22, 1847, Abraham Lincoln Papers, LOC; "'Spot' Resolutions in the United States House of Representatives," Basler, *Collected Works*, vol. 1, 420–22; Beale, *Diary of Edward Bates*, 122; Bartlett, *Presidential Candidates*.

37. Beale, *Diary of Edward Bates*, 129, 131.

38. McCormack, *Memoirs of Gustave Koerner*, vol. 2, 87–89; Schurz, *Reminiscences of Carl Schurz*, vol. 2, 180; Achorn, *Lincoln Miracle*.

39. Schurz, *Reminiscences*, vol. 2, 178, 183–84; Paludan, *Presidency of Abraham Lincoln*, 15; AL to Lyman Trumbull, April 29, 1860, Basler, *Collected Works*, vol. 4, 45; Schurz, *Reminiscences*, vol. 2, 184–85; Donald, *Lincoln*, 249–50.

40. Schurz, *Reminiscences*, 128.

41. EB to Schuyler Colfax, May 25, 1860, Bates Collection, ALPLM.
42. "Letter of Judge Bates, Pledging his Support to the Republican Ticket," *New York Times*, June 23, 1860.
43. Ibid.
44. Beale, *Diary of Edward Bates*, 152.
45. James McPherson, *Ordeal by Fire*, 138.
46. Petition from Kinsley S. Bingham, Solomon Foot, and Zachariah Chandler to AL, January 21, 1861, Abraham Lincoln Papers, LOC.
47. Burlingame, *With Lincoln in the White House*, 17.
48. Beale, *Diary of Edward Bates*, 162–65.
49. Ibid., 153, 165.
50. Burlingame, *With Lincoln in the White House*, 19.
51. EB to James Rollins, January 23, 1861, Bates Family Papers, MOHIST.

7. The Union Dissolved; The Union Defended

1. William Carr Lane to EB, December 14, 1860, William Carr Lane Papers, MOHIST.
2. William Carr Lane to EB, December 14, 1860; EB to Wyndham Robertson, November 3, 1860, Cain, "Lincoln's Attorney General," 20–21.
3. Ibid., 21.
4. AL, "Speech in Independence Hall," February 22, 1861, Basler, *Collected Works*, vol. 4, 241–42.
5. Crofts, *Lincoln and the Politics of Slavery*.
6. EB to AL, January 1861, Manuscript Division, LOC.
7. Primm, *Lion of the Valley*, 244; Phillips, *Missouri's Confederate*; "From Jefferson City" *Missouri Republican*, January 4, 1861, 2; Gerteis, *Civil War St. Louis*, 77–78.
8. Gerteis, *Civil War St. Louis*, 77–82.
9. Beale, *Diary of Edward Bates*, 173–74; Bowman, *Lincoln's Resolute Unionist*.
10. Gerteis, *Civil War St. Louis*, 82–85.
11. EB to AL, January 30, 1861, Abraham Lincoln Papers, LOC.
12. Gerteis, *Civil War St. Louis*, 85.
13. Primm, *Lion of the Valley*, 247.
14. John G. Nicolay to EB, February 5, 1861; EB to John G. Nicolay, February 9, 1861, Abraham Lincoln Papers, LOC; Beale, *Diary of Edward Bates*, 175.
15. Beale, *Diary of Edward Bates*, 175.
16. AL, "First Inaugural Address," March 4, 1861, in Reynolds, *Lincoln's Selected Writings*, 230–33 (emphasis in original).
17. Beale, *Diary of Edward Bates*, 176.
18. Niven, *Gideon Welles*.

19. Smith, "Meanest Man," 195.
20. Conway, *Omitted Chapters*, 135; Learned, "Attorney-General and the Cabinet," 444.
21. Learned, "Attorney-General and the Cabinet," 451–57.
22. Joseph Holt and Winfield Scott to AL, March 5, 1861, Abraham Lincoln Papers, LOC; James McPherson, *Battle Cry of Freedom*, 264–66.
23. Beale, *Diary of Edward Bates*, 177.
24. Ibid., 177–78.
25. EB to AL, March 16, 1861, Abraham Lincoln Papers, LOC.
26. GW to AL, March 15, 1861; WHS to AL, March 16, 1861; SC to AL, March 16, 1861, Abraham Lincoln Papers, LOC.
27. SPC to AL, March 16, 1861; MB to AL, March 15, 1861, ibid.
28. EB to AL, March 16, 1861, ibid; Gerteis, *Civil War St. Louis*, 89; McPherson, *Battle Cry of Freedom*, 255.
29. McPherson, *Battle Cry of Freedom*, 269–70; Beale, *Diary of Edward Bates*, 180; EB to AL, March 29, 1861, Abraham Lincoln Papers, LOC.
30. Paludan, *Presidency of Abraham Lincoln*, 58–61; Beale, *Diary of Edward Bates*, 181.
31. McPherson, *Battle Cry of Freedom*, 273–74.
32. EB to Onward Bates, March 22, 1861, Bates Family Papers, MOHIST.

8. Constitutional Scruples

1. EB to BB, March 22, 1861, Bates Family Papers, MOHIST; AL to EB, March 9, 1861; AL to EB, March 11, 1862; AL to EB, March 18, 1861; AL to EB, March 27, 1861; Basler, *Collected Works*, vol. 4, 279, 281, 290–91, 299, 323.
2. EB, "Opinion on the Power to the President to Create a Militia Bureau in the War Department" in Ashton, *Official Opinions*, vol., 14, 11.
3. AL, Proclamation Calling Militia and Convening Congress, April 15, 1861, Abraham Lincoln Papers, LOC.
4. Neely, *Fate of Liberty* and *Lincoln and the Triumph of the Nation*; as well as Farber, *Lincoln's Constitution*, and White, *Abraham Lincoln and Treason*.
5. Beale, *Diary of Edward Bates*, 183.
6. AL, "First Inaugural Address," March 4, 1861, Reynolds, *Lincoln's Selected Writings*, 230.
7. Holt, *Political Crisis of the 1850s*, 220.
8. EB to AL, April 15, 1861, Abraham Lincoln Papers, LOC.
9. Winfield Scott to AL, April 15, 1861, ibid.; AL, "Proclamation of a Blockade," April 19, 1861, Basler, *Collected Works*, vol. 4, 338–39; McPherson, *Battle Cry of Freedom*, 313–14.
10. Gerteis, *Civil War St. Louis*, 236–41.

11. Lincoln's First Inaugural Address, March 4, 1861, Reynolds, *Lincoln's Selected Writings*, 230; "Proclamation of a Blockade," April 19, 1861, Basler, *Collected Works*, vol. 4, 338–39

12. Beale, *Diary of Edward Bates*, 183 (emphasis in original); Beale, *Diary of Gideon Welles*, vol. 1, 86; GW to AL, August 5, 1861, The Papers of Abraham Lincoln, LOC; Beale, *Diary of Edward Bates*, 265–66.

13. Lamon, *Recollections*, 266.

14. *New York Times*, April 20, 1861; Neely, *Fate of Liberty*, 4–5.

15. Beale, *Diary of Edward Bates*, 185 (emphasis in original).

16. AL to Winfield Scott, April 25, 1861, Basler, *Collected Works*, vol. 4, 344.

17. AL to General Winfield Scott, April 27, 1861, Ibid., 347.

18. "Important from Key West," *National Republican* (Washington, DC), May 21, 1861; AL, "Proclamation Suspending the Writ of Habeas Corpus in Florida," May 10, 1861, Basler, *Collected Works*, vol. 4, 364.

19. "The Case of Mr. John Merryman in Baltimore," *Evening Star* (Washington, DC), May 28, 1861; *New York Times*, June 4, 1861; Neely, *Fate of Liberty*, 10–11.

20. United States Constitution, article I, section 9, clause 2; Taney, *Ex Parte Merryman*; AL to EB, May 30, 1861, Basler, *Collected Works*, vol. 4, 390.

21. Titian J. Coffey to AL, April 19, 1861, Abraham Lincoln Papers, LOC (emphasis in original).

22. Johnson, *Power of the President*.

23. EB, Journal of Legal Studies (1847), Bates Family Papers, MOHIST; Hurd, *Treatise on the Right*, 192–94.

24. EB to AL, July 5, 1861, Abraham Lincoln Papers, LOC.

25. Ibid.

26. EB, *Diary: 1846–1852*, March 13, 1848.

27. Dirck, *Lincoln and the Constitution*, 55; AL, Message to Congress in Special Session, July 4, 1861, Basler, *Collected Works*, vol. 4, 431.

28. Randall, "Indemnity Act of 1863," 589–613; *American Annual Cyclopedia*, vol. 1, 234; Byrd, *Senate, 1789–1989*, vol. 1, 245; McGinty, *Body of John Merryman*, 122.

29. EB to AL, June 5, 1863, Abraham Lincoln Papers, LOC.

9. Waging War

1. Tilly Bates to Hester Bates, May 23, 1861, Abraham Lincoln Papers, LOC.

2. *OR*, ser. 3, vol. 1, 82–83; McPherson, *Ordeal by Fire*, 169.

3. Catton, *Coming Fury*, 374–75; Gerteis, *Civil War St. Louis*, 89; Clayborne Fox Jackson to Jefferson Davis, April 17, 1861; Jefferson Davis to Claiborne Fox Jackson, April 23, 1861, in Crist and Dix, *Papers of Jefferson Davis*, vol. 7, 107, 117; "Gov. Jackson's Message," *Missouri Republican*, May 4, 1861, 2.

4. Gerteis, *Civil War in Missouri*, 12, 82–86.

5. Gerteis, *Civil War St. Louis*, 90–93.

6. Ibid., 95–96.

7. Ibid., 100–101; Johnson, *Broken Heart of America*, 110–27; Adamson, *Rebellion in Missouri*, 63; William S. Harney and Sterling Price, "To the People of the State of Missouri," *OR*, ser. 1, vol. 3, 375.

8. EB to SC, April 27, 1861, *OR*, ser. 1, vol. 1, 671; John Rodgers to EB, May 14, 1861, Abraham Lincoln Papers, LOC; BB to EB, June 3, 1861, Bates Family Papers, MOHIST.

9. BB to EB, June 3, 1861, Bates Family Papers, MOHIST.

10. Catton, *Coming Fury*, 387; Adamson, *Rebellion in Missouri*, 92–94; Gerteis, *Civil War St. Louis*, 122.

11. EB, Memorandum on Missouri Affairs, May 20, 1861, Edward Bates Papers, LOC.

12. Adamson, *Rebellion in Missouri*, 106; Snead, *Fight for Missouri*, 197–200; "The Conference," *Missouri Republican*, June 12, 1861, 2; Gerteis, *Civil War St. Louis*, 123–24.

13. Snead, *Fight for Missouri*, 201; Adamson, *Rebellion in Missouri*, 123–27; Gerteis, *Civil War in Missouri*, 34–39; *Journal of the Missouri State Convention, Held at Jefferson City, July, 1861*, 132–33.

14. EB to HRG, August 2, 1861; EB to Charles Gibson, August 4, 1861; EB to HRG, August 12, 1861, Hamilton R. Gamble Papers, MOHIST.

15. JCB to Onward Bates, August 21, 1861, Bates Family Papers, MOHIST.

16. James McPherson, *Ordeal by Fire*, 227; Dickens, *American Notes*, vol. 1, 139; JCB to Onward Bates, August 21, 1861, Bates Family Papers, MOHIST; Brooks, *Washington, D.C.*, 15–16.

17. McPherson, *Ordeal by Fire*, 228, 339–45; Davis, *Battle at Bull Run*; *OR*, ser. 1, vol. 2, 327, 570; Henry Adams to Charles Francis Adams Jr., August 5, 1861, in Levenson et al., *Letters of Henry Adams*, vol. 1, 248.

18. Diary of JCB, July 1861, Bates Family Papers, MOHIST.

19. Ibid.; Donald, *Lincoln*, 307; Beale, *Diary of Edward Bates*, 188.

20. Miers, *Lincoln Day by Day*, 56; AL, Memoranda of Military Policy Suggested by the Bull Run Defeat, July 24, 1861, Basler, *Collected Works*, vol. 4, 457.

21. Catton, *Terrible Swift Sword*, 12–13; Gerteis, *Civil War in Missouri*, 73–76; Piston and Hatcher, *Wilson's Creek*.

22. Beale, *Diary of Edward Bates*, 194.

23. McPherson, *Battle Cry of Freedom*, 362; Beale, *Diary of Edward Bates*, 196–97.

24. McPherson, *Battle Cry of Freedom*, 324; Beale, *Diary of Edward Bates*, 196–7.

25. McPherson, *Battle Cry of Freedom*, 353–56; Beale, *Diary of Edward Bates*, 211.

26. McPherson, *Battle Cry of Freedom*, 352–54.

27. Williams, "Frémont and the Politicians," 179–83; Paludan, *Presidency of Abraham Lincoln*, 86–87; Foner, *Fiery Trial*, 176–80; AL to John C. Frémont, September 11, 1861, Abraham Lincoln Papers, LOC.

28. BB to EB, October 10, 1861, Bates Family Papers, MOHIST.

29. Williams, "Frémont and the Politicians," 183; "GEN. FRÉMONT'S COLUMN," *New York Times*, September 17, 1861.

30. EB to HRG, October 3, 1861, Hamilton R. Gamble Papers, MOHIST; Beale, *Diary of Edward Bates*, 198–99 (emphasis in original).

31. Williams, "Frémont and the Politicians," 184.

32. Ibid., 199.

33. AL to George B. McClellan, November 1, 1861, Basler, *Collected Works*, vol. 5, 10; Mathew B. Brady, *Gen'l Geo. B. McClellan*, photograph (Washington, DC, 1861), LOC; McPherson, *Battle Cry of Freedom*, 348–50, 358–60.

34. McPherson, "Lincoln as Commander-in-Chief," in Simon and Holtzer, *Rediscovering Abraham Lincoln*; Beale, *Diary of Edward Bates*, 200.

35. George B. McClellan to Mary Ellen McClellan, July 27, 1862, in Sears, *Civil War Papers*, 70.

36. Sears, *Young Napoleon*, 116.

37. Beale, *Diary of Edward Bates*, 202

38. Ibid., 200–201.

39. Marzalek, *Commander of All Lincoln's Armies*, and Ambrose, *Halleck*; Beale, *Diary of Edward Bates*, 201.

40. McPherson, *Battle Cry of Freedom*, 389–91.

41. Ibid.

42. Adams, *Trent Affair*, 5; "Thanks to Commodore Wilkes," *Congressional Globe* (Washington, DC), December 6, 1861, 5.

43. Welles, "Capture and Release," 270; Cain, *Lincoln's Attorney General*, 242–44.

44. Cain, *Lincoln's Attorney General*, 276.

45. Donald, *Inside Lincoln's Cabinet*, 55.

46. Welles, "Capture and Release," 274–75.

47. Beale, *Diary of Edward Bates*, 202, 205–6, 213–15.

48. Donald, *Lincoln*, 320–23.

49. Ibid.

50. Sears, *George B. McClellan*, 135–36.

51. Beale, *Diary of Edward Bates*, 218.

52. Ibid., 219 (emphasis in original).

10. Best and Worst of Times

1. Beale, *Diary of Edward Bates*, 221.
2. Ibid.
3. Ibid., 222.
4. Ibid.; Grier, *Glasgow et al. vs. Hortiz et al.*
5. Beale, *Diary of Edward Bates*, 223–34 (emphasis in original); Miers, *Lincoln Day by Day*, vol. 3, 88–89.
6. Beale, *Diary of Edward Bates*, 224.
7. Ibid.
8. Meigs, "General Meigs on the Conduct of the War," 292; Miers, *Lincoln Day by Day*, vol. 3, 89.
9. AL, "President's General War Order No. 1," Basler, *Collected Works*, vol. 5, 111.
10. Ibid., 228; Marvel, *Lincoln's Autocrat*, 138–39; Beale, *Diary of Edward Bates*, 226.
11. Beale, *Diary of Edward Bates*, 227–34
12. Ibid., 232, 228; WHS to AL, April 1, 1861, Abraham Lincoln Papers, LOC; Paludan, *Presidency of Abraham Lincoln*, 72–73; Goodwin, *Team of Rivals*, 341–43; Neely, *Fate of Liberty*, 19–22.
13. Beale, *Diary of Edward Bates*, 230.
14. Ibid., Neely, *Fate of Liberty*, 19.
15. "From Jefferson City," *Missouri Republican*, January 16, 1862; EB to AL, February 28, 1862, Abraham Lincoln Papers, LOC; Beale, *Diary of Edward Bates*, 227–29, 237–38; Neely, *Fate of Liberty*, 19; McPherson, *Ordeal by Fire*, 243–44.
16. McPherson, *Battle Cry of Freedom*, 397–402.
17. Beale, *Diary of Edward Bates*, 233–35; Shea and Hess, *Pea Ridge*; McPherson, *Ordeal of Fire*, 247–53.
18. Beale, *Diary of Edward Bates*, 248; McPherson, *Ordeal by Fire*, 254.
19. McPherson, *Battle Cry of Freedom*, 423; Beale, *Diary of Edward Bates*, 240; AL, "President's War Order No. 3," Basler, *Collected Works*, vol. 5, 155; Sears, *George B. McClellan*, 164–65.
20. Foner, *Fiery Trial*, 191–93; Beale, *Diary of Edward Bates*, 233–34; Foner, *Fiery Trial*, 194; William Lee Miller, "The President and the Slave Trader" in Simon, Holzer, and Vogel, *Lincoln Revisited*, 148.
21. AL, "Message to Congress," March 6, 1862, Basler, *Collected Works*, vol. 5, 145; Foner, *Fiery Trial*, 196.
22. Foner, *Fiery Trial*, 197; Beale, *Diary of Edward Bates*, 241.
23. Striner, *Summoned to Glory*, 292–93; McPherson, *Battle Cry of Freedom*,

499; Proclamation by Abraham Lincoln, 19 May 1862, #90, *Presidential Proclamations*, ser. 23 Record Group 11, NARA.

24. McPherson, *Ordeal by Fire*, 257–58.

25. Beale, *Diary of Edward Bates*, 248–49.

26. Ibid., 253; McPherson, *Ordeal by Fire*, 258–59.

27. McPherson, *Ordeal by Fire*, 254, 257, 258–62; Dowdey, *Seven Days*.

28. McPherson, *Ordeal by Fire*, 264–72.

29. Donald, *Lincoln*, 357–58; George B. McClellan to AL, July 7, 1862, Sears, *Civil War Papers*, 228–29, 344; Paludan, *Presidency of Abraham Lincoln*, 146–47.

30. Witt, *Lincoln's Code*, 228.

31. Paludan, *Presidency of Abraham Lincoln*, 147; McPherson, *Battle Cry of Freedom*, 499–500.

32. AL to Henry W. Halleck, July 11, 1862, Basler, *Collected Works*, vol. 5, 312–13.

33. EB to WHS, September 23, 1861, William H. Seward Papers, LOC; EB, Tenth Opinion of the Attorney General, *US Attorney General Opinions*, November 6, 1861, LexisNexis Academic, www.lexisnexis.com (last accessed October 28, 2014); McPherson, *Battle Cry of Freedom*, 353, 356.

34. Thaddeus Stevens, "Attack on General Hunter," July 5, 1862, in Palmer and Ochoa, *Selected Papers of Thaddeus Stevens*, vol. 1, 317; John Hay to Mary Jay, July 20, 1862, in Burlingame, *At Lincoln's Side*, 23; Gienapp and Gienapp, *Civil War Diary*, 4; Donald, *Inside Lincoln's Cabinet*, 97–100; AL, Emancipation Proclamation—First Draft, July 22, 1862, Basler, *Collected Works*, vol. 5, 337.

35. AL, Appeal to Border State Representatives to Favor Compensated Emancipation, Basler, *Collected Works*, vol. 5, 318; Donald, *Inside Lincoln's Cabinet*, 99.

36. Carpenter, *Six Months*, 20–22.

37. Cain, *Lincoln's Attorney General*, 175.

38. William T. Sherman to EB, May 5, 1862; EB to AL, May 22, 1862; John C. Pope to EB, June 28, 1862; EB to EMS, June 30, 1862, Abraham Lincoln Papers, LOC.

39. EMS to EB, July 2, 1862, Abraham Lincoln Papers, LOC; AL, Order Extending the Pacific Railroad, Basler, *Collected Works*, vol. 5, 314–15.

40. McPherson, *Ordeal by Fire*, 281–82; Petition of EB and others to AL, September 9, 1862, Manuscript Division, LOC.

41. Gienapp and Gienapp, *Civil War Diary*, 24–26; Donald, *Inside Lincoln's Cabinet*, 117–19; Cain, *Lincoln's Attorney General*, 177–79; McPherson, *Ordeal by Fire*, 304, 310–11.

42. EB to HRG, September 22, 1862, Bates Family Papers, MOHIST; Sears, *Landscape Turned Red*, 307, 326–27; AL, Preliminary Emancipation Proclamation, September 22, 1862, Basler, *Collected Works*, vol. 5, 433–36.

43. Basler, *Collected Works*, vol. 5, 151; Gienapp and Gienapp, *Civil War Diary*, 54–55; Beale, *Diary of Edward Bates*, 263–64.

44. Gienapp and Gienapp, *Civil War Diary of Gideon Welles*, 60–61.

45. EB to AL, September 19, 1862; EB to AL, September 23, 1862, Abraham Lincoln Papers, LOC.

46. Goodwin, *Team of Rivals*, 464–65; Cain, *Lincoln's Attorney General*, 213; Neels, "Lincoln's Conservatives"; AL, Address on Colonization to a Deputation of Negroes, August 14, 1862, Basler, *Collected Works*, vol. 5, 371.

47. Beale, *Diary of Edward Bates*, 267; AL, Executive Order Concerning the Confiscation Act, November 13, 1862, Basler, *Collected Works*, vol. 5, 496; Neely, *Fate of Liberty*, and Marvel, *Lincoln's Autocrat*.

48. McPherson, *Battle Cry of Freedom*, 568–75; O'Reilly, *Fredericksburg Campaign*, and Rable, *Fredericksburg! Fredericksburg!*

49. Donald, *Lincoln*, 400–405; Beale, *Diary of Edward Bates*, 270 (misspellings in the original); Beale, *Diary of Gideon Welles*, vol. 1, 199–200.

50. EB, Opinion on Citizenship, November 29, 1862, in Ashton, *Official Opinions*, vol. 10, 382–413; McClure et al., "Circumventing the Dred Scott Decision," 279–83.

51. McClure et al., "Circumventing the Dred Scott Decision," 283; EB to AL, Memorandum on Emancipation Proclamation, 31 December 31, 1862; AL, Annual Message to Congress, December 1, 1862; AL, Preliminary Draft of Final Proclamation with Changes Suggested by EB, December 30, 1862, Abraham Lincoln Papers, LOC; Donald, *Lincoln*, 396.

52. Carpenter, *Six Months at the White House*, 270; Mazur, *Lincoln's Hundred Days*, 206.

53. Gienapp and Gienapp, *Civil War Diary*, 115; Burlingame, *With Lincoln in the White House*, 99–101.

54. Beale, *Diary of Edward Bates*, 113, 262–64; Vorenberg, "Abraham Lincoln and the Politics of Black Colonization," 22–24.

11. Radicalism Ascendent

1. EB to Hester Bates, February 21, 1863, Bates Family Papers, MOHIST.

2. Beale, *Diary of Edward Bates*, 281; Witt, *Lincoln's Code*, 150.

3. McGinty, *Lincoln and the Court*, 142.

4. EB to District Attorneys and Marshals, January 8, 1863, Abraham Lincoln Papers, LOC; Beale, *Diary of Edward Bates*, 280.

5. Blair, *On the Revolutionary Schemes*.

6. Shea and Hess, *Pea Ridge*, 305–6.

7. Beale, *Diary of Edward Bates*, 276, 279.

8. Neels, "'I Will Continue to Make," 6–7; Bowman, *Lincoln's Resolute Unionist*, 211–12; Beale, *Diary of Edward Bates*, 276.

9. EB to General Sumner, March 7, 1863; March 14, 1863, Bates Family Papers, MOHIST.

10. EB to HRG, March 19, 1863; EB to HRG, April 23, 1863, Bates Family Papers, MOHIST; Gerteis, *Civil War St. Louis*, 276.

11. Beale, *Diary of Edward Bates*, 275–77, 283–90; McPherson, *Battle Cry of Freedom*, 639–45.

12. McPherson, *Battle Cry of Freedom*, 283–89, 296.

13. Ibid., 295–300; Guelzo, *Gettysburg*, and Sears, *Gettysburg*; as well as Ballard, *Vicksburg*.

14. Beale, *Diary of Edward Bates*, 301; Donald, *We Are Lincoln Men*, 101–39.

15. Ibid., 291-93, 302.

16. James S. Reynolds to Edward Bates, September 13, 1863, Abraham Lincoln Papers, LOC; Beale, *Diary of Edward Bates*, 294; Gerteis, *Civil War in Missouri*, 141–49; Parrish, *Missouri under Radical Rule*, 4–8; Bowman, *Lincoln's Resolute Unionist*, 227–31.

17. AL to Charles D. Drake and Others, October 5, 1863, in Basler, *Collected Works*, vol. 6, 499; Bowman, *Lincoln's Resolute Unionist*, 231–32; Beale, *Diary of Edward Bates*, 308; EB to HRG, October 10, 1863, Bates Family Papers, MOHIST.

18. Beale, *Diary of Edward Bates*, 308, 447.

19. EB to HRG, April 23, 1863, HRG to EB, August 10, 1863, Bates Family Papers, MOHIST.

20. Beale, *Diary of Edward Bates*, 308; HRG to EB, October 17, 1863, Bates Family Papers, MOHIST.

21. EB to AL, October 22, 1863, Abraham Lincoln Papers, LOC; HRG to EB, October 17, 1863, Bates Family Papers, MOHIST; Beale, *Diary of Edward Bates*, 310.

22. EB to HRG, October 24, 1863, Bates Family Papers, MOHIST.

23. Parrish, *Missouri under Radical Rule*, 8; Cain, *Lincoln's Attorney General*, 280.

24. Beale, *Diary of Edward Bates*, 315.

25. Ibid., 317–21.

26. Ibid.

27. Boman, *Lincoln's Resolute Unionist*, 237.

28. Beale, *Diary of Edward Bates*, 328–29.

29. Gerteis, *Civil War St. Louis*, 280–91.

30. Beale, *Diary of Edward Bates*, 331.

31. Waugh, *Reelecting Lincoln*, 50–53; Gienapp and Gienapp, *Civil War Diary*, 336; Beale, *Diary of Edward Bates*, 333–34.

32. Beale, *Diary of Edward Bates*, 330, 336.

33. Ibid., 337–38, 341; Gienapp and Gienapp, *Civil War Diary*, 282.

34. Williams, *Lincoln and the Radicals*, 306–12, 336–38; Waugh, *Reelecting Lincoln*, 101–24; Beale, *Diary of Edward Bates*, 345.

35. Ascher, "Lincoln's Administration," 38–51; Cain, *Lincoln's Attorney General*, 297–300.

36. Beale, *Diary of Edward Bates*, 342, 354.

37. Harris, *Lincoln and the Border States*, 312–13; Gerteis, *Civil War St. Louis*, 182–86; Beale, *Diary of Edward Bates*, 350–51; AL to William S. Rosecrans, April 4, 1864, Basler, *Collected Works*, vol. 7, 283–84.

38. Beale, *Diary of Edward Bates*, 346, 355, 361–63; BB to EB, May 13, 1864, Bates Family Papers, MOHIST.

39. McPherson, *Ordeal by Fire*, 444–70

40. Beale, *Diary of Edward Bates*, 366–67; McPherson, *Battle Cry of Freedom*, 478–92, 756–57; Gienapp and Gienapp, *Civil War Diary*, 435–36; Gerteis, *Civil War in Missouri*, 196–203.

41. Beale, *Diary of Edward Bates*, 375, 381; Williams, *Lincoln and the Radicals*, 313–16.

42. Beale, *Diary of Edward Bates*, 413.

43. Ibid., 408–9; Williams, *Lincoln and the Radicals*, 317–31; McPherson, *Ordeal by Fire*, 492; Waugh, *Reelecting Lincoln*.

44. Ibid., 394; EB to AL, May 4, 1864, Abraham Lincoln Papers, LOC; Beale, *Diary of Edward Bates*, 372, 393, 395.

45. Beale, *Diary of Edward Bates*, 343, 381–418.

46. Niven, *Salmon P. Chase*, 374.

47. Beale, *Diary of Edward Bates*, 427–28; Gienapp and Gienapp, *Civil War Diary*, 534; EB to AL, November 25, 1864, Abraham Lincoln Papers, LOC.

12. Final Battles

1. Beale, *Diary of Edward Bates*, 428–29.

2. Phillips, *Rivers Ran Backward*, 182–85; Gerteis, *Civil War St. Louis*, 170–80; Parrish, *Missouri under Radical Rule*, 12–13.

3. March, *History of Missouri*, vol. 2, 998; Astor, *Rebels on the Border*, 170–72.

4. Beale, *Diary of Edward Bates*, 349, 443–44, 450–51; Cain, *Lincoln's Attorney General*, 319.

5. Astor, *Rebels on the Border*, 174–77.

6. Beale, *Diary of Edward Bates*, 430–32.

7. "An Ordinance Abolishing Slavery in Missouri" passed in Convention, January 11, 1865, MOHIST.

8. Beale, *Diary of Edward Bates*, 439–41.

9. Ibid., 450.

10. Ibid., 452–53.

11. AL to Thomas C. Fletcher, February 20, 1865, Abraham Lincoln Papers, LOC.

12. Thomas C. Fletcher to AL, February 27, 1865, ibid.

13. John C. Pope to Thomas C. Fletcher, as printed in the *Missouri Republican*, March 8, 1865.

14. "Proclamation by the Governor of Missouri," *Missouri Democrat*, March 8, 1865.

15. *Missouri Democrat*, March 9, 1865, March 17, 1865; John C. Pope, *Special Orders No. 15*, as printed in the *Missouri Democrat*, March 20, 1865; Beale, *Diary of Edward Bates*, 463, 467.

16. Beale, *Diary of Edward Bates*, 467.

17. *Missouri Republican*, April 7, 1865.

18. Beale, *Diary of Edward Bates*, 473.

19. Ibid., 475, 483.

20. *Missouri Republican*, April 13, 1865.

21. Ibid.

22. *Missouri State Constitution of 1865*, Article II, Sections 3–6, adopted by Convention, April 10, 1865, ratified by the people of Missouri, June 6, 1865; *"An Ordinance Providing for the Vacating of Certain Civil Offices in the State, Filling the Same Anew, and Protecting the Citizens from Injury and Harassment,"* Passed in Convention, March 17, 1865, MOHIST.

23. *Missouri Democrat*, April 10, 1865.

24. Cain, *Lincoln's Attorney General*, 319–24.

25. *Missouri Democrat*, April 18, 1865; *Missouri Republican*, April 29, 1865.

26. *Missouri Democrat*, May 11, 1865.

27. Ibid., April 18, 1865.

28. Ibid., April 21, 1865: Beale, *Diary of Edward Bates*, 475.

29. *Missouri Republican*, May 26, 1865; *Missouri Democrat*, June 3, 1865.

30. *Missouri Democrat*, June 2–6, 1865.

31. Louis Fusz, *Diary*, vol. 3, 92, MOHIST.

32. Beale, *Diary of Edward Bates*, 486; "Proclamation of Governor Thomas Fletcher upon the Results of Ratification," *Missouri Republican*, July 1, 1865; Parrish, *Missouri under Radical Rule*, 46–48.

33. Parrish, *Missouri under Radical Rule*, 48; Beale, *Diary of Edward Bates*, 490–95.

34. Beale, *Diary of Edward Bates*, 504, 521.

35. EB to Andrew Johnson, February 10, 1866, in Bergeron, *Papers of Andrew Johnson*, vol. 10, 71; "Edward Bates and the President—An Impressive Scene,"

Daily News and Herald (Savannah, GA), September 19, 1866; Astor, *Rebels on the Border*, 179.

36. Parrish, *Missouri under Radical Rule*, 261–66; Beale, *Diary of Edward Bates*, 512, 519.

37. Summers, *Ordeal of the Reunion*, 347–48; March, "Charles Daniel Drake," Christensen et al., *Dictionary of Missouri Biography*, 256; Astor, *Rebels on the Border*, 168–207.

38. Ross, *Liberal Republican Movement*, 48, 57, 62.

39. Slap, *Doom of Reconstruction*; *Constitution of the State of Missouri of 1875*; Astor, *Rebels on the Border*, 215.

40. Astor, *Rebels on the Border*, 181.

41. BB to James Eads, December 23, 1869, Hester Bates to Caroline Matilda Bates, March 27, 1869, Bates Family Papers, MOHIST; Cain, *Lincoln's Attorney General*, 332–33; Theising, "Lincoln's Man in Florissant," 7; Record of Internments in Receiving Tomb, 1869, Bellefontaine Cemetery and Arboretum, St. Louis; "Will of the Late Ex-Attorney-General Bates," *New York Times*, May 28, 1869.

42. "The Late Edward Bates," Second Meeting of the Members of the Bar, Resolutions of Respect, March 1869, Bates Family Papers, MOHIST.

43. Ibid.

44. "Forest Park," *St. Louis Post Dispatch*, June 24, 1876; Gerteis, *Civil War St. Louis*, 336–37.

45. "Attorney-General Bates's Widow," *New York Times*, October 24, 1880; Certificate of Death Outside of St. Louis and Burial Permit for Edward Bates, May 12, 1906, City of St. Louis Health Department in the records of Bellefontaine Cemetery and Arboretum, St. Louis.

Conclusion

1. Owen Lovejoy, "Is the President Slandered by his Friends?" in Burr, *Old Guard*, 274.

2. AL, "Annual Message to Congress," December 1, 1862, Basler, *Collected Works*, vol. 5, 537.

3. Smith, *Stormy Present*, 228.

4. AL, First Inaugural Address, March 4, 1861, Basler, *Collected Works*, vol. 4, 271.

5. *Bangor Daily Whig and Courier*, August 9, 1865: Gienapp and Gienapp, *Civil War Diary*, 518.

BIBLIOGRAPHY

Manuscript Collections

Bates Family Papers, MOHIST
Hamilton Rowan Gamble Papers, MOHIST
James O. Broadhead Collection, MOHIST
William Greenleaf Eliot Collection, MOHIST
Thomas Jefferson Papers, LOC
St. Louis Circuit Court Records, Washington University, St. Louis
Thomas Hart Benton Papers, MOHIST
Missouri State Constitution, MOARC
Missouri Marriage Records, MOARC
Switzler Collection, MOHIST
Duels Collection, MO HIST
Edward Bates Papers, VHS
Edward Bates Collection, ALPLM
Leonard Collection, SHSMO
Swekosky Notre Dame College Collection, MOHIST
St. Louis Fires Collection, MOHIST
Easterly Daguerreotype Collection, MOHIST
Missouri History Papers, MOHIST

Schuyler Colfax Collection, ALPLM
Edward Bates Collection, ALPLM
Abraham Lincoln Papers, LOC
William Carr Lane Papers, MOHIST
Manuscript Division, LOC
William H. Seward Papers, LOC
Circuit Court Records, WASHU
Swekosky Notre Dame College Collection, MOHIST

Journals, Memoirs, Papers, Proceedings, and Speeches

Adams, Charles Francis. *The Trent Affair: An Historical Retrospect.* Boston: Massachusetts Historical Society, 1912.

Ashton, J. Hubley, ed. *Official Opinions of the Attorneys General of the United States.* 12 vols. Washington, DC: W. H. & O. H. Morrison, 1868.

Bartlett, D. W. *Presidential Candidates Containing Sketches, Biographical, Personal and Political, of Prominent Candidates for the Presidency in 1860.* New York: A. B. Burdick, Publishers, 1859.

Basler, Roy P., ed. *The Collected Works of Abraham Lincoln.* 9 vols. New Brunswick, NJ: Rutgers University Press, 1953.

Beale, Howard K., ed. *The Diary of Gideon Welles.* 3 vols. New York: Houghton Mifflin Company, 1911.

———. *The Diary of Edward Bates, 1859–1866.* Washington, DC: United States Government Printing Office, 1933.

Bergeron, Paul H., ed. *The Papers of Andrew Johnson.* 16 vols. Knoxville: University of Tennessee Press, 1992.

Blair, Montgomery. *On the Revolutionary Schemes of the Ultra Abolitionists, and in Defense of the Policy of the President.* New York: D. W. Lee, 1863.

Boernstein, Henry. *Memoirs of a Nobody: The Missouri Years of an Austrian Radical, 1849–1866.* Translated by Steven Rowan. St. Louis: Missouri Historical Society Press, 1997.

Burlingame, Michael, ed. *At Lincoln's Side: John Hay's Civil War Correspondence and Selected Writings.* Carbondale: Southern Illinois University Press, 2000.

———. *With Lincoln in the White House: Letters, Memoranda, and Other Writings of John G. Nicolay, 1860–1865.* Carbondale: Southern Illinois University Press, 2000.

Carpenter, Francis Bicknell. *Six Months at the White House.* New York: Hurd and Houghton, 1866.

Carter, Clarence Edwin, ed., *The Territorial Papers of the United States.* Vol. XIV. Washington, DC: Government Printing Office, 1949.

Colfax, Schuyler. *Kansas—The Lecompton Constitution, March 20, 1858.* Washington, DC: Buell & Blanchard, 1858.

Collections of the Pioneer Society of the State of Michigan Together with Reports of County Pioneers Societies. Vol VIII. Lansing, MI: Wynkoop, Hallenbeck Crawford Co., 1907.

Crist, Lynda Lasswell, and Mary Seaton Dix, eds. *The Papers of Jefferson Davis.* 14 vols. Baton Rouge: Louisiana State University Press, 1992.

Donald, David Herbert, ed. *Inside Lincoln's Cabinet: The Civil War Diaries of Salmon P. Chase.* New York: Longmans, Green and Co., 1954.

Fergus, Robert, ed. *Chicago River and Harbor Convention: An Account of Its Origins and Proceedings.* Chicago: Fergus Printing Company, 1882.

Gienapp, William E., and Erica L. Gienapp, eds. *The Civil War Diary of Gideon Welles, Lincoln's Secretary of the Navy: The Original Manuscript Edition.* Chicago: University of Illinois Press, 2014.

Gordon, John Wesley. *The Honorable Edward Bates, of Missouri: Is He Fit-Is He Available, as the Republican Candidate for the Presidency?* Indianapolis: Capital Job Office Steam Press Print, 1860.

Howard, Benjamin C. *A Report of the Decision of the Supreme Court of the United States, and the Opinions of the Judges Thereof, in the Case of Dred Scott versus John F. A. Sandford.* New York: D. Appleton & Co., 1857.

Hurd, Rollin C. *A Treatise on the Right of Personal Liberty: And on the Writ of Habeas Corpus and the Practice Connected With It—With a View of Law of Extradition of Fugitives.* 2nd ed. Albany: W. C. Little & Co., 1876.

Johnson, Charles W., ed. *Proceedings of the First Three Republican National Conventions of 1856, 1860, and 1864.* Minneapolis: Harrison & Smith, 1893.

Johnson, Reverdy. *Power of the President to Suspend the Habeas Corpus Writ.* New York, 1861.

Levenson, J. C., Ernest Samuels, Charles Vandersee, Viola Hopkins Winner, Jayne N. Samuels, and Eleanor Pearre Abbot, eds. *The Letters of Henry Adams.* 6 vols. Cambridge, MA: Harvard University Press, 1982.

Leopard, Buel, and Floyd C. Shoemaker, eds. *The Messages and Proclamations of the Governors of the State of Missouri.* 20 vols. Columbia: State Historical Society of Missouri, 1922.

Marshall, Thomas Maitland, ed. *The Life and Papers of Frederick Bates.* 2 vols. St. Louis: Missouri Historical Society, 1926.

McCormack, Thomas J., ed. *The Memoirs of Gustave Koerner, 1809–1896: Life-Sketches Written at the Suggestion of His Children.* 2 vols. Cedar Rapids, IA: The Torch Press, 1909.

Mordell, Albert, ed. *Selected Essays of Gideon Welles: Civil War and Reconstruction.* New York: Twayne Publishers, 1959.

Palmer, Beverly Wilson, and Holly Byers Ochoa, eds. *The Selected Papers of Thaddeus Stevens*. 2 vols. Pittsburgh: University of Pittsburgh Press, 1997.

Peters, Gerhard, and John T. Wooley, eds. *The American Presidency Project*, http://www.presidency.ucsb.edu.

Phillips, Wendell. *The Freedom Speech of Wendell Phillips*. Boston: Wendell Phillips Hall Association, 1891.

Richardson, James D. ed. *A Compilation of the Messages and Papers of the Presidents*. 11 vols. Washington, DC: Government Printing Office, 1900.

Reynolds, David S., ed. *Lincoln's Selected Writings*. New York: W. W. Norton & Company, 2015.

Sears, Stephen W., ed. *The Civil War Papers of George B. McClellan*. New York: Da Capo Press, 1992.

Schurz, Carl. *The Reminiscences of Carl Schurz*. 2 vols. New York: The McClure Company, 1908.

Government Documents

Appointment Records, Commissions, Miscellaneous Permanent and Temporary Presidential Commissions, 1789–1972, National Archives and Records Administration, Washington, DC.

Byrd, Robert C., ed. *The Senate, 1789–1989: Addresses on the History of the United States Senate*. 4 vols. Washington, DC: Government Printing Office, 1988.

Congress. House Committee on Roads and Canals. Harbor at St. Louis: To accompany bill, H.R. No. 451. 23rd Cong., 1st Sess., January 2, 1834.

———. House Committee on Roads and Canals. *Report of Charles Gratiot, Chief Engineer, Army Corps of Engineers attached to House Report No. 425*. 23rd Cong., 1st Sess., April 16, 1834.

———. House Committee on Commerce. *Letter from the Secretary of War transmitting the information required by a resolution of the House of Representatives respecting the Harbor of St. Louis*. 25th Cong., 2nd Sess., April 4, 1838.

Constitution of the State of Missouri of 1875. Jefferson City: The Hugh Stephens Printing Company, 1909.

Grier, Robert Cooper, and Supreme Court of The United States. *U.S. Reports: Glasgow et al. vs. Hortiz et al.*, 66 U.S. 1 Black 595. 1861.

Heads of Families at the First Census of the United States Taken in the Year 1790. Washington, DC: Government Printing Office, 1908.

"Inventory for Thornhill," *National Register of Historic Places*, National Park Service, United States Department of the Interior, October 17, 1973.

Journal of the House of Representatives of the Second General Assembly of the State of Missouri. St. Charles: Nathaniel Paschall, 1823.

Journal of the House of Representatives of the State of Missouri at the first session of the Seventh General Assembly. St. Louis: John Steele, 1833.

Journal of the House of Representatives of the United States of America. Vol. 21. Washington, DC: Gales & Seaton, 1827.

Journal of the Missouri State Convention. St. Louis: I. N. Henry & Co., 1820.

Journal of the Missouri State Convention, Held at Jefferson City, July 1861. St. Louis: George Knapp & Co., 1861.

Journal of the Senate of the Second General Assembly of the State of Missouri. St. Charles: Nathaniel Paschall, 1823.

Journal of the Senate of the State of Missouri at the first session of the Seventh General Assembly. Jefferson City: Calvin Gunn, 1833.

Journal of the Executive Proceedings of the Senate of the United States of America, Volume 11. Washington, DC: Government Printing Office, 1887.

Presidential Proclamations, series 23 Record Group 11, NARA.

Taney, Roger B. *Opinion of Chief Justice Taney in the Case of Ex Parte John Merryman, Applying for a Writ of Habeas Corpus.* New Orleans: George Ellis, Publisher, 1861.

U.S. Census of Population and Housing, 1810. Washington, DC: Government Printing Office, 1811.

U.S. Census of Population and Housing, 1830. Washington, DC: Government Printing Office, 1831.

U.S. Census of Population and Housing, 1820. Washington, DC: Government Printing Office, 1821.

U.S. Census of Population and Housing, 1840. Washington, DC: Government Printing Office, 1841.

U.S. Census of Population and Housing, 1850. Washington, DC: Government Printing Office, 1851.

U.S. War Department. *The War of the Rebellion: A Compilation of the Official Records of the Union and Confederate Armies.* 128 vols. Washington, DC: Government Printing Office, 1880–1901.

Newspapers

The Alexandria Gazette and Virginia Advertiser
Boon's Lick Times
Charleston, Missouri Courier
The Congressional Globe (Washington, D.C.)
Evansville Daily Journal
Evening Star (Washington, D.C.)
The Hannibal Journal
The Missouri Daily Republican
The Missouri Democrat

The Missouri Gazette and Public Advertiser
The Missouri Glasgow Weekly Times
The Missouri Intelligencer
The National Republican (Washington, D.C.)
The New York Daily Tribune
The New York Times
Palmyra Weekly Whig
The Republic (Washington, D.C.)
The St. Charles Republican Intelligencer
St. Louis Intelligencer
St. Louis Post Dispatch

Articles

Ascher, Leonard. "Lincoln's Administration and the New Almaden Scandal." *Pacific Historical Review* 5, no. 1 (March 1936).

Bailyn, Bernard. "Political Experience and Enlightenment Ideas in Eighteenth-Century America." *American Historical Review* 67 (1961–62).

Benson, Lee, and Cushing Strout. "Causation and the American Civil War: Two Appraisals." *History and Theory* 1 (1960–61).

Bonner, Thomas N. "Civil War Historians and the 'Needless War.'" *Journal of the History of Ideas* 17, no. 2 (April 1956).

Brinkley, Alan. "Conservatism as a Growing Field of Scholarship." *Journal of American History* 98, no. 3 (December 2011).

Booth, Don. "Archeology at the Arch." *The Confluence* 9, no. 2 (Spring/Summer 2018).

Broadhead, Garland C. "A Few of the Leading People and Events of Missouri History." *Missouri Historical Review* 1, no. 4 (July 1907).

Cain, Marvin, ed. "Lincoln's Attorney General Views the Secession Crisis: Edward Bates's Letters to Wyndham Robertson." *Bulletin of the Missouri Historical Society* 21, no. 1 (October 1964).

Critchlow, Donald T. "Rethinking American Conservatism: Toward a New Narrative." *Journal of American History* (December 2011).

Dearinger, Ryan L. "Violence, Masculinity, Image, and Reality on the Antebellum Frontier." *Indiana Magazine of History* 100 (March 2004).

Gaines, Philip. "The 'True Lawyer' in America: Discursive Construction of the Legal Profession in the Nineteenth Century." *American Journal of Legal History* 45, no. 2 (April 2001).

Gerteis, Louis S. "Salmon P. Chase, Radicalism, and the Politics of Emancipation, 1861–1864." *Journal of American History* 60, no. 1 (June 1973).

Horder, Eric. "The Duel and the English Law of Homicide." *Oxford Journal of Legal Studies* 12, no. 3 (1992).

Keller, Kenneth W. "Alexander McNair and John B. C. Lucas: The Background of Early Missouri Politics." *Bulletin of the Missouri Historical Society* 33, no. 4 (1977).

Learned, Henry Barrett. "The Attorney-General and the Cabinet." *Political Science Quarterly* 24, no. 3 (September 1909).

Les Benedict, Michael. "Preserving the Constitution: The Conservative Basis of Radical Reconstruction." *Journal of American History* 61, no. 1 (June 1974).

———. "Southern Democrats in the Crisis of 1876–1877: A Reconstruction of Reunion and Reaction." *Journal of Southern History* 46, no. 4 (November 1980).

Marshall, Lynn L. "The Strange Stillbirth of the Whig Party." *American Historical Review* 72, no. 2 (January 1967).

McClure, James P., Leigh Johansen, Kathleen Norman, and Michael Vanderlan, eds. "Circumventing the Dred Scott Decision: Edward Bates, Salmon P. Chase, and the Citizenship of African Americans." *Civil War History* 43, no. 4 (December 1997).

Meerse, David E. "Buchanan, Corruption and the Election of 1860." *Civil War History* 12, no. 2 (June 1966): 116–31.

Meigs, Montgomery C. "General Meigs on the Conduct of the War." *American Historical Review* 26, no. 2 (January 1921).

Moore, Bob. "New Perspectives on the Great Fire of 1849." *The Confluence* 10, no. 2 (Spring/Summer 2019).

Neels, Mark A. "'We Shall Be Literally Sold to the Dutch': Nativist Suppression of German Radicals in Antebellum St. Louis, 1852–1861." *The Confluence* 1, no. 1 (Fall 2009).

———. "The Barbarous Custom of Dueling: Death and Honor on St. Louis' Bloody Island." *The Confluence* 2, no. 1 (Fall/Winter 2010).

———. "'I Will Continue to Make the Best Defense I Can': Edward Bates and the Battle over the Missouri Constitution of 1865." *The Confluence* 5, no. 1 (Fall/Winter 2013).

Randall, James G. "The Indemnity Act of 1863: A Study in the Wartime Immunity of Governmental Officers." *Michigan Law Review* 20, no. 6 (April 1922).

———. "Has the Lincoln Theme Been Exhausted?" *American Historical Review* 41, no. 2 (January 1936).

———. "The Blundering Generation." *Mississippi Valley Historical Review* 27, no. 1 (June 1940): 3–28.

Shoemaker, Floyd C. "David Barton, John Rice Jones and Edward Bates: Three Missouri State and Statehood Founders." *Missouri Historical Review* 65, no. 4 (1971).

Smith, Michael Thomas. "The Meanest Man in Lincoln's Cabinet: A Reappraisal of Montgomery Blair." *Maryland Historical Magazine* 95, no. 2 (2000).

Smith, Willard H. "Schuyler Colfax and the Political Upheaval of 1854–1855." *Mississippi Valley Historical Review* 28, no. 3 (December 1941).

Stevens, Walter B. "Alexander McNair." *Missouri Historical Review* 17, no. 1 (1922).

Viles, Jonas. "Missouri Capitals and Capitols: Second Article." *Missouri Historical Review* 13, no. 3 (1919).

Vorenberg, Michael. "Abraham Lincoln and the Politics of Black Colonization." *Journal of the Abraham Lincoln Association* 14, no. 2 (1993).

Wiecek, William M. "Missouri Statehood: The Second Crisis of the Union." *The Sources of Anti-slavery Constitutionalism in America, 1760–1848.* London: Cornell University Press, 1977.

Williams, Mentor L. "The Chicago River and Harbor Convention, 1847." *Mississippi Valley Historical Review* 35, no. 4 (March 1949).

Williams, T. Harry. "Frémont and the Politicians." *Journal of the American Military Foundation* 2, no. 4 (Winter 1938).

Books, Dissertations, and Theses

Achorn, Edward. *The Lincoln Miracle: Inside the Republican Convention That Changed History.* New York: Atlantic Monthly Press, 2023.

Adamson, Hans Christian. *Rebellion in Missouri: 1861, Nathaniel Lyon and His Army of the West.* Philadelphia: Chilton Company, 1961.

Ambrose, Stephen E. *Halleck: Lincoln's Chief of Staff.* Baton Rouge: Louisiana State University Press, 1962.

The American Almanac and Repository of Useful Knowledge for the Year 1844. Boston: David H. Williams, 1843.

The American Annual Cyclopedia and Register of Important Events of the Year 1861. Vol. 1. New York: D. Appleton & Co., 1870.

Anbinder, Tyler. *Nativism and Slavery: The Northern Know Nothings and the Politics of the 1850s.* New York: Oxford University Press, 1992.

Appleby, Joyce. *Inheriting the Revolution: The First Generation of Americans.* Cambridge, MA: Harvard University Press, 2001.

Astor, Aaron. *Rebels on the Border: Civil War, Emancipation, and the Reconstruction of Kentucky and Missouri.* Baton Rouge: Louisiana State University Press, 2012.

Bailyn, Bernard. *The Ideological Origins of the American Revolution.* Cambridge, MA: Harvard University Press, 1967.

Baker, Jean H. *Affairs of Party: The Political Culture of Northern Democrats in the Mid-nineteenth Century.* Ithaca, NY: Cornell University Press, 1983.

Ballard, Michael B. *Vicksburg: The Campaign That Opened the Mississippi.* Chapel Hill: University of North Carolina Press, 2004.

Banning, Lance. *The Jeffersonian Persuasion: Evolution of a Party Ideology.* Ithaca, NY: Cornell University Press, 1978.

Bates, Onward, ed. *Bates et al of Virginia and Missouri.* Chicago: P. F. Pettibone & Company, 1914.

Bay, William Van Ness. *Reminiscences of the Bench and Bar of Missouri.* St. Louis: F. H. Thomas and Company, 1878.

Benedict, Michael Les. *The Impeachment and Trial of Andrew Johnson.* New York: W. W. Norton & Company, 1973.

———. *Preserving the Constitution: Essays on Politics and the Constitution in the Reconstruction Era.* New York: Fordham University Press, 2006.

Benson, Lee. *The Concept of Jacksonian Democracy: New York as a Test Case.* Princeton, NJ: Princeton University Press, 1961.

Billon, Frederic L. *Annals of St. Louis in Its Territorial Days from 1804 to 1821.* St. Louis: Frederic L. Billon, 1888.

Blue, Frederick J. *The Free Soilers: Third Party Politics, 1848–54.* Urbana: University of Illinois Press, 1973.

———. *Salmon P. Chase: A Life in Politics.* Kent, OH: The Kent State University Press, 1987.

Borneman, Walter R. *Polk: The Man Who Transformed the Presidency and America.* New York: Random House, 2008.

Bowman, Dennis K. *Lincoln's Resolute Unionist: Hamilton Gamble, Dred Scott Dissenter and Missouri's Civil War Governor.* Baton Rouge: Louisiana State University Press, 2006.

Breen, T. H. *The Character of the Good Ruler: Puritan Political Ideas in New England, 1630–1730.* New York: W. W. Norton & Company, 1970.

Brooks, Noah. *Washington, D.C., in Lincoln's Time: A Memoir of the Civil War Era by the Newspaperman Who Knew Lincoln Best.* Edited by Herbert Mitgang. Athens: University of Georgia Press, 1958.

Brown, Bertram Wyatt. *Southern Honor: Ethics and Behavior in the Old South.* New York: Oxford University Press, 1982.

Burke, Edmund. *Reflections on the Revolution in France.* Edited by Conor Cruise O'Brien. New York: Penguin Books, 1969.

Burr, C. Chauncey, ed. *The Old Guard, a Monthly Journal, Devoted to the Principles of 1776 and 1787.* Vol. 1. New York: Chauncy Burr & Co., 1863.

Cain, Marvin. *Lincoln's Attorney General: Edward Bates of Missouri.* Columbia: University of Missouri Press, 1965.

Carwardine, Richard. *Lincoln: A Life of Purpose and Power.* New York: Random House, Inc., 2006.

Catton, Bruce. *The Coming Fury.* New York: Doubleday, 1961.

———. *Terrible Swift Sword*. New York: Random House, Inc., 1963.

Chambers, William Nisbet. *Old Bullion Benton: Senator from the West*. Boston: Little, Brown and Company, 1956.

Christensen, Lawrence O., William E. Foley, Gary R. Kremer, and Kenneth H. Winn, eds. *Dictionary of Missouri Biography*. Columbia: University of Missouri Press, 1999.

Clary, David A. *Eagles and Empire: The United States, Mexico, and the Struggle for a Continent*. New York: Random House, 2009.

Clinton, Catherine. *Mrs. Lincoln: A Life*. New York: Harper Perennial, 2009.

Cobb, Thomas R. R. *An Inquiry into the Law of Negro Slavery in the United States of America*. Vol. 1. Philadelphia: T. & J. W. Johnson & Co., 1858.

Conway, Moncure Daniel. *Omitted Chapters of History Disclosed in the Life and Papers of Edmund Randolph*. New York: G. P. Putnam's Sons, 1888.

Cook, Robert J. *Civil War Senator: William Pitt Fessenden and the Fight to Save the American Republic*. Baton Rouge: Louisiana State University Press, 2011.

Craven, Avery. *The Coming of the Civil War*. Chicago: University of Chicago Press, 1942.

Crofts, Daniel. *Lincoln and the Politics of Slavery: The Other Thirteenth Amendment and the Struggle to Save the Union*. Chapel Hill: University of North Carolina Press, 2016.

Cronon, William. *Nature's Metropolis: Chicago and the Great West*. New York: W. W. Norton & Company, 1991.

Culmer, Frederic Arthur. *A New History of Missouri*. Mexico, MO: The McIntyre Publishing Company, 1938.

Cunningham, Noble E. *The Jeffersonian Republicans: The Formation of Party Organization, 1789–1801*. Chapel Hill: University of North Carolina Press, 1957.

———. *In Pursuit of Reason: The Life of Thomas Jefferson*. New York: Ballantine Books, 1987.

Current, Richard N. *Lincoln and the First Shot*. New York: J. B. Lippincott Company, 1963.

Dangerfield, George. *The Era of Good Feelings*. New York: Harcourt Brace & World, 1952.

Darby, John F. *Personal Recollections*. St. Louis: G. I. Jones and Company, 1880.

Davis, Virginia Lee Hutcheson. *Tidewater Virginia Families*. Baltimore: Genealogical Publishing Company, 1989.

Davis, Walter Bickford, and Daniels Durrie. *An Illustrated History of Missouri*. St. Louis: A. J. Hall and Company, 1876.

Davis, William C. *Battle at Bull Run: A History of the First Major Campaign of the Civil War*. Baton Rouge: Louisiana State University Press, 1977.

Delaney, Lucy A. *From the Darkness Cometh the Light or Struggles for Freedom*. Project Gutenberg, http://www.gutenberg.org/files/17820/17820-h/17820-h.htm (last accessed 27 April 2019).

Dickens, Charles. *American Notes for General Circulation*. Boston: Ticknor and Fields, 1867.

Dirck, Brian R. *Lincoln and the Constitution*. Carbondale: Southern Illinois University Press, 2012.

Donald, David Herbert. *Lincoln Reconsidered: Essays on the Civil War Era*. 2nd ed. New York: Random House, 1956.

———. *Lincoln's Herndon*. New York: Da Capo Press, 1989.

———. *Lincoln*. New York: Simon & Schuster, 1995.

———. *We Are Lincoln Men: Abraham Lincoln and His Friends*. New York: Simon & Schuster, 2003.

Dowdey, Clifford. *The Seven Days: The Emergence of Lee*. Lincoln: University of Nebraska Press, 1964.

Dubin, Michael J. *United States Gubernatorial Elections, 1776–1860: The Official Results by State and County* (Jefferson, NC: McFarland & Co., 2003.

Egerton, Douglas R. *The Wars of Reconstruction: The Brief, Violent History of America's Most Progressive Era*. New York: Bloomsbury Press, 2014.

Earle, Jonathan H. *Jacksonian Antislavery and the Politics of Free Soil, 1824–1854*. Chapel Hill: University of North Carolina Press, 2004.

Egnal, Marc. *Clash of Extremes: The Economic Origins of the Civil War*. New York: Hill and Wang, 2009.

Ellis, Joseph. *American Sphinx: The Character of Thomas Jefferson*. New York: Random House, 1996.

Emerson, Jason. *Giant in the Shadows: The Life of Robert Todd Lincoln*. Carbondale: Southern Illinois University Press, 2012.

Epstein, Daniel Mark. *Lincoln's Men: The President and His Private Secretaries*. New York: HarperCollins, 2009.

Erwin, James W. *St. Charles, Missouri: A Brief History*. Charleston, NC: History Press, 2017.

Farber, Daniel. *Lincoln's Constitution*. University of Chicago Press, 2004.

Fehrenbacher, Don E. *The Dred Scott Case: Its Significance in American Law and Politics*. New York: Oxford University Press, 1978.

Foner, Eric. *Free Soil, Free Labor, Free Men: The Ideology of the Republican Party before the Civil War*. New York: Oxford University Press, 1970.

———. *Reconstruction: America's Unfinished Revolution: 1863–1877*. New York: Oxford University Press, 1988.

———, ed. *Our Lincoln: New Perspectives on Lincoln and His World*. New York: W. W. Norton & Company, 2008.

———. *The Fiery Trial: Abraham Lincoln and American Slavery*. New York: W. W. Norton & Company, 2010.

Freeman, Joanne B. *The Field of Blood: Violence in Congress and the Road to Civil War*. New York: Farrar, Straus and Giroux, 2018.

Gerteis, Louis S. *Morality and Utility in American Antislavery Reform*. Chapel Hill: University of North Carolina Press, 1987.

———. *Civil War St. Louis*. Lawrence: University Press of Kansas, 2001.

———. *The Civil War in Missouri: A Military History*. Columbia: University of Missouri Press, 2012.

Gienapp, William. *The Origins of the Republican Party, 1852–1856*. New York: Oxford University Press, 1987.

Goodwin, Doris Kearns. *Team of Rivals: The Political Genius of Abraham Lincoln*. New York: Simon & Schuster, 2005.

Greenberg, Amy S. *A Wicked War: Polk, Clay, Lincoln, and the 1846 U.S. Invasion of Mexico*. New York: Alfred A. Knopf, 2012.

Grimsley, Mark. *The Hard Hand of War: Union Military Policy toward Southern Civilians, 1861–1865*. New York: Cambridge University Press, 1995.

Guelzo, Allen C. *Emancipation Proclamation: The End of Slavery in America*. New York: Simon & Schuster, 2004.

———. *Fateful Lightning: A New History of the Civil War and Reconstruction*. New York: Oxford University Press, 2012.

———. *Gettysburg: The Last Invasion*. New York: Alfred A. Knopf, 2013.

Hamilton, Holman. *Prologue to Conflict: The Crisis and Compromise of 1850*. New York: W. W. Norton & Company, 1964.

Harris, William C. *Lincoln and the Border States: Preserving the Union*. Lawrence: University Press of Kansas, 2011.

Harrold, Stanley. *Border War: Fighting Over Slavery before the Civil War*. Chapel Hill: University of North Carolina Press, 2010.

Hendrick, Burton Jesse. *Lincoln's War Cabinet*. New York: Little, Brown and Company, 1946.

History of St. Charles, Montgomery and Warren Counties, Missouri. St. Louis: National Historical Company, 1885.

Hofstadter, Richard. *The American Political Tradition and the Men Who Made It*. New York: Alfred Knopf, 1948

Holmberg, James J., and Jay H. Buckley, eds. *By His Own Hand: The Mysterious Death of Meriwether Lewis*. Norman: University of Oklahoma Press, 2006.

Holt, Michael F. *The Political Crisis of the 1850s*. New York: W. W. Norton & Company, 1978.

———. *The Rise and Fall of the American Whig Party: Jacksonian Politics and the Onset of the Civil War*. New York: Oxford University Press, 1999.

Howe, Daniel Walker. *The Political Culture of the American Whigs*. Chicago: University of Chicago Press, 1984.

———. *What Hath God Wrought: The Transformation of America, 1815–1848*. New York: Oxford University Press, 2007.

Humphreys, Frederick. *The Cholera, and Its Homeopathic Treatment*. New York: William Radde, 1849.

Huton, Mary Louise Marshall. *Seventeenth Century Colonial Ancestors of members of the National Society Colonial Dames, XVII Century*. Baltimore: Genealogical Publishing Co., 1984.

Hyde, William, and Howard L. Conard, eds. *Encyclopedia of the History of St. Louis*. 2 vols. St. Louis: The Southern History Company, 1899.

Irving, Washington. *Astoria or Anecdotes of an Enterprise beyond the Rocky Mountains*. 2 vols. Philadelphia: Carey, Lea, & Blanchard, 1836.

Jefferson, Thomas. *Notes on the State of Virginia*. Boston: Lilly and Wait, 1832.

Johannsen, Robert W. *Stephen A. Douglas*. New York: Oxford University Press, 1973.

Johnson, Paul E. *A Shopkeeper's Millennium: Society and Revivals in Rochester, New York, 1815–1837*. New York: Hill and Wang, 1978.

Johnson, Steven. *The Ghost Map: The Story of London's Most Terrifying Epidemic and How It Changed Science, Cities, and the Modern World*. New York: Penguin Group, 2006.

Johnson, Walter. *Soul by Soul: Life inside the Antebellum Slave Market*. Cambridge, MA: Harvard University Press, 1999.

———. *River of Dark Dreams: Slavery and Empire in the Cotton Kingdom*. Cambridge, MA: Harvard University Press, 2013.

———. *The Broken Heart of America: St. Louis and the Violent History of the United States*. New York: Basic Books, 2021.

Jones, Landon Y. *William Clark and the Shaping of the West*. Lincoln: University of Nebraska Press, 2004.

Jones, Martha S. *Birthright Citizens: A History of Race and Rights in Antebellum America*. Cambridge: Cambridge University Press, 2018.

Kahan, Paul. *Amiable Scoundrel: Simon Cameron, Lincoln's Scandalous Secretary of War*. Lincoln, NE: Potomac Books, 2016.

Kohl, Lawrence Frederick. *The Politics of Individualism: Parties and the American Character in the Jacksonian Era*. New York: Oxford University Press, 1989.

Kolchin, Peter. *American Slavery, 1619–1877*. New York: Hill and Wang, 1993.

Konig, David Thomas, Paul Finkelman, and Christopher Alan Bracey, eds. *The Dred Scott Case: Historical and Contemporary Perspectives on Race and Law*. Athens: Ohio University Press, 2010.

Lamon, Ward Hill. *Recollections of Abraham Lincoln*. Edited by Dorothy Lamon Teillard. Lincoln: University of Nebraska Press, 1994.

Lewis, Tom. *Washington: A History of Our National City*. New York: Basic Books, 2015.

Levine, Bruce. *Half Slave and Half Free: The Roots of Civil War*. New York: Hill and Wang, 1992.

Long, David. *The Jewel of Liberty: Abraham Lincoln's Re-election and the End of Slavery*. New York: DaCapo Press, 1997.

Luthin, Reinhard H. *The First Lincoln Campaign*. Gloucester: Peter Smith, 1964.

Lynn, Joshua A. *Preserving the White Man's Republic: Jacksonian Democracy, Race, and the Transformation of American Conservatism*. Charlottesville: University of Virginia Press, 2019.

Magness, Philip W., and Sebastian N. Page. *Colonization after Emancipation: Lincoln and the Movement for Black Resettlement*. Columbia: University of Missouri Press, 2011.

March, Daniel D. *The History of Missouri*. 4 vols. New York: Lewis Historical Publishing Company, 1967.

Marvel, William. *Lincoln's Autocrat: The Life of Edwin Stanton*. Chapel Hill: University of North Carolina Press, 2015.

Marzalek, John F. *Commander of All Lincoln's Armies: A Life of General Henry W. Halleck*. Cambridge, MA: Harvard University Press, 2004.

Mason, Matthew. *Apostle of Union: A Political Biography of Edward Everett*. Chapel Hill: University of North Carolina Press, 2016.

Masur, Louis P. *Lincoln's Hundred Days: The Emancipation Proclamation and the War for the Union*. Cambridge, MA: Harvard University Press, 2012.

Meyers, Marvin. *The Jacksonian Persuasion: Politics and Belief*. Stanford, CA: Stanford University Press, 1957.

McGinty, Brian. *Lincoln and the Court*. Cambridge, MA: Harvard University Press, 2008.

———. *The Body of John Merryman: Abraham Lincoln and the Suspension of Habeas Corpus*. Cambridge, MA: Harvard University Press, 2011.

McPherson, James. *Ordeal by Fire: The Civil War and Reconstruction*. New York: Alfred A. Knopf, 1982.

———. *Battle Cry of Freedom: The Civil War Era*. New York: Oxford University Press, 1988.

Mering, John Volmer. *The Whig Party in Missouri*. Columbia: University of Missouri Press, 1967.

Miers, Earl Schenk. *Lincoln Day by Day: A Chronology*. 3 vols. Washington, DC: Lincoln Sesquicentennial Commission, 1960.

Mutti Burke, Diane. *On Slavery's Border: Missouri's Small-Slaveholding House-holds, 1815–1865.* Athens: University of Georgia Press, 2010.

Nagel, Paul C. *Missouri: A History.* New York: W. W. Norton & Company, 1977.

Neels, Mark A. "Lincoln's Conservatives: Conservative Unionism and Political Tradition in the Civil War Era." PhD diss., Southern Illinois University, 2015.

Neely, Mark E. *The Fate of Liberty: Abraham Lincoln and Civil Liberties.* New York: Oxford University Press, 1991.

———. *Lincoln and the Triumph of the Nation: Constitutional Conflict in the American Civil War.* Chapel Hill: University of North Carolina Press, 2011.

Nevins, Allan, ed. *Polk: The Diary of a President: 1845–1849.* New York: Capricorn Books, 1968.

Niven, John. *Gideon Welles: Lincoln's Secretary of the Navy.* New York: Oxford University Press, 1973.

———. *Salmon P. Chase: A Biography.* New York: Oxford University Press, 1995.

Oates, Stephen B. *The Fires of Jubilee: Nat Turner's Fierce Rebellion.* New York: Harper Perennial, 2016.

O'Reilly, Francis Augustin. *The Fredericksburg Campaign: Winter War on the Rappahannock.* Baton Rouge: Louisiana State University Press, 2003.

Parrish, William E. *Missouri under Radical Rule: 1865–1870.* Columbia: University of Missouri Press, 1965.

———. *Frank Blair: Lincoln's Conservative.* Columbia: University of Missouri Press, 1998.

Paludan, Philip Shaw. *The Presidency of Abraham Lincoln.* Lawrence: University of Kansas Press, 1994.

Pessen, Edward. *Jacksonian America: Society, Personality, and Politics.* Homewood, IL: Dorsey Press, 1978.

Phillips, Christopher. *Missouri's Confederate: Claiborne Fox Jackson and the Creation of Southern Identity in the Border West.* Columbia: University of Missouri Press, 2000.

———. *The Rivers Ran Backward: The Civil War and the Remaking of the American Middle Border.* New York: Oxford University Press, 2016.

Piston, William Garrett, and Richard W. Hatcher. *Wilson's Creek: The Second Battle of the Civil War and the Men Who Fought It.* Chapel Hill: University of North Carolina Press, 2004.

Potter, David M. *The Impending Crisis: 1848–1861.* New York: Harper & Row, 1976.

Pratt, Fletcher. *Stanton: Lincoln's Secretary of War.* New York: W. W. Norton & Company, 1953.

Primm, James Neal. *Lion of the Valley: St. Louis, Missouri*. Boulder, CO: Pruett Publishing Company, 1981.

Rable, George C. *Fredericksburg! Fredericksburg!* Chapel Hill: University of North Carolina Press, 2002.

Rader, Perry S. *The Civil Government of the United States and the State of Missouri and the History of Missouri from the Earliest Times to the Present*. Columbia: E. W. Stephens, 1898.

Randall, James G., ed. *The Diary of Orville Hickman Browning*. 2 vols. Springfield: Illinois State Historical Library, 1925.

———. *Constitutional Problems under Lincoln*. New York: D. Appleton and Company, 1926.

Remini, Robert V. *Henry Clay: Statesman for the Union*. New York: W. W. Norton & Company, 1993.

———. *Daniel Webster: The Man and His Time*. New York: W. W. Norton & Company, 1997.

———. *John Quincy Adams*. New York: Henry Holt and Company, 2002.

———. *The House: The History of the House of Representatives*. New York: HarperCollins, 2006.

Richardson, Heather Cox. *To Make Men Free: A History of the Republican Party*. New York: Basic Books, 2014.

Robinson, Michael D. *A Union Indivisible: Secession and the Politics of Slavery in the Border South*. Chapel Hill: University of North Carolina Press, 2017.

Rosenberg, Charles E. *The Cholera Years: The United States in 1832, 1849, and 1866*. Chicago: University of Chicago Press, 1962.

Ross, Earl Dudley. *The Liberal Republican Movement*. Seattle: University of Washington Press, 1910.

Said, Edward. *Orientalism*. New York: Random House Press, 1978.

Scott, John M. *An Address Delivered to the Law Academy of Philadelphia, at the Opening of the Session in September 1830*. Philadelphia: Mifflin & Parry, 1830.

Sears, Stephen W. *Gettysburg*. New York: Houghton Mifflin Company, 2003.

Sellers, Charles. *The Market Revolution: Jacksonian America, 1815–1846*. New York: Oxford University Press, 1994.

Shea, William L., and Earl J. Hess. *Pea Ridge: Civil War Campaign in the West*. Chapel Hill: University of North Carolina Press, 1992.

Shoemaker, Floyd C. "The First Constitution of Missouri: A Study of Its Origins." Master's thesis, University of Missouri, Columbia, 1911.

———. *Missouri's Struggle for Statehood, 1804–1821*. Jefferson City: Hugh Stephens Printing Co., 1916.

Silbey, Joel H. *A Respectable Minority: The Democratic Party in the Civil War Era, 1860–1868*. New York: W. W. Norton & Company, 1977.

———. *Storm over Texas: The Annexation Controversy and the Road to Civil War*. New York: Oxford University Press, 2005.

Simon, John Y. and Harold Holtzer, eds. *Rediscovering Abraham Lincoln*. New York: Fordham University Press, 2002.

Simon, John Y., Harold Holtzer, and Dawn Vogel, eds. *Lincoln Revisited*. New York: Fordham University Press, 2007.

Simon, Paul. *Freedom's Champion: Elijah Lovejoy*. Carbondale: Southern Illinois University Press, 1994.

Slap, Andrew L. *The Doom of Reconstruction: The Liberal Republicans in the Civil War Era*. New York: Fordham University Press, 2006.

Smith, Adam I. P. *No Party Now: Politics in the Civil War North*. New York: Oxford University Press, 2006.

———. *The Stormy Present: Conservatism and the Problem of Slavery in Northern Politics, 1846–1865*. Chapel Hill: University of North Carolina Press, 2017.

Smith, Elbert B. *The Presidency of James Buchanan*. Lawrence: University Press of Kansas, 1975.

———. *Francis Preston Blair*. New York: Free Press, 1980.

Smith, William E. *The Francis Preston Blair Family in Politics*. 2 vols. New York: The MacMillan Company, 1933.

Snead, Thomas L. *The Fight for Missouri: From the Election of Lincoln to the Death of Lyon*. New York: Charles Scribner's Sons, 1886.

Snow, John. *On the Mode of Communication of Cholera*. 2nd ed. London: John Churchill, New Burlington Street, 1854.

Stahr, Walter. *Seward: Lincoln's Indispensable Man*. New York: Simon & Schuster, 2012.

———. *Stanton: Lincoln's War Secretary*. New York: Simon & Schuster, 2017.

———. *Salmon P. Chase: Lincoln's Vital Rival*. New York: Simon & Schuster, 2021.

Stampp, Kenneth. *The Era of Reconstruction, 1865–1877*. New York: Alfred A. Knopf, Inc., 1965.

Stevens, Walter B. *St. Louis: The Fourth City, 1764–1911*. St. Louis: S. J. Clarke Publishing Co., 1911.

———. *Centennial History of the Missouri (The Center State): One Hundred Years in the Union, 1820–1921*. St. Louis: S. J. Clarke Publishing Company, 1921.

Stone, Thomas P. *The Martyr of Freedom: A Discourse*. Boston: Isaac Knapp, 1838.

Striner, Richard. *Summoned to Glory: The Audacious Life of Abraham Lincoln*. New York: Rowman & Littlefield, 2020.

Summers, Mark Wahlgren. *A Dangerous Stir: Fear, Paranoia, and the Making of Reconstruction*. Chapel Hill: University of North Carolina Press, 2009.

———. *The Ordeal of the Reunion: A New History of Reconstruction*. Chapel Hill: University of North Carolina Press, 2014.

Summers, Joseph, and Dottie Summers Dallmeyer. *Jefferson City, Missouri*. Chicago: Arcadia Publishing, 2000.

Tefft, Benjamin Franklin, ed. *Speeches of Daniel Webster*. New York: A. L. Burt Company, 1854.

Thomas, Benjamin. *Abraham Lincoln: A Biography*. New York: A. A. Knopf, 1952.

Thomas, Benjamin, and Harold Hyman. *Stanton: The Life and Times of Lincoln's Secretary of War*. New York: A. A. Knopf, 1962.

Thomas, Emory. *The Dogs of War: 1861*. New York: Oxford University Press, 2011.

Trefousse, Hans L. *Impeachment of a President: Andrew Johnson, the Blacks, and Reconstruction*. Knoxville: University of Tennessee Press, 1975.

———. *Carl Schurz: A Biography*. Knoxville: University of Tennessee Press, 1982.

———. *Andrew Johnson: A Biography*. New York: W. W. Norton & Company, 1989.

Tyler, Alice Felt. *Freedom's Ferment: Phases of American Social History from the Colonial Period to the Outbreak of the Civil War*. New York: Harper & Row, 1944.

Van Atta, John R. *Wolf by the Ears: The Missouri Crisis, 1819–1821*. Baltimore: Johns Hopkins University Press, 2015.

Van Deusen, Glyndon G. *William Henry Seward*. New York: Oxford University Press, 1967.

VanderVelde, Lea. *Redemption Songs: Suing for Freedom before Dred Scott*. New York: Oxford University Press, 2014.

Violette, Eugene Morrow. *A History of Missouri*. New York: D. C. Heath & Co., 1918.

Wade, Richard C. *Slavery in the Cities: The South, 1820–1860*. New York: Oxford University Press, 1964.

Waldrep, Christopher, ed. *Lynching in America: A History in Documents*. New York: New York University Press, 2006.

Ward, John William. *Andrew Jackson: Symbol for an Age*. New York: Oxford University Press, 1962.

Watson, Harry L. *Liberty and Power: The Politics of Jacksonian America*. New York: Hill and Wang, 1990.

Waugh, John C. *Reelecting Lincoln: The Battle for the 1864 Presidency.* New York: Crown Publishers, 1997.

Weber, Jennifer L. *Copperheads: The Rise and Fall of Lincoln's Opponents in the North.* New York: Oxford University Press, 2008.

White, Jonathan W. *Abraham Lincoln and Treason in the Civil War: The Trials of John Merryman.* Baton Rouge: Louisiana State University Press, 2011.

White, Richard. *The Republic for Which It Stands: The United States during Reconstruction and the Gilded Age, 1865–1896.* New York: Oxford University Press, 2017.

Wilentz, Sean. *The Rise of American Democracy: Jefferson to Lincoln.* New York: W. W. Norton & Company, 2005.

Williams, Robert C. *Horace Greeley: Champion of American Freedom.* New York: New York University Press, 2006.

Williams, T. Harry. *Lincoln and the Radicals.* Madison: University of Wisconsin Press, 1941.

———. *Lincoln and his Generals.* New York: Alfred A. Knopf, 1952.

Witt, John Fabian. *Lincoln's Code: The Laws of War in American History.* New York: Free Press, 2012.

Work, David. *Lincoln's Political Generals.* Chicago: University of Illinois Press, 2009.

Zeitz, Joshua. *Lincoln's Boys: John Hay, John Nicolay, and the War for Lincoln's Image.* New York: Penguin Group, 2014.

INDEX

Italicized page numbers indicate figures.

Ashley, William, 21, 24–25, 35
Atchison, David Rice, 67, 68

Baltimore, Maryland, 115–16
Bangor (Maine) Daily Whig and Courier, 192–93
banking industry, 21–22, 33, 35
Barton, David, 13, 17–18, 32, 34
Barton, Joshua, 14, 15, 23–24
Bates, Barton. *See* Bates, Joshua Barton
Bates, Caroline Matilda Woodson (mother), 6, 8–10, 11, 44
Bates, Charles Woodson (son), 121, 143, 175
Bates, Coalter (John) (son), 121, 127, 152, 162–63, 167, 172
Bates, Dick (Richard) (son), 7, 105, 139, 163, 166–67, 171
Bates, Edward, *91, 95, 99, 100*; birth and origin family, 6, 8–11, 44, 185, 186; commemorative statue, *100,* 189; death and eulogies, 188–89; descriptions, 14, 88, *91, 95,* 170, 188–89; education, 11, 13–14; enslaved people of, 9, 19, 29, 51, 52–53, 81, 193; gap in scholarship on, 4–5, 194; illnesses, 110, 163, 171, 185–86, 188; influences on, 10, 13, 26; legal career, 14–15, 21–22, 24, 36, 63, 69, 178; as orator, 14, 38, 69–70; personal losses, 24, 26, 167, 181; professional disappointments, 84–86, 174; religious faith, 45, 63, 65, 110, 170–71, 186
Bates, Edward, marriage and family life of: challenges, 44, 123, 127, 163, 166–67; comfort and support from, 44–45, 62–63, 143, 171, 174; family tree, 7; with Julia Coalter, 7, 22–23, 62–63, *91,* 188; residences, 36–37, 57, 105, 121, 176–77

Bates, Edward, in Missouri politics: as attorney, 14–15, 21–22, 178; as District Attorney, 24; at 1820 constitution convention, 17–19; as 1865 constitution opposition, 176, 177–78, 179–80, 181–85; and election of 1850, 60–62; influence of, 17–19, 32, 161–62, 184, 185; judgeships of, 51–52, 69; on "radicals," 177; at River and Harbor Convention, 37–40, 56; in state assembly (1822, 1830), 22, 23, 32; as Whig Party leader, 33, 36, 38, 53, 60–62, 67–68, 189
Bates, Edward, in national politics (pre-1860): attorney general prospects (1849), 55–56; and Lincoln's 1860 election, 86–90; as presidential candidate (1860) (*see* Bates, Edward, as presidential candidate); as U.S. representative (1826), 26–30, 33–34; U.S. senate prospects (1850s), 67–68; vice presidential prospects (1848, 1852), 53, 54, 66; as Whig Party leader, 33, 36, 45, 53–54, 56, 69–70, 71, 87
Bates, Edward, political philosophy of: on civilian rights, 149, 160, 178, 179–80, 181, 193; conservatism, overview of, 192–94; on Emancipation Proclamation/emancipation, 2, 99, 146, 149, 152–53, 155–58, 177, 194; on enslaved labor, 18–19, 28–29, 46, 50–53, 54, 56, 66, 73–75, 78, 85, 102–3, 129, 193; of honest governance, 22, 27, 28, 29–30, 39–40, 88, 110; Jeffersonian roots of, 3–4, 26–27, 189; with opposition to populism, 27, 29–31, 33–34, 36, 192; of placing principles over constituents, 61–62; on racial separation, 153–54, 157–58, 188,

193; on unionism and secession, 60, 63–64, 70, 78–79, 88–89, 101–3, 105; on war and executive power, 48–49, 56, 111–12, 116–20, 181–82, 194

Bates, Edward, as presidential candidate, 75–87; loss of, 85–87, 90; opposition to, 80, 81; at Republican convention, 81–84; strategy of, 78, 79; support for, 75–76, 77–78, 79, 80–82

Bates, Edward, as U.S. attorney general: acceptance of offer, 88–90, 96, 104–5, 106–7; accolades for, 170, 188–89; advice to Lincoln on Civil War, 108, 112, 113, 117–20, 124, 131, 136, 137–38, 140–42, 151, 154, 193–94; advice to Lincoln on slavery and emancipation, 145–46, 152–53, 155–58; cabinet infighting, 142–43, 154–55, 164, 193; and Civil War legal issues (*see* legal issues in Civil War); on Civil War strategy (*see* Civil War); demands of office, 111, 139–40, 159, 163, 171; disagreements with Lincoln, 141, 158, 173, 174; effectiveness of, 193–94; and federal land grant case, 140; passed over for U.S. Supreme Court, 174; and railroad in Missouri, 150–51; resignation of, 174, 175; on thirteenth amendment, 156–57, 168–69; Washington D.C. life, 104–5, 121, 126–27, 139, 167, 175

Bates, Fleming (son), 7, 45, 123, 127, 167, 188, 190

Bates, Frederick (brother), 9, 10–11, 12–13, 23, 24–26, 92

Bates, John (fourth great-grandfather), 8

Bates, John Coalter (son), 121, 127, 152, 162–63, 167, 172

Bates, Joshua Barton (son), *93*; birth of, 7, 24; legal work of, 63, *93*; marriage and family of, 45, 63; on Missouri Supreme Court, *93*, 143; support for Edward by, 111, 123, 130, 143, 171, 176, 188; Union support, 134

Bates, Julia Davenport Coalter (wife), *91*; children of, 24, 45, 163, 166–67; description, 23, *91*, 190; illness and death, 188, 189–90; marriage, 7, 22–23, 62–63, 188; in Washington, D.C., 121, 125–27, 139, 167, 175

Bates, Julian (son), 7, 24, 45, 63, 163, 171, 188, 190

Bates, Matilda "Tilly" (daughter), 7, 121, 139, 159, 163, 175

Bates, Nancy (daughter), 7, 24, 45, 139, 175, 185–86, 188, 190

Bates, Onward (grandson), 9–10, 45, 110, 121, 125, 163

Bates, Richard "Dick" (son), 7, 105, 139, 163, 166–67, 171

Bates, Thomas Fleming (father), 6, 8–11, 192

Bates, Woodson (Charles) (son), 121, 143, 175

Battle of Antietam, 151–52, 154

Battle of Ball's Bluff, 128

Battle of Chancellorsville, 162–63

Battle of Fredericksburg, 154–55

Battle of Gettysburg, 163, 167

Battle of Manassas, First and Second, 126–27, 146, 151

Battle of Pea Ridge, 144, 161

Battle of Shiloh, 144

Battle of the Seven Days, 147–48

Battle of Wilson's Creek, 127

Beauregard, P. G. T., 109–10, 126, 147

Bell, John, 88

Bell, William H., 103, 104, 122

civilian courts: for confiscation cases, 129, 149, 154, 160–61, 194; vs. martial law, 178–82, 184, 187, 194

Civil War: Bates' military strategy, 113, 124, 125, 127–28, 131, 133, 137, 140–42, 146, 151, 161–63; Bates' opinion on progress of, 127–28, 144, 146–47, 162; beginning and end, 107–10, 172, 178–79, 180–81; blockade of Southern coastline, 113–15, 134, 136, 159–60, 194; Confederate victories, 125–28, 130, 154–55, 162–63; international implications, 114, 134–37, 138; legal issues (see legal issues in Civil War); military tribunals, 120; militias, 103–4, 111–12, 122–23, 148, 164, 179; in Missouri, 103–4, 121–25, 127, 129–31, 133–34, 161–62, 172; riverboat flotilla in west, 113–14, 140, 163, 194; scholarship on, 4–5; secession crisis before, 88–89, 101–3, 105, 107; Seward's prediction of, 77; and suspension of habeas corpus, 112, 116–20, 142–43, 160, 181, 194; Union leadership problems, 122–24, 128–31, 137–38, 140–41, 162; Union victories, 133, 143–44, 152, 163, 172, 180–81; and U.S. Constitution, 112, 117–19, 132; and Washington, D.C., 125–26

Clark, John Bullock, 36

Clark, William, 13, 14, 20–21

Clay, Henry, 18, 29, 38, 59

Coalter, Julia. See Bates, Julia

Coffey, Titian J., 117, 171

Colfax, Schuyler, 71, 76–77, 78–79, 86

colonization, 28–29, 51, 52–53, 146, 152–53, 155, 156–58

Colonization Society, American, 28–29, 51, 52–53, 157

commander in chief title, 132, 137

compensated emancipation, 146, 149–50, 152, 155–57, 166, 191

Compromise of 1850, 59–60, 66–67

Confederate States of America, 113–15, 134–37

Confiscation Acts of 1861 and 1862, 129–30, 148–49, 152

confiscation cases and civilian courts, 129, 149, 154, 160–61, 194

conservatism, overview of, 192–94

Constitutional Union Party, 87, 88, 89

corruption in Union leadership, 128–31

cotton fiasco, 161, 169, 173

Crittenden, John J., 102

currency, paper, 21–22

Curtis, Samuel R., 144, 161–62, 170–71

Dana, Richard Henry, Jr., 159–60

Davis, David, 86

Davis, Henry Winter, 81, 83, 172

Davis, Jefferson, 109, 122, 134, 147

Dayton, William L., 83, 88, 134

Democratic Party: Bates on, 87; on Civil War issues, 137, 145; on emancipation, 145; Jacksonian roots of, 3, 34, 106; in Missouri, 34, 35–36, 59–60, 61, 67, 70–71, 103; Northern, 38, 48, 49, 54, 58, 68, 74; in presidential elections, 54, 67, 70, 77, 82, 172–73, 188; on public works, 37–39; schisms in, 34, 35, 49, 54, 58, 59–61, 74, 82; on slavery, 49, 54, 59–61, 67, 68, 70, 74, 76–77, 81; Southern, 48, 49, 54, 58, 67, 74, 76; on war with Mexico, 47–49

Department of the Missouri, 161

Department of the West, 122, 127, 130

District of Columbia, emancipation in, 146

Doolittle, James R., 186

Douglas, Stephen A., 59, 74, 78, 82, 84–85, 88, 103, 163

Drake, Charles Daniel, *94*, 161, 164–65, 166, 167, 182–85, 186–87

Dred Scott case, 73–74, 106, 156

dueling, 13, 14–16, 23–24, 25–26, 34–35

Eads, James, 113–14, 140, 167, 188, 189

Eames, Charles, 160

Early, Jubal, 172

Easton, Rufus, 13, 22

election fraud, 72

elections. *See* presidential elections

emancipation: and colonization, 28–29, 51, 52–53, 146, 152, 155, 156–58; compensated, 146, 149–50, 152, 155–57, 166, 191; in District of Columbia, 146; gradual, 16, 75, 145–46, 149, 152, 164, 177, 191; Lincoln's journey to, 130, 145–46, 149; in Missouri, 18–19, 176, 177; voluntary, 29

Emancipation Proclamation: Bates' opinion on, 152–53, 155–58; cabinet members' opinions on, 1–2, 149–50, 152–58, 164; Lincoln's drafts of, 149–50, 152–54; signing of, 1–2, *99*, 154, 157–58

enslaved people: in Bates family, 9–10, 19, 29, 51, 52–53, 81, 193; Bates on, 18–19, 28–29, 46, 50–53, 54, 56, 66, 73–75, 78, 85, 102–3, 129, 193; and Confiscation Acts (1861, 1862), 129–30, 148–49, 152, 154, 160–61, 194; conviction of trader in, 145; and freedom suits, 51–52, 73–74; in Goochland County, Virginia,

9–10; international trade in, 28; and Mexican-American War, 46, 49; in Missouri, 12, 16–17, 18–19, 29, 49–50, 51–53, 59–62, 168, 176; in new territories, 54, 58–62, 66–68, 72–74, 102–3; Northern states vs. Southern states on, 28, 49, 58–59, 64, 74, 77; and thirteenth amendment proposal, 156, 168–69; uprisings, 28–29; and violence, 49–50, 73, 79. *See also* antislavery movement; emancipation

equal rights for Black persons, 168, 172, 173, 186–87, 193

Evansville Daily Journal, 76

Evarts, William, 83, 159–60

executive power during war, 48–49, 56, 111–12, 116–20, 159–60, 181–82, 194

Ex Parte Merryman, 117

federal public works projects, 37–40, 44, 45

Fessenden, William Pitt, 5, 173

Field, David Dudley, 39

Fillmore, Millard, 54, 58, 59, 66–67, 69, 70

First Battle of Bull Run, 126–27, 142

First Battle of Lexington, 130

First Confiscation Act of 1861, 129–30, 149

First Reading of the Emancipation Proclamation of Abraham Lincoln, The (Carpenter), 1–2, *99*

Fletcher, Thomas C., 176, 177, 178–80, 184, 185

Foote, Andrew H., 114, 143

Fort Monroe, Virginia, 129

Fort Pickens, Florida, 108, 109

Fort Sumter, South Carolina, 107–10, 113, 115

France, 134–37

National Republicans, 33. *See also* Whig Party
National Whig Party Convention, 69–70
nativists, 65–66, 85, 90
New Mexico, 58, 61
New Orleans, Louisiana, 42, 144
New York Daily Tribune, 75, 81
New York Times, 81, 82, 87, 156, 190
Nicolay, John G., 5, 88, 89, 104, 157
nonagitation stance on slavery, 75, 78, 85, 90, 192
Norfolk, Virginia, 8, 147

Ohio River, 113
Oregon, 47, 61, 77, 88
ousting ordinance, Missouri, 182, 183, 185

Panic of 1819, 21, 33
paper currency, 21–22
Peninsula Campaign, 146–48
Pettis, Spencer, 29–30, 33, 34–35
Phillips, Wendell, 50, 145
Pickens, Francis, 109
Pierce, Franklin, 67, 73
Polk, James K., 37, 47–49, 56, 84, 119, 193
Pope, John C., 144, 151, 178, 179–80
popular sovereignty, 54, 59, 62, 72–74, 103
populism, Jacksonian, 27, 29–30, 31, 33–34, 36, 192
ports, closing of, 113–15, 134–37
Potomac River, 128
Presbyterian Church (St. Louis), 45, 63, 65, 170–71
presidential elections: of 1848, 53–54; of 1852, 66–67; of 1856, 68–70, 77; of 1860, 75–88, 90; 1860 convention for, 81–84; of 1864, 165–66, 168, 169–70, 172–73

Price, Sterling: and Bates' son Fleming, 138, 167; in Missouri politics, 104; as Missouri State Guard commander, 123, 124–25, 127, 130, 144, 172, 179
Prize Cases, 159–60
property seizures, 129–30, 148, 149, 152, 154, 160–61
public works projects, 29, 33, 37–40, 44, 45

Quakerism (Society of Friends), 8, 9–10

racial prejudice, 18–19, 52–53, 153–54, 157–58, 173, 188, 193. *See also* enslaved people
radical Republicans. *See* Republican Party radicals
railroad, Missouri, 150–51
Randolph, Edmund, 106
rebel sympathizers, treatment of, 120, 170–71, 176, 182, 183, 187
Rector, Thomas, 23–24
Rector, William C., 23–24
republicanism (Jeffersonian), 10–11, 26–27, 33, 83, 189
Republican Party: Bates as new member of, 76, 80–84, 87; 1860 convention of, 81–84; in 1860 presidential election, 75–78, 80–88; Germans in, 85; Missouri, origins in, 69, 76–80, 81, 187; as Northern party, 74; origins of, 3, 68, 71, 76; scholarship on, 3; on slavery, 68, 70, 72–73, 77, 78, 80, 81, 82, 84–85, 90, 145; and Whig Party, 68, 69, 71, 86
Republican Party radicals: and cabinet infighting, 155, 164; vs. conservatives, 2, 145, 187, 191–92; vs. conservatives in Missouri, 130–31,

Cabinet as secretary of navy, 88, *98*, 105–6, 108, 114, 134–36, 142, 147, 149, 151, 154–55, 164; on Emancipation Proclamation, 1, *99*, 149, 152, 153, 157

Western expansion, 54, 58–62, 64, 66–68, 72–74, 102–3

Whig Party: Bates as leader in, 33, 36, 45, 53–54, 56, 60–62, 67–68, 69–70, 71, 87, 189; characteristics and platform of, 33, 35; decline of, 62, 66–68, 69–70, 71, 86, 87; in Missouri, 33, 35–36, 37, 38, 44, 45, 53, 60–62, 67, 80, 189; nativism of, 65, 66; Northern, 3, 58, 62, 68, 69; on public works, 37–39, 44, 45; on slavery, 49, 58, 60, 62, 66, 70, 74–75, 77; Southern, 3, 62, 64, 69; on war with Mexico, 47–49

White, Adam, 52–53

White House, New Year's Day at, 139, 157–58

white supremacist views, 18–19, 52–53, 153–54, 157–58, 173, 188, 193

Wilkes, Charles, 134–37

Wilmot, David, 58, 82–83

Wilmot Proviso, 58, 82

Wilson, Robert, 80

Woods, William T., 80

Woodson, John, 8

MARK A. NEELS teaches history in St. Louis, Missouri. Previous positions include assistant research associate at the Papers of Abraham Lincoln and assistant professor of history at Western Wyoming Community College.